Family Bible

Andrew Knowles was born in London in 1946 and educated at Dulwich College. He studied history and theology at St Catharine's College Cambridge before training for the priesthood of the Church of England at St John's College Nottingham.

After ordination in 1971, he served churches in Leicester, Cambridge and Woking, and was made the first Vicar of the newly created parish of Goldsworth Park in Surrey in 1981.

Andrew Knowles has written several books on biblical subjects, as well as the text of the Fount Children's Bible, and a number of scripts for television.

He and his wife, Diane, have two young children, Hannah and Matthew.

Available in Fount Paperbacks
by Andrew Knowles

FOUNT CHILDREN'S BIBLE

For Diane, Hannah and Matthew

Andrew Knowles

Family Bible Readings

Using the text of the Good News Bible

Illustrations by
Edward Mortelsmans

Collins
FOUNT PAPERBACKS

First published by Fount Paperbacks, London in 1984

Reproduced, printed and bound in Great Britain by
Hazell Watson & Viney Limited,
Member of the BPCC Group,
Aylesbury, Bucks

Introduction

This book of Bible Readings is intended for the young family that has already enjoyed some of the favourite Bible stories and is now ready to dip into the Bible itself.

The days of the head of the house reading long chapters to the rest of the family are gone, and today's breakfast is generally eaten on the run. But for the family that can manage to pause for two minutes, here is a reading, comment and prayer for each day of the year. They are dated, not in order to become a burden, but to make it easy to start again when you get out of the habit!

Goldsworth Park
Easter 1984

Andrew Knowles

A Psalm for
January

Happy are those
who reject the advice of evil men,
who do not follow the example of sinners
or join those who have no use for God.
Instead, they find joy in obeying the
Law of the LORD,
and they study it day and night.
They are like trees that grow beside a stream,
that bear fruit at the right time,
and whose leaves do not dry up.
They succeed in everything they do.

But evil men are not like this at all;
they are like straw that the wind blows away.
Sinners will be condemned by God
and kept apart from God's own people.
The righteous are guided and protected
by the LORD,
but the evil are on the way to their doom.

Psalm 1

January 1

Every year the parents of Jesus went to Jerusalem for the Passover Festival.

When Jesus was twelve years old, they went to the festival as usual. When the festival was over, they started back home, but the boy Jesus stayed in Jerusalem. His parents did not know this; they thought that he was with the group, so they travelled a whole day and then started looking for him among their relatives and friends. They did not find him, so they went back to Jerusalem looking for him.

Luke 2:41–45

✠

This glimpse of Jesus and his parents is like a precious snapshot in the family album.

Indeed, it is the only picture we have of Jesus as a boy – and what a clear one it is!

We see a family that does things together. Every year they go to the Passover festival. And this year is the most important so far for Jesus, because he is twelve. Next year, at thirteen, he will become a "Son of the Law" and a full member of the Jewish church.

Not surprisingly, Jesus takes off by himself to find out all he can. Like most twelve-year-olds, he gets carried away in what he is doing – or simply doesn't think! But of course Mary and Joseph, like most parents, are worried to death when they realize he is missing.

Even in together-families there are difficulties and misunderstandings!

✠

Lord, as we grow and change, help us still to think of each other.

✠ ✠ ✠ ✠ ✠

January 2

On the third day they found him in the Temple, sitting with the Jewish teachers, listening to them and asking questions. All who heard him were amazed at his intelligent answers. His parents were astonished when they saw him, and his mother said to him, "My son, why have you done this to us? Your father and I have been terribly worried trying to find you."

He answered them, "Why did you have to look for me? Didn't you know that I had to be in my Father's house?" But they did not understand his answer.

So Jesus went back with them to Nazareth, where he was obedient to them. His mother treasured all these things in her heart. Jesus grew both in body and in wisdom, gaining favour with God and men.

Luke 2:46–52

✠

Another snapshot of Jesus. Bright as a button, and surrounded by astonished teachers.

Joseph and Mary haven't seen this side of him before either. Maybe they assumed it would be many more years before he realized what it meant to be God's Son. But here he is in the Temple, soaking up the teaching of the elders, and calling it his Father's house. Jesus is quite surprised that they hadn't looked for him there in the first place.

The story of Jesus getting lost has a happy outcome. Jesus learns obedience and responsibility at home, as we all must do. We learn far more about life through our families and homes than we ever do at school. And, like Jesus, we may discover that growing towards God means living for others as well – not leaving them out.

✠

Lord, thank you for our home.

✠ ✠ ✠ ✠ ✠

Now we leap back in time – two thousand years in fact – to read the story of Abraham (or Abram as he was at first). Abraham lived in the Bronze Age – as many years before the time of Jesus as we are since. Both Jews and Arabs look to Abraham as their forefather. And so, in a strange way, do Christians. So he's the Daddy of us all!

✠

January 3

The LORD said to Abram, "Leave your native land, your relatives, and your father's home, and go to a country that I am going to show you. I will give you many descendants, and they will become a great nation. I will bless you and make your name famous, so that you will be a blessing.

I will bless those who bless you,
But I will curse those who curse you.
And through you I will bless all the
nations."

When Abram was seventy-five years old, he started out from Haran, as the LORD had told him to do; and Lot went with him. Abram took his wife Sarai, his nephew Lot, and all the wealth and all the slaves they had acquired in Haran, and they started out for the land of Canaan.

Genesis 12:1–5a

✠

Abram lived in a busy city, with three-storey houses and all mod cons. But God had other plans for him than to live to a ripe old age in the comfort of Ur. Instead, God called him to step out on the desert life of a wandering herdsman – a life in which he would simply have to trust God to lead and provide.

But this wasn't just a plan for Abram. It was a plan to give him a family which would become a great nation (the Jews) and to bless the whole world.

✠

Lord, thank you that whether we are young or old, every day of our life is important to you, and every day you can bless others through us.

✠ ✠ ✠ ✠ ✠

January 4

When they arrived in Canaan, Abram travelled through the land until he came to the sacred tree of Moreh, the holy place at Shechem. (At that time the Canaanites were still living in the land.) The LORD appeared to Abram and said to him, "This is the country that I am going to give to your descendants." Then Abram built an altar there to the LORD, who had appeared to him. After that, he moved on south to the hill-country east of the city of Bethel and set up his camp between Bethel on the west and Ai on the east. There also he built an altar and worshipped the LORD. Then he moved on from place to place, going towards the southern part of Canaan.

Genesis 12:5b–9

So Abram gets his first glimpse of Canaan – a beautiful, fertile land, occupied by a pagan people. The Canaanites worshipped idols of wood or stone, believing that this was what made their crops grow and their women have babies. Most of what they did would revolt us by its bloodthirstiness and vulgarity.

And what could Abram do to change all that? He quietly travelled from place to place, worshipping the Living God as he went. And he had the steady conviction that this was the land God was going to give him and his descendants. Over the years, he staked out the land by building altars – just as Edmund Hillary and Sherpa Tenzing placed the Union Jack on the summit of Mount Everest, or Neil Armstrong planted the Stars and Stripes on the surface of the moon.

✠

Lord, help us to make places special by praying in them. We look forward to the wonderful things you want to do in our homes, in our church, at our work, and in our neighbourhood.

✠ ✠ ✠ ✠ ✠

January 5

Abram had a vision and heard the LORD say to him, "Do not be afraid, Abram. I will shield you from danger and give you a great reward."

But Abram answered, "Sovereign LORD, what good will your reward do me, since I have no children? My only heir is Eliezer of Damascus. You have given me no children, and one of my slaves will inherit my property."

Then he heard the LORD speaking to him again: "This slave Eliezer will not inherit your property; your own son will be your heir." The LORD took him outside and said, "Look at the sky and try to count the stars; you will have as many descendants as that."

Abram put his trust in the LORD, and because of this the LORD was pleased with him and accepted him.

Genesis 15:1–6

✠

The one thing which made Abram great was his faith. Step by step, he trusted God. And that wasn't easy.

For one thing, God had promised him a whole nation of descendants, but now he was an old man with an elderly wife, and he hadn't a single child!

One night, when he was pouring out his heart to God, he received a marvellous promise. God spoke to him through the greatness of the night sky, and gave his solemn word that Abram's descendants would be as countless as the stars.

It's when we pause to remember how great God is, that our problems dwindle – and our new-found trust always delights the Lord.

✠

Lord, thank you that your promises are always greater than our problems.

✠ ✠ ✠ ✠ ✠

As a token of his plan for them, God gave Abram and Sarai new names – Abraham and Sarah. Names are often special in the Bible, saying something important about who a person is, or God's plan for their life.

For all their faith in God, Abraham and Sarah decide to help him by having a child through one of their slave girls. So Ishmael was born. But God's purpose was still that they should have a son of their own – despite the fact that Abraham was a hundred years old and Sarah ninety!

✠

January 6

God said to Abraham, "You must no longer call your wife Sarai; from now on her name is Sarah. I will bless her, and I will give you a son by her. I will bless her, and she will become the mother of nations, and there will be kings among her descendants."

Abraham bowed down with his face touching the ground, but he began to laugh when he thought, "Can a man have a child when he is a hundred years old? Can Sarah have a child at ninety?" He asked God, "Why not let Ishmael be my heir?"

But God said, "No. Your wife Sarah will bear you a son and you will name him Isaac. I will keep my covenant with him and with his descendants for ever. It is an everlasting covenant."

Genesis 17:15–19

✠

Now Sarah is to be called to trust God too. God has a blessing for her, and the priceless gift of a son. Her long years of childlessness and shame and failure are coming to an end. And, together, Abraham and Sarah will realize that God can be trusted absolutely to keep his word. His promise to bless, protect and guide his people will run until the end of the world.

✠

Lord, help us to trust you. Thank you that you never break your promises. Help us to keep our promises to you.

✠ ✠ ✠ ✠ ✠

January 7

The LORD appeared to Abraham at the sacred trees of Mamre. As Abraham was sitting at the entrance of his tent during the hottest part of the day, he looked up and saw three men standing there. As soon as he saw them, he ran out to meet them. Bowing down with his face touching the ground, he said, "Sirs, please do not pass by my home without stopping; I am here to serve you. Let me bring some water for you to wash your feet; you can rest here beneath this tree. I will also bring a bit of food; it will give you strength to continue your journey. You have honoured me by coming to my home, so let me serve you."

They replied, "Thank you; we accept."

Abraham hurried into the tent and said to Sarah, "Quick, take a sack of your best flour, and bake some bread." Then he ran to the herd and picked out a calf that was tender and fat, and gave it to a servant, who hurried to get it ready. He took some cream, some milk, and the meat, and set the food before the men. There under the tree he served them himself, and they ate.

Then they asked him, "Where is your wife Sarah?"

"She is there in the tent," he answered.

One of them said, "Nine months from now I will come back, and your wife Sarah will have a son."

Genesis 18:1–10

✠

When we call on somebody unexpectedly, we sometimes feel uneasy that we aren't really welcome. But Abraham was never like that. To this very day, desert people offer the best hospitality they can manage. Welcoming strangers is a lifeline in the desert.

As it turned out, these were very special visitors. Indeed, this is one of the very few places in the Old Testament where God himself comes to call. The good news he brings is that by the time he returns, Sarah will have her longed-for son.

✠

Lord, help us to give special care to strangers – not to brush them off as a nuisance and an interruption, but to welcome them for your sake.

✠ ✠ ✠ ✠ ✠

January 8

The LORD blessed Sarah, as he had promised, and she became pregnant and bore a son to Abraham when he was old. The boy was born at the time God had said he would be born. Abraham named him Isaac, and when Isaac was eight days old, Abraham circumcised him, as God had commanded. Abraham was a hundred years old when Isaac was born. Sarah said, "God has brought me joy and laughter. Everyone who hears about it will laugh with me." Then she added, "Who would have said to Abraham that Sarah would nurse children? Yet I have borne him a son in his old age."

The child grew, and on the day that he was weaned, Abraham gave a great feast.

Genesis 21:1–8

✠

By the time Isaac is born, we feel that we already know him rather well! We've been looking forward to his arrival for so long. All the same, let's pause to realize what a miracle this is. It was unheard of for two such elderly people to have a baby. It was only a fifty-fifty chance that it would be a boy. And without the medical care we take for granted today, it was by no means a foregone conclusion that he would survive.

Sarah is all smiles – and Abraham holds a feast. Isaac's very name means "He who laughs". Welcome, Smiler!

✠

Lord, open our eyes to the miracles around us. May we be glad today because of the great things you do.

January 9

One day Ishmael, whom Hagar the Egyptian had borne to Abraham, was playing with Sarah's son Isaac. Sarah saw them and said to Abraham, "Send this slave-girl and her son away. The son of this woman must not get any part of your wealth, which my son Isaac should inherit." This troubled Abraham very much, because Ishmael was also his son. But God said to Abraham, "Don't be worried about the boy and your slave Hagar. Do whatever Sarah tells you, because it is through Isaac that you will have the descendants I have promised. I will also give many children to the son of the slave-girl, so that they will become a nation. He too is your son."

Early the next morning Abraham gave Hagar some food and a leather bag full of water. He put the child on her back and sent her away.

Genesis 21:9–14

✠

When Abraham and Sarah had tried to help God's plan along, they made a lot of trouble.

Ishmael was already Abraham's son, and that meant that there was jealousy between him and Isaac, to say nothing of teasing and bullying.

In the end, the time came when Ishmael and his mother had to leave. But God knew all about it. He had a plan to take care of Hagar and Ishmael, and Abraham simply had to trust that all would be well. But what a lot of heartache! And what a difficult choice for Abraham.

✠

Lord, forgive us when we go against your will. Thank you that you use even our mistakes to build up our trust in you.

✠ ✠ ✠ ✠ ✠

January 10

Hagar left and wandered about in the wilderness of Beersheba. When the water was all gone, she left the child under a bush and sat down about a hundred metres away. She said to herself, "I can't bear to see my child die." While she was sitting there, she began to cry.

God heard the boy crying, and from heaven the angel of God spoke to Hagar, "What are you troubled about, Hagar? Don't be afraid. God has heard the boy crying. Get up, go and pick him up, and comfort him. I will make a great nation out of his descendants." Then God opened her eyes, and she saw a well. She went and filled the leather bag with water and gave some to the boy. God was with the boy as he grew up; he lived in the wilderness of Paran and became a skilful hunter. His mother found an Egyptian wife for him.

Genesis 21:14–21

✠

What a wonderful God we have!

Things couldn't have been worse for Hagar. She had been driven away from home, had wandered in the desert until she was exhausted, and then half-dragged, half-carried Ishmael to the shelter of a bush. She had left him to die.

But God heard Ishmael's cry, and reached out to comfort Hagar and show her a well of life-giving water.

Why is it so often only when we are in desperate need that we turn to God?

✠

Lord, thank you that even when the worst happens, you are close to help.

✠ ✠ ✠ ✠ ✠

January 11

Some time later God tested Abraham; he called to him, "Abraham!" And Abraham answered, "Yes, here I am!"

"Take your son," God said, "your only son, Isaac, whom you love so much, and go to the land of Moriah. There on a mountain that I will show you, offer him as a sacrifice to me."

Early the next morning Abraham cut some wood for the sacrifice, loaded his donkey, and took Isaac and two servants with him. They started out for the place that God had told him about. On the third day Abraham saw the place in the distance. Then he said to the servants, "Stay here with the donkey. The boy and I will go over there and worship, and then we will come back to you."

Abraham made Isaac carry the wood for the sacrifice, and he himself carried a knife and live coals for starting the fire. As they walked along together, Isaac said, "Father!"

He answered, "Yes, my son?"

Isaac asked, "I see that you have the coals and the wood, but where is the lamb for the sacrifice?"

Abraham answered, "God himself will provide one." And the two of them walked on together.

Genesis 22:1–8

✠

This was surely Abraham's greatest test.

Maybe he had looked at the tribes around, where some people showed their fear of God by sacrificing their children. Maybe he had wondered, "Could I ever do that – or does my son mean more to me than God?"

So God tested Abraham. But never with a view to getting him to kill his precious son. He only wanted to strengthen his faith.

✠

Lord, when you ask us to go through with something hard, or call us to give up something we treasure, help us to trust that you know best.

✠ ✠ ✠ ✠ ✠

January 12

When they came to the place which God had told him about, Abraham built an altar and arranged the wood on it. He bound his son and placed him on the altar, on top of the wood. Then he picked up the knife to kill him. But the angel of the LORD called to him from heaven, "Abraham, Abraham!"

He answered, "Yes, here I am."

"Don't hurt the boy or do anything to him," he said. "Now I know that you fear God, because you have not kept back your only son from him."

Abraham looked round and saw a ram caught in a bush by its horns. He went and got it and offered it as a burnt-offering instead of his son. Abraham named that place "The LORD Provides".

Genesis 22:9–14

✠

The only way to know whether God is to be trusted is to follow his promptings.

Abraham had learned over many years that God could be trusted – absolutely. "The Lord provides" was not just the name of a place – it was Abraham's family motto.

To offer God any sacrifice will never do us harm. God will never allow any sacrifice to hurt us. All that happens, when we obey the Lord's prompting, is that he brings us through his testing into a new place of assurance and blessing.

✠

Lord, thank you that you are always on our side, and want the very best for us.

✠ ✠ ✠ ✠ ✠

January 13

Abraham was now very old, and the LORD had blessed him in everything he did. He said to his oldest servant, who was in charge of all that he had, "I want you to make a vow in the name of the LORD, the God of heaven and earth, that you will not choose a wife for my son from the people here in Canaan. You must go back to the country where I was born and get a wife for my son Isaac from among my relatives."

The servant took ten of his master's camels and went to the city where Nahor had lived in northern Mesopotamia. When he arrived, he made the camels kneel down at the well outside the city. It was late afternoon, the time when women came out to get water. He prayed, "LORD, God of my master Abraham, give me success today and keep your promise to my master. Here I am at the well where the young women of the city will be coming to get water. I will say to one of them, 'Please, lower your jar and let me have a drink.' If she says, 'Drink, and I will also bring water for your camels,' may she be the one that you have chosen for your servant Isaac. If this happens, I will know that you have kept your promise to my master."

Genesis 24:1–4,10–13

✠

When you think about it, we don't choose our parents. Nor do we choose our brothers, sisters – or children. But we *do* choose whom we marry.

The time has come for Isaac to choose a wife, and Abraham is concerned that he should meet and marry the right girl. It was important to find *God's* choice, and that Isaac's wife should be a woman of faith in the Living God.

Abraham's servant is a wonderful man. He really puts his master's interests before his own. And, after all, if Abraham had had no child, that servant would have inherited his master's wealth – so he is being doubly selfless.

✠

Lord, help us to make our life-choices in a careful and prayerful way, looking for your choice for us.

✠ ✠ ✠ ✠ ✠

January 14

Before Abraham's servant had finished praying, Rebecca arrived with a water-jar on her shoulder. She was the daughter of Bethuel, who was the son of Abraham's brother Nahor and his wife Milcah. She was a very beautiful young girl and still a virgin. She went down to the well, filled her jar, and came back. The servant ran to meet her and said, "Please give me a drink of water from your jar."

She said, "Drink, sir," and quickly lowered her jar from her shoulder and held it while he drank. When he had finished, she said, "I will also bring water for your camels and let them have all they want." She quickly emptied her jar into the animals' drinking-trough and ran to the well to get more water, until she had watered all his camels. The man kept watching her in silence, to see if the LORD had given him success.

When she had finished, the man took an expensive gold ring and put it in her nose and put two large gold bracelets on her arms. He said, "Please tell me who your father is. Is there room in his house for my men and me to spend the night?"

"My father is Bethuel son of Nahor and Milcah," she answered. "There is plenty of straw and fodder at our house, and there is a place for you to stay."

Then the man knelt down and worshipped the LORD. He said, "Praise the LORD, the God of my master Abraham, who has faithfully kept his promise to my master. The LORD has led me straight to my master's relatives."

Genesis 24:15–27

✠

When we ask God to guide our choices, he doesn't tease us or play hard to get.

In all the teeming population, God leads Abraham's servant straight to Rebecca, and we immediately begin to see that she is as hard-working as she is beautiful.

Many servants would have been tempted to congratulate themselves on their sharp wits and good taste – but not Abraham's servant. He falls on his knees and praises God. He is delighted for Abraham, pleased for Isaac, and thankful that he has been of use.

✠

Lord, please show us the ways in which we can be useful to others today.

✠ ✠ ✠ ✠ ✠

January 15

At Rebecca's home, Abraham's servant meets her crafty brother Laban. Laban has already noticed the bracelets and jewels on his sister's arms and neck, and is keen to arrange the marriage. Abraham's servant faithfully tells them of his errand.

✠

Laban and Bethuel answered, "Since this matter comes from the LORD, it is not for us to make a decision. Here is Rebecca; take her and go. Let her become the wife of your master's son, as the LORD himself has said." When the servant of Abraham heard this, he bowed down and worshipped the LORD. Then he brought out clothing and silver and gold jewellery, and gave them to Rebecca. He also gave expensive gifts to her brother and to her mother.

But Rebecca's brother and her mother said, "Let the girl stay with us a week or ten days, and then she may go."

But he said, "Don't make us stay. The LORD has made my journey a success; let me go back to my master."

They answered, "Let's call the girl and find out what she has to say." So they called Rebecca and asked, "Do you want to go with this man?"

"Yes," she answered.

So they let Rebecca and her old family servant go with Abraham's servant and his men. And they gave Rebecca their blessing in these words:

> "May you, sister, become the mother of millions!
> May your descendants conquer the cities of their
> enemies!"

Then Rebecca and her young women got ready and mounted the camels to go with Abraham's servant, and they all started out.

Genesis 24:50–53,55–61

✠

When Laban and his mother try to play for time, Abraham's servant refuses to stay. When we're clear about God's way for us, it's best to get on with it. No good can come of delay.

✠

Lord, please help us both to find out your will for us, and to do it.

✠ ✠ ✠ ✠ ✠

January 16

And so we say goodbye to Abraham. Today we have two readings which look back at his life.

✠

Abraham died at the ripe old age of a hundred and seventy-five. His sons Isaac and Ishmael buried him in Machpelah Cave. It was the field that Abraham had bought from the Hittites; both Abraham and his wife Sarah were buried there.

It was faith that made Abraham obey when God called him to go out to a country which God had promised to give him. He left his own country without knowing where he was going. By faith he lived as a foreigner in the country that God had promised him. He lived in tents, as did Isaac and Jacob, who received the same promise from God. For Abraham was waiting for the city which God has designed and built, the city with permanent foundations.

It was faith that made Abraham able to become a father, even though he was too old and Sarah herself could not have children. He trusted God to keep his promise. Though Abraham was practically dead, from this one man came as many descendants as there are stars in the sky, as many as the numberless grains of sand on the sea-shore.

It was in faith that all these persons died. They did not receive the things God had promised, but from a long way off they saw them and welcomed them, and admitted openly that they were forcigners and refugees on earth.

Genesis 25:7–10
Hebrews 11:8–13

✠

In everything Abraham had learned to look to God – discovering the same God was Lord wherever he went. Indeed, earthly cities might come and go, but Abraham looked forward to life in God's heavenly city, which stands for ever.

On the face of it, Abraham's life was almost a failure. He left behind Isaac (who was hardly a great nation), and a small piece of land (in which his wife was buried). But with God everything is possible, and from that slender start sprang the nation of Israel and the Promised Land. And we, as Christian people, look back to Abraham as our father. He was the first to trust

God simply and completely, and we are truly his descendants when we do the same.

✠

Lord, thank you for the life and example of Abraham. Help us to have faith like his.

✠ ✠ ✠ ✠ ✠

January 17

This is the story of Abraham's son Isaac. Isaac was forty years old when he married Rebecca, the daughter of Bethuel and sister of Laban. Because Rebecca had no children, Isaac prayed to the LORD for her. The LORD answered his prayer, and Rebecca became pregnant. She was going to have twins, and before they were born, they struggled against each other in her womb. She said, "Why should something like this happen to me?" So she went to ask the LORD for an answer.

The LORD said to her,

> "Two nations are within you;
> You will give birth to two rival peoples.
> One will be stronger than the other;
> The older will serve the younger."

The time came for her to give birth, and she had twin sons. The first one was reddish, and his skin was like a hairy robe, so he was named Esau. The second one was born holding on tightly to the heel of Esau, so he was named Jacob.

Genesis 25:19–26

As Isaac comes out from underneath Abraham's shadow, we realize we know very little about him. He seems a quiet, prayerful person. Was he too shy to go in search of his own wife? Or wasn't he really bothered?

And yet Isaac is a vital link in the chain of God's purpose. He and Rebecca are part of the long family line which will run all the way from Abraham to Jesus. Like all families, it will take all sorts and include all sorts, as we shall see.

Meanwhile, Rebecca is expecting twins – and they are at odds with each other before they are even born. And that's the shape of things to come as well!

✠

Lord, thank you that you have made us all different, and that there is a place in your plan for everyone.

✠ ✠ ✠ ✠ ✠

January 18

The boys grew up, and Esau became a skilled hunter, a man who loved the outdoor life, but Jacob was a quiet man who stayed at home. Isaac preferred Esau, because he enjoyed eating the animals Esau killed, but Rebecca preferred Jacob.

One day while Jacob was cooking some bean soup, Esau came in from hunting. He was hungry and said to Jacob, "I'm starving; give me some of that red stuff."

Jacob answered, "I will give it to you if you give me your rights as the first-born son."

Esau said, "All right! I am about to die; what good will my rights do me then?"

Jacob answered, "First make a vow that you will give me your rights."

Esau made the vow and gave his rights to Jacob. Then Jacob gave him some bread and some of the soup. He ate and drank and then got up and left. That was all Esau cared about his rights as the first-born son.

Genesis 25:27–34

✠

Although Esau and Jacob are twins, born on the same day, Esau was born first. It is he who will inherit the lion's share of his father's wealth, and receive the special blessing from Isaac – a blessing which can only be given once.

Esau and Jacob are as different as chalk from cheese. Esau is a man of action, who speaks first and thinks afterwards. Jacob is a schemer, who prefers to stay at home with his mother. Unfortunately, Jacob and Rebecca spend most of their time plotting against Esau. Jacob is determined to steal the birthright, and Rebecca has plans to steal the blessing.

✠

Lord, help us to be thankful for our brothers and sisters, rather than spiteful or jealous. As you have made us all different, may we use our differences to help each other.

✠ ✠ ✠ ✠ ✠

January 19

Isaac was now old and had become blind. He sent for his elder son Esau and said to him, "My son!"

"Yes," he answered.

Isaac said, "You see that I am old and may die soon. Take your bow and arrows, go out into the country, and kill an animal for me. Cook me some of that tasty food that I like, and bring it to me. After I have eaten it, I will give you my final blessing before I die."

While Isaac was talking to Esau, Rebecca was listening. So when Esau went out to hunt, she said to Jacob, "I have just heard your father say to Esau, 'Bring me an animal and cook it for me. After I have eaten it, I will give you my blessing in the presence of the LORD before I die.' Now, my son," Rebecca continued, "listen to me and do what I say. Go to the flock and pick out two fat young goats, so that I can cook them and make some of that food your father likes so much. You can take it to him to eat, and he will give you his blessing before he dies."

But Jacob said to his mother, "You know that Esau is a hairy man, but I have smooth skin. Perhaps my father will touch me and find out that I am deceiving him; in this way I will bring a curse on myself instead of a blessing."

His mother answered, "Let any curse against you fall on me, my son; just do as I say, and go and get the goats for me."

Genesis 27:1–13

✠

We begin to see where Jacob gets his scheming nature and crafty ideas. They come from his mum!

Jacob is to become one of the Bible's greatest men. One day his name will be Israel, and a whole nation will be called his children.

But the Bible tells us bluntly that he was a very unpleasant character – jealous, deceitful, and willing to go to great lengths to get his own way. But in God's good time, Jacob will grow in faith and change his ways.

✠

Lord, you know that not one of us is perfect. Thank you that you start from where we are – greedy, mean and selfish – and offer us your wonderful new life.

✠ ✠ ✠ ✠ ✠

January 20

So Jacob went to get the goats and brought them to his mother, Rebecca and she cooked the kind of food that his father liked. Then she took Esau's best clothes, which she kept in the house, and put them on Jacob. She put the skins of the goats on his arms and on the hairless part of his neck. She handed him the tasty food, together with the bread she had baked.

Then Jacob went to his father and said, "Father!"

"Yes," he answered. "Which of my sons are you?"

Jacob answered, "I am your elder son Esau; I have done as you told me. Please sit up and eat some of the meat that I have brought you, so that you can give me your blessing."

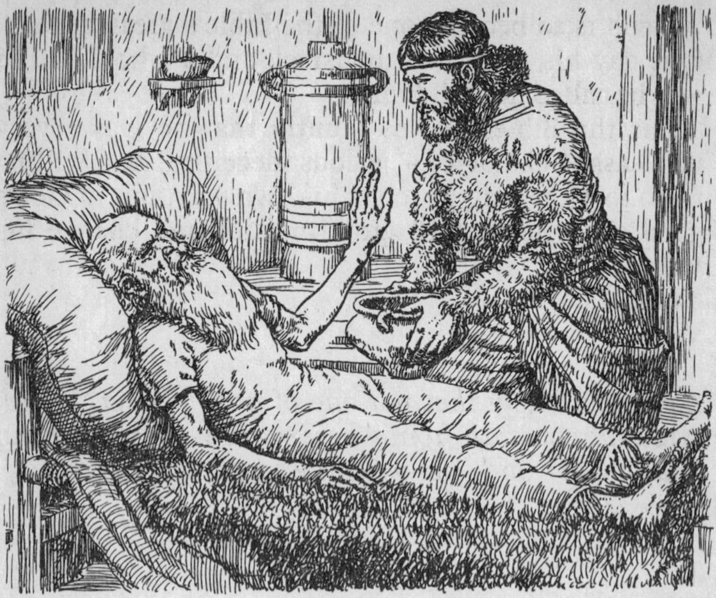

Isaac said, "How did you find it so quickly, my son?"

Jacob answered, "The LORD your God helped me to find it."

Isaac said to Jacob, "Please come closer so that I can touch you. Are you really Esau?" Jacob moved closer to his father, who felt him and said, "Your voice sounds like Jacob's voice, but your arms feel like Esau's arms." He did not recognize Jacob, because his arms were hairy like Esau's. He was about to give him his blessing, but asked again, "Are you really Esau?"

"I am," he answered.

Isaac said, "Bring me some of the meat. After I have eaten it, I will give you my blessing." Jacob brought it to him and he also brought him some wine to drink. Then his father said to him, "Come closer and kiss me, my son." As he came up to kiss him, Isaac smelt his clothes – so he gave him his blessing.

Genesis 27:14–27

✠

It would be funny if it weren't so terrible. Jacob pretending to be Esau – putting on a husky voice and smelling like a goat. And old Isaac not even able to tell the difference!

But to hear Jacob telling one lie after another, and dragging God's name in for good measure – well, that seems dreadful.

But that's how we all are when we want to get our own way, isn't it?

✠

Lord, please forgive us. Forgive us the lies we tell and the mean tricks we play. Forgive us when we pretend to be better than we are. Help us instead to live open and truthful lives, so that others can trust us, and so that we bring credit to you.

✠ ✠ ✠ ✠ ✠

January 21

Isaac finished giving his blessing, and as soon as Jacob left, his brother Esau came in from hunting. He also cooked some tasty food and took it to his father. He said, "Please, father, sit up and eat some of the meat that I have brought you, so that you can give me your blessing."

"Who are you?" Isaac asked.

"Your elder son Esau," he answered.

Isaac began to tremble and shake all over, and he asked, "Who was it, then, who killed an animal and brought it to me? I ate it just before you came. I gave him my final blessing, and so it is his for ever."

When Esau heard this, he cried out loudly and bitterly and said, "Give me your blessing also, father!"

Isaac answered, "Your brother came and deceived me. He has taken away your blessing."

Esau said, "This is the second time that he has cheated me. He took my rights as the first-born son, and now he has taken away my blessing. Haven't you saved a blessing for me?"

Then Isaac said to him,

"No dew from heaven for you,
No fertile fields for you.
You will live by your sword,
But be your brother's slave.
Yet when you rebel,
You will break away from his control."

Esau hated Jacob, because his father had given Jacob the blessing. He thought, "The time to mourn my father's death is near; then I will kill Jacob."

Genesis 27:30–36,39–41

✠

Poor Esau! He has been well and truly robbed – and perhaps he only values the blessing now that he can't have it.

We really don't know why God preferred Jacob to Esau, choosing Jacob to be the father of the Israelites and the ancestor of Jesus. But we see that God is the champion of the outsider, and that he can bring good out of evil. And he can change lives – even someone like Jacob, a nasty little stay-at-home mummy's boy, can become a mighty man of God.

✠

Lord, you are a great God who can change lives. Please change our selfishness to love today, and our anger to kindness.

✠ ✠ ✠ ✠ ✠

January 22

Jacob has had to run for his life, with Esau's threats still ringing in his ears.

✠

Jacob left Beersheba and started towards Haran. At sunset he came to a holy place and camped there. He lay down to sleep, resting his head on a stone. He dreamt that he saw a stairway reaching from earth to heaven, with angels going up and coming down on it. And there was the LORD standing beside him. "I am the LORD, the God of Abraham and Isaac," he said. "I will give to you and to your descendants this land on which you are lying. They will be as numerous as the specks of dust on the earth. They will extend their territory in all directions, and through you and your descendants I will bless all the nations. Remember, I will be with you and protect you wherever you go, and

I will bring you back to this land. I will not leave you until I have done all that I have promised you."

Genesis 28:10–15

✠

Alone and far from home, Jacob lies down to sleep. And in his dream he meets with God.

For many of us it's only when we leave home – to travel, or go to college, or get a job – that we begin to think twice about God. Is he real? Does he care about me?

Jacob found without a shadow of doubt that the answer to both these questions is "yes". The God of his father and grandfather was to be his God too. The land which had been promised to them was now promised to him as well.

✠

Lord, thank you that there's nowhere in the world that we can go where we are away from you. And thank you that you can use even our lonely moments to speak to us in a new way.

✠ ✠ ✠ ✠ ✠

January 23

Jacob woke up and said, "The LORD is here! He is in this place, and I didn't know it!" He was afraid and said, "What a terrifying place this is! It must be the house of God; it must be the gate that opens into heaven."

Jacob got up early next morning, took the stone that was under his head, and set it up as a memorial. Then he poured olive-oil on it to dedicate it to God. He named the place Bethel. (The town there was once known as Luz.) Then Jacob made a vow to the LORD: "If you will be with me and protect me on the journey I am making and give me food and clothing, and if I return safely to my father's home, then you will be my God. This memorial stone which I have set up will be the place where you are worshipped, and I will give you a tenth of everything you give me."

Genesis 28:16–22

✠

Jacob has come face to face with the Living God, but it doesn't stop him being both crafty and shrewd!

He drives a hard bargain. In return for food, clothing and safe travel, Jacob promises to worship God and give him a tenth of all his possessions.

What a cheek! But at least Jacob knows that most important principle of prayer – that we should come to God just as we are, and not try to deceive him with pious talk.

✠

Lord, help us to be honest with you, talking heart to heart, and giving you your due.

✠ ✠ ✠ ✠ ✠

F.B.R.—3

January 24

At the end of his journey, Jacob arrives at the house of his uncle Laban. And there he meets his match!

✠

Laban said to Jacob, "You shouldn't work for me for nothing just because you are my relative. How much pay do you want?" Laban had two daughters; the elder was named Leah, and the younger Rachel. Leah had lovely eyes, but Rachel was shapely and beautiful.

Jacob was in love with Rachel, so he said, "I will work seven years for you, if you will let me marry Rachel."

Laban answered, "I would rather give her to you than to anyone else; stay here with me." Jacob worked seven years so that he could have Rachel, and the time seemed like only a few days to him, because he loved her.

Then Jacob said to Laban, "The time is up; let me marry your daughter." So Laban gave a wedding-feast and invited everyone. But that night, instead of Rachel, he took Leah to Jacob. Not until the next morning did Jacob discover that it was Leah. He went to Laban and said, "Why did you do this to me? I worked to get Rachel. Why have you tricked me?"

Laban answered, "It is not the custom here to give the younger daughter in marriage before the elder. Wait until the week's marriage celebrations are over, and I will give you Rachel, if you will work for me another seven years."

Genesis 29:15–23,25–27

✠

Laban can out-manoeuvre Jacob any time with the lovely Rachel as his bargaining counter. He squeezes fourteen years of hard labour out of Jacob, as well as getting him to take both daughters off his hands. And again we have to laugh – this time at Jacob, in the darkness of the night and the haze of the wedding feast, reeling off to his room with the wrong wife!

And yet Leah wasn't the wrong wife for Jacob. She may not have been as shapely as Rachel, but she was to be the mother of many fine sons – indeed, half the children of Israel.

✠

Lord, thank you for overruling in all our affairs, and harnessing our desires to your perfect plan.

✠ ✠ ✠ ✠ ✠

January 25

In the end, Jacob and his wives had to run away from Laban – it was the only way to escape so powerful and cunning a man.

But looming ahead was Esau. Esau who was last heard of threatening to murder his little brother Jacob!

✠

Jacob sent messengers ahead of him to his brother Esau in the country of Edom. He instructed them to say: "I, Jacob, your obedient servant, report to my master Esau that I have been staying with Laban and that I have delayed my return until now. I own cattle, donkeys, sheep, goats, and slaves. I am sending you word, sir, in the hope of gaining your favour."

When the messengers came back to Jacob, they said, "We went to your brother Esau, and he is already on his way to meet you. He has four hundred men with him." Jacob was frightened and worried. He divided into two groups the people who were with him, and also his sheep, goats, cattle, and camels. He thought, "If Esau comes and attacks the first group, the other may be able to escape."

Then Jacob prayed, "God of my grandfather Abraham and God of my father Isaac, hear me! You told me, LORD, to go back to my land and to my relatives, and you would make everything go well for me. I am not worth all the kindness and faithfulness that you have shown me, your servant. I crossed the Jordan with nothing but a walking-stick, and now I have come back with these two groups. Save me, I pray, from my brother Esau. I am afraid – afraid that he is coming to attack us and destroy us all, even the women and children."

Genesis 32:3–11

✠

Jacob has changed over the years. He gives God much more credit for his success and well-being. But the biggest test is yet to come, and Jacob is terrified.

In his fear, he prays as he has never prayed before. No hard bargaining this time, but a heartfelt cry that God will do what only he can do – save him from the wrath of Esau.

✠

Lord, thank you that in our need we can always turn to you. Please forgive us when we forget to be in touch in between times.

January 26

That same night Jacob got up, took his two wives, his two concubines, and his eleven children, and crossed the River Jabbok. After he had sent them across, he also sent across all that he owned, but he stayed behind, alone.

Then a man came and wrestled with him until just before daybreak. When the man saw that he was not winning the struggle, he struck Jacob on the hip, and it was thrown out of joint. The man said,"Let me go; daylight is coming."

"I won't, unless you bless me," Jacob answered.

"What is your name?" the man asked.

"Jacob," he answered.

The man said, "Your name will no longer be Jacob. You have struggled with God and with men, and you have won; so your name will be Israel."

Jacob said, "Now tell me your name."

But he answered, "Why do you want to know my name?" Then he blessed Jacob.

Jacob said, "I have seen God face to face, and I am still alive"; so he named the place Peniel. The sun rose as Jacob was leaving Peniel, and he was limping because of his hip.

Genesis 32:22–31

✠

All through the night Jacob wrestles.

He wonders what will happen to him the following day, and what will become of his family. Are the promises of God and the years of hard work to come to nothing?

But Jacob is a fighter. All night he struggles, not just with his conscience or his problems, but with God.

And in the morning, God gives him a new name – Israel: "He who struggles with God".

From time to time we all have nights of doubt and sorrow, fear and self-pity. But even in the darkness and loneliness we can begin to glimpse God's future, and the way he can use our problems for his glory.

✠

Lord, when we make a mess of things, thank you that you don't say, "I told you so", or give up on us. And thank you that after dark nights of doubt, there are bright mornings of joy.

✠ ✠ ✠ ✠ ✠

January 27

Jacob saw Esau coming with his four hundred men, so he divided the children among Leah, Rachel, and the two concubines. He put the concubines and their children first, then Leah and her children, and finally Rachel and Joseph at the rear. Jacob went ahead of them and bowed down to the ground seven times as he approached his brother. But Esau ran to meet him, threw his arms round him and kissed him. They were both crying. When Esau looked round and saw the women and the children, he asked, "Who are these people with you?"

"These, sir, are the children whom God has been good enough to give me," Jacob answered. Then the concubines came up with their children and bowed down; then Leah and her children came, and last of all Joseph and Rachel came and bowed down.

Esau asked, "What about that other group I met? What did that mean?"

Jacob answered, "It was to gain your favour."

But Esau said, "I have enough, my brother; keep what you have."

Jacob said, "No, please, if I have gained your favour, accept my gift. To see your face is for me like seeing the face of God, now that you have been so friendly to me. Please accept this gift which I have brought for you; God has been kind to me and given me everything I need." Jacob kept on urging him until he accepted.

Genesis 33:1–11

✠

In the end, all Jacob's heart-searching and planning prove quite unnecessary.

Esau has long since forgiven Jacob (or, knowing Esau, simply forgotten all about it!). Instead, he is deeply moved to meet his twin brother again, and to discover two sisters-in-law and eleven nephews he never knew he had.

And Jacob? Maybe he began to wonder what all the panic had been about.

✠

Lord, help us to trust you with our problems, and to look confidently for your provision and safe keeping.

✠ ✠ ✠ ✠ ✠

January 28

Now we leave Abraham, Isaac and Jacob, and leap forward two thousand years to the time of Jesus. Jesus is now about thirty years old, having lived with his family in the north country town of Nazareth for the whole of that time. Meanwhile, his cousin John has turned out to be a fiery preacher.

✠

At that time John the Baptist came to the desert of Judaea and started preaching. "Turn away from your sins," he said, "because the Kingdom of heaven is near!" John was the man the prophet Isaiah was talking about when he said,

> "Someone is shouting in the desert,
> 'Prepare a road for the Lord;
> make a straight path for him to travel!'"

John's clothes were made of camel's hair; he wore a leather belt round his waist, and his food was locusts and wild honey. People came to him from Jerusalem, from the whole province of Judaea, and from all the country near the River Jordan. They confessed their sins, and he baptized them in the Jordan.

Matthew 3:1–6

✠

John was nicknamed "the Baptist" because he plunged people in the river Jordan. It was a kind of public wash to show that the person was turning away from his old selfishness and sins, and getting clean – ready to meet with God.

John is every inch a prophet – dressed like Elijah of old, and calling on people to make room in their hearts and lives for the coming King, the Messiah.

No prophet has appeared in Israel for hundreds of years, and John is big news. People travel from far and wide to hear him, and many respond to his preaching by being baptized.

✠

Lord, thank you for those who dare to preach your message boldly, so that many people can turn to you for a new start in life.

✠ ✠ ✠ ✠ ✠

January 29

The people asked John, "What are we to do, then?"

He answered, "Whoever has two shirts must give one to the man who has none, and whoever has food must share it."

Some tax collectors came to be baptized, and they asked him, "Teacher, what are we to do?"

"Don't collect more than is legal," he told them.

Some soldiers also asked him, "What about us? What are we to do?"

He said to them, "Don't take money from anyone by force or accuse anyone falsely. Be content with your pay."

People's hopes began to rise, and they began to wonder whether John perhaps might be the Messiah. So John said to all of them, "I baptize you with water, but someone is coming who is much greater than I am. I am not good enough even to untie his sandals. He will baptize you with the Holy Spirit and fire. He has his winnowing shovel with him, to thresh out all the grain and gather the wheat into his barn; but he will burn the chaff in a fire that never goes out."

Luke 3:10–17

✠

After people have been baptized, John gives them advice on how to live in a way that pleases God. He tells those who are well off to share with those who are poor. He tells tax collectors to be fair, and soldiers not to be greedy or bullying.

Although John is the man of the moment, with thousands of admirers, he remains humble and poor. All the time he looks out for the arrival of the Messiah. And he warns that when God's King comes, there will be a dreadful day of reckoning – like the sorting out at harvest time, with the good grain gathered in and the chaff destroyed.

✠

Lord, please help us to share the good things we have, and to be honest and fair – so that you can be pleased with the harvest of our lives.

✠ ✠ ✠ ✠ ✠

January 30

At that time Jesus arrived from Galilee and came to John at the Jordan to be baptized by him. But John tried to make him change his mind. "I ought to be baptized by you," John said, "and yet you have come to me!"

But Jesus answered him, "Let it be so for now. For in this way we shall do all that God requires." So John agreed.

As soon as Jesus was baptized, he came up out of the water. Then heaven was opened to him, and he saw the Spirit of God coming down like a dove and alighting on him. Then a voice said from heaven, "This is my own dear Son, with whom I am pleased."

Matthew 3:13–17

✠

When Jesus comes to be baptized, John can hardly believe his eyes. After all, what has Jesus done that he should have to wade into the muddy waters of the Jordan for a wash? But Jesus insists. he wants to be counted with God's people in everything, including repentance.

And when he is baptized, God the Father sends his Spirit afresh on his Son. And he announces who Jesus is, so that Jesus can now begin his public work.

✠

Lord, thank you that Jesus came to be one of us, with no special treatment, and no shortcuts.

✠ ✠ ✠ ✠ ✠

January 31

The next day John saw Jesus coming to him, and said, "There is the Lamb of God, who takes away the sin of the world! This is the one I was talking about when I said, 'A man is coming after me, but he is greater than I am, because he existed before I was born.' I did not know who he would be, but I came baptizing with water in order to make him known to the people of Israel."

And John gave this testimony: "I saw the Spirit come down like a dove from heaven and stay on him. I still did not know that he was the one, but God, who sent me to baptize with water, had said to me, 'You will see the Spirit come down and stay on a man; he is the one who baptizes with the Holy Spirit.' I have seen it," said John, "and I tell you that he is the Son of God."

John 1:29–34

✠

When John sees Jesus coming, he says, "There is the Lamb of God!" For us, a lamb is an adorable, cuddly creature. But for the Jews, it was an animal they often used as a sacrifice. Once a year, each family would kill one of its very best lambs, to show God how sorry they were for the wrong things they had done.

When John calls Jesus "the Lamb of God", it shows that he understands that Jesus has come to die – to lay down his life as a sacrifice for the sins of the world.

✠

Dear God our Father, help us to be sure about Jesus, to recognize him as our Saviour and serve him as our Lord.

A Psalm for
February

O LORD, our Lord,
  your greatness is seen in all the world!
Your praise reaches up to the heavens;
  it is sung by children and babies.
You are safe and secure from all your enemies;
  you stop anyone who opposes you.

When I look at the sky, which you have made,
  at the moon and the stars, which you
    set in their places –
what is man, that you think of him;
  mere man, that you care for him?

Yet you made him inferior only to yourself;
  you crowned him with glory and honour.
You appointed him ruler over
    everything you made;
  you placed him over all creation:
  sheep and cattle, and the wild animals too;
  the birds and the fish
  and the creatures in the seas.

O LORD, our Lord,
  your greatness is seen in all the world!

Psalm 8

February 1

The next day John was standing there again with two of his disciples, when he saw Jesus walking by. "There is the Lamb of God!" he said.

The two disciples heard him say this and went with Jesus. Jesus turned, saw them following him, and asked, "What are you looking for?"

They answered, "Where do you live, Rabbi?" (This word means "Teacher".)

"Come and see," he answered. (It was then about four o'clock in the afternoon.) So they went with him and saw where he lived, and spent the rest of that day with him.

One of them was Andrew, Simon Peter's brother. At once he found his brother Simon and told him, "We have found the Messiah." (This word means "Christ".) Then he took Simon to Jesus.

Jesus looked at him and said, "Your name is Simon son of John, but you will be called Cephas." (This is the same as Peter and means "a rock".)

John 1:35–42

✠

Andrew is the very first disciple – and a very good one, too. We often find him being the link between other people and Jesus. For example, as soon as he finds out where Jesus lives, he is off to fetch his brother Simon. Before long, Simon is meeting Jesus for himself, and being given a surprising nickname – Peter, or "Rocky". From now on Andrew will always be in Peter's shadow, but without him Jesus and Peter might never have met.

✠

Lord Jesus, help us to bring our friends to you in a happy and unselfish way – not keeping you from them because we're jealous nor keeping them from you because we're shy.

✠ ✠ ✠ ✠ ✠

February 2

Jesus returned from the Jordan full of the Holy Spirit and was led by the Spirit into the desert, where he was tempted by the Devil for forty days. In all that time he ate nothing, so that he was hungry when it was over.

The Devil said to him, "If you are God's Son, order this stone to turn into bread."

But Jesus answered, "The scripture says, 'Man cannot live on bread alone.'"

Then the Devil took him up and showed him in a second all the kingdoms of the world. "I will give you all this power and all this wealth," the Devil told him. "It has all been handed over to me, and I can give it to anyone I choose. All this will be yours, then, if you worship me."

Jesus answered, "The scripture says, 'Worship the Lord your God and serve only him!'"

Luke 4:1–8

✠

Whenever God does something special, the Devil tries to spoil it. No sooner is Jesus baptized and his public life beginning, than the Devil mounts a savage attack.

The temptations were *real*, and Jesus is sorely tested. But through them he learns vital lessons about the kind of Messiah he is to be.

He refuses to turn stones to bread despite his hunger, because God's power can never be used for magic or for selfish greed.

He refuses to worship the Devil, because Satan is the very one whose power he has come to destroy. Of course, Jesus would have loved to rule the world, with all the armies and navies at his command. But if that meant teaming up with the Devil, he could never do it.

And do you notice that Jesus fights off Satan's attacks with verses from scripture? Maybe that's something we can learn to do.

✠

Lord Jesus, thank you for standing firm in the face of all the Devil's attacks. Please stand with us in our battles, so that we may do the same.

✠ ✠ ✠ ✠ ✠

February 3

Then the Devil took him to Jerusalem and set him on the highest point of the Temple, and said to him, "If you are God's Son, throw yourself down from here. For the scripture says, 'God will order his angels to take good care of you.' It also says, 'They will hold you up with their hands so that not even your feet will be hurt on the stones.'"

But Jesus answered, "The scripture says, 'Do not put the Lord your God to the test.'"

When the Devil finished tempting Jesus in every way, he left him for a while.

Then Jesus returned to Galilee, and the power of the Holy Spirit was with him. The news about him spread throughout all that territory. He taught in the synagogues and was praised by everyone.

Luke 4:9–15

✠

Satan is getting desperate. He even tries to quote a bit of the Bible himself, as he challenges Jesus to a daring publicity stunt.

But Jesus knows that God's way is never sensational. He can never draw people to God's love through tricks and gimmicks.

In the end, the Devil leaves Jesus for a while. But only for a while. He knows he has pressed Jesus very hard, and he will be back with the same temptations in different disguises in the coming months and years.

✠

Lord Jesus, we are going to be tempted in some way or other every day of our life. Please keep us in these times of trial, so that Satan may never have his way.

February 4

Then Jesus went to Nazareth, where he had been brought up, and on the Sabbath he went as usual to the synagogue. He stood up to read the scriptures and was handed the book of the prophet Isaiah. He unrolled the scroll and found the place where it is written,

"The Spirit of the Lord is upon me,
  because he has chosen me to bring
    good news to the poor.
  He has sent me to proclaim liberty to
    the captives
  and recovery of sight to the blind;
  to set free the oppressed
  and announce that the time has come
  when the Lord will save his people."

Jesus rolled up the scroll, gave it back to the attendant, and sat down. All the people in the synagogue had their eyes fixed on him, as he said to them, "This passage of scripture has come true today, as you heard it being read."

Luke 4:16–21

✠

It is hard for Jesus to be back in Nazareth. So many people know him – or think they do. Most of his family and friends are there, as well as those who were at school with him, and those who used to come to his workshop.

When he reads the words from Isaiah about God's Servant bringing good news of freedom and healing, they listen carefully. After all, there may be something in it for them. If Jesus is going to be famous, then Nazareth will be famous too.

Lord Jesus, we are often too full of ourselves to give you our full attention. Please hush the noise of our wilfulness and pride, and help us to give you first place in our lives.

✠ ✠ ✠ ✠ ✠

February 5

They were all well impressed with him and marvelled at the eloquent words that he spoke. They said, "Isn't he the son of Joseph?"

He said to them, "I am sure that you will quote this proverb to me, 'Doctor, heal yourself.' You will also tell me to do here in my home town the same things you heard were done in Capernaum. I tell you this," Jesus added, "a prophet is never welcomed in his home town.

"Listen to me: it is true that there were many widows in Israel during the time of Elijah, when there was no rain for three and a half years and a severe famine spread throughout the whole land. Yet Elijah was not sent to anyone in Israel, but only to a widow living in Zarephath in the territory of Sidon. And there were many people suffering from a dreaded skin-disease who lived in Israel during the time of the prophet Elisha; yet not one of them was healed, but only Naaman the Syrian."

When the people in the synagogue heard this, they were filled with anger. They rose up, dragged Jesus out of the town, and took him to the top of the hill on which their town was built. They meant to throw him over the cliff, but he walked through the middle of the crowd and went his way.

Luke 4:22–30

The people of Nazareth are all agog. They want to see Jesus do something exciting to prove he is the Messiah. To prove that prophecy is being fulfilled before their very eyes.

But Jesus explains that he hasn't come to perform tricks for them. Nor is he their personal property. Like Elijah and Elisha, the prophets of long ago, Jesus will be helping and healing some very unlikely people, some of whom will be outside the Jewish faith altogether.

This makes the Nazareth folk see red! In fact they are so angry and jealous that they try to kill Jesus there and then. But somehow he simply walks through the crowd and goes on his way.

✠

Lord Jesus, thank you that you didn't come to save an in-crowd or a clique. You came for people who were far away from God. People like us.

✠ ✠ ✠ ✠ ✠

February 6

Then Jesus went to Capernaum, a town in Galilee, where he taught the people on the Sabbath. They were all amazed at the way he taught, because he spoke with authority. In the synagogue was a man who had the spirit of an evil demon in him; he screamed out in a loud voice, "Ah! What do you want with us, Jesus of Nazareth? Are you here to destroy us? I know who you are: you are God's holy messenger!"

Jesus ordered the spirit, "Be quiet and come out of the man!" The demon threw the man down in front of them and went out of him without doing him any harm.

The people were all amazed and said to one another, "What kind of words are these? With authority and power this man gives orders to the evil spirits, and they come out!" And the report about Jesus spread everywhere in that region.

Luke 4:31–37

✠

Jesus makes his home in the seaside town of Capernaum. And the people there really appreciate him. There is something very striking about the way he teaches. Power seems to come from inside him, and what he says rings true.

They find with Jesus that his talk and his life go together. He doesn't just talk about the power of God's Kingdom – he shows it. As when he orders the demon to come out of a man and leave him alone. They have never seen anything like it!

✠

Lord Jesus, you are the living truth. Truth in action. Truth which sets us free. Thank you!

✠ ✠ ✠ ✠ ✠

February 7

Jesus left the synagogue and went to Simon's house. Simon's mother-in-law was sick with a high fever, and they spoke to Jesus about her. He went and stood at her bedside and ordered the fever to leave her. The fever left her, and she got up at once and began to wait on them.

After sunset all who had friends who were sick with various diseases brought them to Jesus; he placed his hands on every one of them and healed them all. Demons also went out from many people, screaming, "You are the Son of God!"

Jesus gave the demons an order and would not let them speak, because they knew that he was the Messiah.

Luke 4:38–41

✠

Jesus has the power of God in his life. He talks to illness and tells it to be off. He gives demons their marching orders. (And notice that evil spirits recognize Jesus as the Son of God, even if human beings don't!)

And when the Sabbath rest ends and people can once more shoulder heavy loads, it's to Jesus that they bring their diseased and paralysed friends.

All the same, Jesus stops the demons from crying out that he is the Messiah. There were some very strange ideas about the Messiah – in particular that he would be a mighty warrior who would lead the Jews to battle against their enemies. Jesus didn't want any such idea about him getting around, because nothing could be further from the truth.

✠

Lord Jesus, as you came to cast out illness and banish evil, give us your saving health today.

✠ ✠ ✠ ✠ ✠

February 8

One day Jesus was standing on the shore of Lake Gennesaret while the people pushed their way up to him to listen to the word of God. He saw two boats pulled up on the beach; the fishermen had left them and were washing the nets. Jesus got into one of the boats – it belonged to Simon – and asked him to push off a little from the shore. Jesus sat in the boat and taught the crowd.

Luke 5:1–3

✠

What a marvellous idea – to use Simon's boat as a pulpit. The people who heard Jesus that day would never forget.

Do we have something Jesus can use? Our legs to run an errand, our hands to help around the house, or our tongues to say a kind word . . .?

✠

Lord Jesus, may we be useful to you today in some way, however small.

✠ ✠ ✠ ✠ ✠

February 9

When Jesus finished speaking, he said to Simon, "Push the boat out further to the deep water, and you and your partners let down your nets for a catch."

"Master," Simon answered, "we worked hard all night long and caught nothing. But if you say so, I will let down the nets." They let them down and caught such a large number of fish that the nets were about to break. So they motioned to their partners in the other boat to come and help them. They came and filled both boats so full of fish that the boats were about to sink. When Simon Peter saw what had happened, he fell on his knees before Jesus and said, "Go away from me, Lord! I am a sinful man!"

He and the others with him were all amazed at the large number of fish they had caught. The same was true of Simon's partners, James and John, the sons of Zebedee. Jesus said to Simon, "Don't be afraid; from now on you will be catching men."

They pulled the boats up on the beach, left everything, and followed Jesus.

Luke 5:4–11

✠

How hard for Peter to take advice on fishing from a carpenter! Especially hard as he has already spent the night out on the lake and caught nothing.

But Simon is learning. When Jesus says he should do something, it's usually well worth doing. And soon they have a record catch which threatens to sink their boats.

Peter immediately realizes that this is none other than the power of God at work. And what can sinful Peter have to do with a holy God? He begs Jesus to go away!

But Jesus has other ideas. He wants these hard-working, all-weather fishermen to come and help him preach the Good News. No more catching fish for food. From now on they'll be catching men for God.

✠

Holy Lord, thank you for coming just where we are, taking us just as we are, and calling us to share in your work.

✠ ✠ ✠ ✠ ✠

February 10

After this, Jesus went out and saw a tax collector named Levi, sitting in his office. Jesus said to him, "Follow me." Levi got up, left everything, and followed him.

Then Levi had a big feast in his house for Jesus, and among the guests was a large number of tax collectors and other people. Some Pharisees and some teachers of the Law who belonged to their group complained to Jesus' disciples. "Why do you eat and drink with tax collectors and other outcasts?" they asked.

Jesus answered them, "People who are well do not need a doctor, but only those who are sick. I have not come to call respectable people to repent, but outcasts."

Luke 5:27–32

✠

Levi is undoubtedly the most unpopular man in town. He is a greedy tax collector who jumps out of his office and confiscates people's money or belongings.

He is definitely the last person you would expect Jesus to choose as a disciple.

But Jesus *does* choose him. The wonderful thing about Jesus is that he doesn't just see what people *are*, but what they can become.

And when the strictly religious people complain that Jesus keeps bad company, Jesus gladly explains that these are the very folk he has come to meet!

✠

Lord Jesus, you are amazing. Fancy making a disciple out of a tax collector! Thank you for the wonderful difference you are making to all our lives.

✠ ✠ ✠ ✠ ✠

February 11

Jesus was walking through some cornfields on the Sabbath. His disciples began to pick the ears of corn, rub them in their hands, and eat the grain. Some Pharisees asked, "Why are you doing what our Law says you cannot do on the Sabbath?"

Jesus answered them, "Haven't you read what David did when he and his men were hungry? He went into the house of God, took the bread offered to God, ate it, and gave it also to his men. Yet it is against our Law for anyone except the priests to eat that bread."

And Jesus concluded, "The Son of Man is Lord of the Sabbath."

Luke 6:1–5

✠

The Sabbath is supposed to be a day of complete rest. No cooking food, no lifting loads, no going places. The idea is to obey the commandment to keep one day in seven as God's day – a holy day.

The religious Pharisees are hopping mad because Jesus takes no notice of all their little Sabbath rules. In their opinion, Jesus and his disciples are breaking God's law by working on the Sabbath – harvesting the corn!

Jesus disagrees. If the Sabbath is God's day, then it should be a day of joy and plenty. A day in which to glimpse the life of heaven. What a tragedy that they have turned the Sabbath into a day for doing nothing – nothing except avoiding breaking the rules.

✠

Lord Jesus, thank you for setting us free from the prison of religious rules and regulations. Thank you for showing us the gladness and freedom of a life with God, and for making holiness exciting.

✠ ✠ ✠ ✠ ✠

February 12

Then Jesus went up a hill and called to himself the men he wanted. They came to him, and he chose twelve, whom he named apostles. "I have chosen you to be with me," he told them. "I will also send you out to preach, and you will have authority to drive out demons."

These are the twelve he chose: Simon (Jesus gave him the name Peter); James and his brother John, the sons of Zebedee (Jesus gave them the name Boanerges, which means "Men of Thunder"); Andrew, Philip, Bartholomew, Matthew, Thomas, James son of Alphaeus, Thaddaeus, Simon the Patriot, and Judas Iscariot, who betrayed Jesus.

Mark 3:13–19

✠

It was rather unusual for Jesus to choose disciples. It was normally disciples who chose their teacher. He appoints twelve (the same number as the tribes of Israel) and calls them apostles (perhaps meaning helmsmen or navigators – they will be the people who steer the Church in the early days).

The twelve are a mixed bunch – all men, but from different backgrounds and with differing views, especially on politics!

Jesus calls them simply to be with him – at least to start with. In due course, they will have a go at preaching themselves – and will have power to drive out demons. Jesus is obviously very fond of them already, judging from the way he gives some of them nicknames. And yet hidden in their number is the one who will eventually betray him.

✠

Lord Jesus, thank you that you know us very well, and love us very dearly, before ever you ask us to do anything for you.

✠ ✠ ✠ ✠ ✠

February 13

Jesus saw the crowds and went up a hill, where he sat down. His disciples gathered round him, and he began to teach them:

"Happy are those who know they are
    spiritually poor;
  the Kingdom of heaven belongs to them!
"Happy are those who mourn;
  God will comfort them!
"Happy are those who are humble;
  they will receive what God has promised!
"Happy are those whose greatest desire
    is to do what God requires;
  God will satisfy them fully!"

Matthew 5:1–6

✠

We all want to be happy, but we look for happiness in all the wrong places. We think that if only we could be more popular, or have more money, or lead an easier life, all would be well.

Jesus takes us by surprise when he says that the poor in spirit, the sad, and those with deep longings for God, will turn out to be the truly happy ones.

Lord, help us to find our happiness in you today.

✠ ✠ ✠ ✠ ✠

February 14

"Happy are those who are merciful to others;
God will be merciful to them!
"Happy are the pure in heart;
they will see God!
"Happy are those who work for peace;
God will call them his children!
"Happy are those who are persecuted
because they do what God requires;
the Kingdom of heaven belongs to them!

"Happy are you when people insult you and persecute you and tell all kinds of evil lies against you because you are my followers. Be happy and glad, for a great reward is kept for you in heaven. This is how the prophets who lived before you were persecuted."

Matthew 5:7–12

✠

We live in a world where evil seems to win. We live in a world where being merciful is sissy and being pure is a waste of time. If we work for peace, we seem to get trampled on. And when we go through persecution, we wonder how God can allow it.

But Jesus assures us with all his heart that God sees us, God knows us, and God will share the life of his Kingdom with those who love him.

✠

Lord Jesus, help us to defy the way the world is, and to live your upside-down, back-to-front, happy way of life.

✠ ✠ ✠ ✠ ✠

February 15

"You are like salt for all mankind. But if salt loses its saltiness, there is no way to make it salty again. It has become worthless, so it is thrown out and people trample on it.

"You are like light for the whole world. A city built on a hill cannot be hidden. No one lights a lamp and puts it under a bowl; instead he puts it on the lampstand, where it gives light for everyone in the house. In the same way your light must shine before people, so that they will see the good things you do and praise your Father in heaven."

Matthew 5:13–16

✠

Jesus says his disciples are like salt. A tangy flavour? Yes. But in those days salt was also used for preserving meat and fish, and for fertilizing the fields.

So when Jesus says that we are "like salt", he means that we help to stop the rottenness of evil spreading in the world, and that we help goodness grow instead.

Jesus says his disciples are like light. Light not only shows things up for what they are, but reveals itself at the same time. That's why Jesus people must live out-in-the-open lives. Lives which drive out the darkness of sin and reflect the glory of God.

✠

Lord Jesus, help us to live your different life – to be your Salt and Light Company where we live.

✠ ✠ ✠ ✠ ✠

February 16

When John's disciples told him about all these things, he called two of them and sent them to the Lord to ask him, "Are you the one John said was going to come, or should we expect someone else?"

When they came to Jesus, they said, "John the Baptist sent us to ask if you are the one he said was going to come, or if we should expect someone else."

At that very time Jesus cured many people of their sicknesses, diseases, and evil spirits, and gave sight to many blind people. He answered John's messengers, "Go back and tell John what you have seen and heard: the blind can see, the lame can walk, those who suffer from dreaded skin-diseases are made clean, the deaf can hear, the dead are raised to life, and the Good

News is preached to the poor. How happy are those who have no doubts about me!"

Luke 7:18–23

✠

John the Baptist has been thrown into prison for daring to criticize the king. Perhaps it hadn't worried him too much at first, because his cousin Jesus was the Messiah who had come to give freedom to captives. But as time went by, and nothing happened, even John began to have his doubts.

When Jesus gets John's message, he doesn't say anything – but he does a lot. As John's disciples watch, Jesus shows them the power of God at work, healing illness, and casting out evil spirits. Then he sends them back to John.

We all have to learn to see Jesus as he really is, and not as we would like him to be. He came to save the world in God's power and in God's time. That meant that John had to be patient and endure suffering, and the same may be true for us.

✠

Lord, give us a patient faith in you. When times are hard for us, may we still have no doubts that you are in control.

✠ ✠ ✠ ✠ ✠

February 17

After John's messengers had left, Jesus began to speak about him to the crowds: "When you went out to John in the desert, what did you expect to see? A blade of grass bending in the wind? What did you go out to see? A man dressed up in fancy clothes? People who dress like that and live in luxury are found in palaces! Tell me, what did you go out to see? A prophet? Yes indeed, but you saw much more than a prophet. For John is the one of whom the scripture says: 'God said, I will send my messenger ahead of you to open the way for you.' I tell you," Jesus added, "John is greater than any man who has ever lived. But he who is least in the Kingdom of God is greater than John."

Luke 7:24–28

✠

Jesus pays the highest tribute to his cousin John. It may look as though John is on the scrap heap – put out of action, and languishing in King Herod's dungeon.

But Jesus says that John is in fact the greatest man who has ever lived. There is nothing fancy about him in the way of fine clothes or good education. But he was none other than the great prophet who paved the way for the Messiah.

Even so, Jesus points out that John is the last of the old order – the Law and the Prophets. Now anyone who comes into the Kingdom of God through Jesus is more privileged than John the Baptist ever was.

✠

Lord Jesus, thank you that we don't live in the old days when people were waiting for you to come.

Thank you that we know what you are like, and can welcome you into our hearts and lives.

✠ ✠ ✠ ✠ ✠

February 18

Then Jesus' mother and brothers arrived. They stood outside the house and sent in a message, asking for him. A crowd was sitting round Jesus, and they said to him, "Look, your mother and your brothers and sisters are outside, and they want you."

Jesus answered, "Who is my mother? Who are my brothers?" He looked at the people sitting round him and said, "Look! Here are my mother and my brothers! Whoever does what God wants him to do is my brother, my sister, my mother."

Mark 3:31–35

✠

Jesus sounds very cruel in not stopping his work to go out and see his family. They must surely have been very hurt by what he said. They may even have begun to believe the reports that he was mad and should be taken home!

But what Jesus is really trying to explain is that he has an urgent task to perform, and very little time in which to accomplish it. The people who listen to his teaching and accept God's healing are as close and important to him as his own mother and brothers.

It was hard for Jesus' family to feel squeezed out a little, but wonderful for people like us to know that we are drawn in.

Lord Jesus, thank you for our families and those who love us. Help us to have good times together, but may we also give good time to the other things you want us to do.

✠ ✠ ✠ ✠ ✠

February 19

People kept coming to Jesus from one town after another; and when a great crowd gathered, Jesus told this parable:

"Once there was a man who went out to sow corn. As he scattered the seed in the field, some of it fell along the path, where it was stepped on, and the birds ate it up. Some of it fell on rocky ground, and when the plants sprouted, they dried up because the soil had no moisture. Some of the seed fell among thorn bushes, which grew up with the plants and choked them. And some seeds fell in good soil; the plants grew and produced corn, a hundred grains each."

And Jesus concluded, "Listen, then, if you have ears!"

Luke 8:4–8

✠

As so many people come to hear Jesus, he wonders whether the things he says to them are really sinking in. He feels that he is like a sower scattering seed, which sometimes grows and sometimes doesn't. It all depends on the kind of ground on which it lands.

And so it is when the Good News of God's love arrives through our ears and lands in our hearts. If our hearts are trampled hard like a Palestinian path, the good news is easily snatched away again. If we're not really serious, then the good news makes us happy for a short while, but there is no lasting growth. If our hearts are already crowded with worries and riches, then the good news has no room to grow.

But if our hearts are open and deep, then God can grow a wonderful harvest of goodness when Jesus plants the good news in us.

✠

Lord Jesus, we open our hearts to your good news today. Please grow a bumper crop of love and joy and peace in us.

✠ ✠ ✠ ✠ ✠

February 20

Later, Jesus explained his parable about the sower.

✠

"This is what the parable means: the seed is the word of God. The seeds that fell along the path stand for those who hear; but the Devil comes and takes the message away from their hearts in order to keep them from believing and being saved. The seeds that fell on rocky ground stand for those who hear the message and receive it gladly. But it does not sink deep into them; they believe only for a while but when the time of testing comes, they fall away. The seeds that fell among thorn bushes stand for those who hear; but the worries and riches and pleasures of this life crowd in and choke them, and their fruit never ripens. The seeds that fell in good soil stand for those who hear the message and retain it in a good and obedient heart, and they persist until they bear fruit."

Luke 8:11–15

✠

The story about the sower was a parable – a story saying something about God and his Kingdom in a way we can easily picture.

Jesus uses the parable of the sower to explain that his preaching is never wasted. Certainly the Devil is a busy enemy, snatching away the message. Certainly some people seem excited by the good news for a while, but never really last. Certainly the good news is crowded out when people fail to give it proper space . . .

But all the same, there are those who *do* receive the good news and allow it to grow in them. And in due course their lives are wonderfully different.

✠

Lord God, please bless the preaching of your Word around the world today. May many people welcome Jesus into their hearts and bear his fruit in their lives. And may we do the same.

✠ ✠ ✠ ✠ ✠

February 21

"What shall we say the Kingdom of God is like?" asked Jesus. "What parable shall we use to explain it? It is like this. A man takes a mustard seed, the smallest seed in the world, and plants it in the ground. After a while it grows up and becomes the biggest of all plants. It puts out such large branches that the birds come and make their nests in its shade."

Jesus preached his message to the people, using many other parables like these; he told them as much as they could understand. He would not speak to them without using parables, but when he was alone with his disciples, he would explain everything to them.

Mark 4:30–34

✠

Jesus told parables nearly all the time, and it's rather fun to try to puzzle them out. This one about the mustard seed is really quite easy.

God's Kingdom is like a tiny seed. At first it is almost invisible, but just see how it grows!

And just as the mustard seed becomes a plant in which birds can shelter and build their nests, so the Kingdom of God offers protection to all, and we can make our hearts at home in it.

✠

Lord God, your Kingdom spreads wherever people love you. We can't take a photo of it or draw it on a map, but we get glimpses of it all around. And thank you that we belong.

✠ ✠ ✠ ✠ ✠

February 22

On the evening of that same day Jesus said to his disciples, "Let us go across to the other side of the lake." So they left the crowd; the disciples got into the boat in which Jesus was already sitting, and they took him with them. Other boats were there too. Suddenly a strong wind blew up, and the waves began to spill over into the boat, so that it was about to fill with water. Jesus was in the back of the boat, sleeping with his head on a pillow. The disciples woke him up and said, "Teacher, don't you care that we are about to die?"

Jesus stood up and commanded the wind, "Be quiet!" and he said to the waves, "Be still!" The wind died down, and there was a great calm. Then Jesus said to his disciples, "Why are you frightened? Have you still no faith?"

But they were terribly afraid and said to one another, "Who is this man? Even the wind and the waves obey him!"

Mark 4:35–41

✠

It's a terrifying experience to get caught in a sudden storm – especially when you're in a boat and the waves start pouring in over the side. When it happens to the disciples on the Sea of Galilee, they can't understand how Jesus can sleep through it all!

When they wake him with their cries for help, they see him perform an awesome miracle. He stands up in the boat and tells the wind and waves to lie down – almost as though they are dogs he has trained to obey him.

Seeing the power of the Son of God at close quarters is almost as terrifying as the storm, and the disciples are afraid. But at the same time, Jesus is worried about them. When they know that God is in control and that they are his servants, why is it that they panic so easily?

✠

Lord God, by your mighty power you are in control of everything. Help us to trust you in every part of our lives.

✠ ✠ ✠ ✠ ✠

February 23

Jesus and his disciples arrived on the other side of Lake Galilee, in the territory of Gerasa. As soon as Jesus got out of the boat, he was met by a man who came out of the burial caves there. This man had an evil spirit in him and lived among the tombs. Nobody could keep him chained up any more; many times his feet and hands had been chained, but every time he broke the chains and smashed the irons on his feet. He was too strong for anyone to control him. Day and night he wandered among the tombs and through the hills, screaming and cutting himself with stones.

He was some distance away when he saw Jesus; so he ran, fell on his knees before him, and screamed in a loud voice, "Jesus, Son of the Most High God! What do you want with me? For God's sake, I beg you, don't punish me!" (He said this because Jesus was saying, "Evil spirit, come out of this man!")

So Jesus asked him, "What is your name?"

The man answered, "My name is 'Mob' – there are so many of us!" And he kept begging Jesus not to send the evil spirits out of that region.

Mark 5:1–10

✠

Everyone is afraid of Mob. He is wild, mad, and amazingly strong. And yet it is not Mob, but an evil spirit within him, which is causing all the trouble.

There is one power on earth which is greater than any evil spirit, and that is the Spirit of Jesus. When the demon in Mob realizes Jesus is at hand, he starts to scream for mercy!

✠

Lord Jesus, thank you that we don't have to be the slaves of evil a moment longer. Thank you that your power at work within us can set us free from even the worst that Satan can do.

✠ ✠ ✠ ✠ ✠

February 24

There was a large herd of pigs near by, feeding on a hillside. So the spirits begged Jesus, "Send us to the pigs, and let us go into them." He let them go, and the evil spirits went out of the man and entered the pigs. The whole herd – about two thousand pigs in all – rushed down the side of the cliff into the lake and was drowned.

The men who had been taking care of the pigs ran away and spread the news in the town and among the farms. People went out to see what had happened, and when they came to Jesus, they saw the man who used to have the mob of demons in him. He was sitting there, clothed and in his right mind; and they were all afraid. Those who had seen it told the people what had happened to the man with the demons, and about the pigs.

So they asked Jesus to leave their territory.

As Jesus was getting into the boat, the man who had had the demons begged him, "Let me go with you!"

But Jesus would not let him. Instead, he told him, "Go back home to your family and tell them how much the Lord has done for you and how kind he has been to you."

So the man left and went all through the Ten Towns, telling what Jesus had done for him. And all who heard it were amazed.

Mark 5:11–20

✠

The best proof that Jesus is real is when we see the change he makes in the life of someone we know. Or, better still, when we let him make changes in *our* lives.

There is certainly an amazing difference in Mob which nobody can deny. It's the talk of the town, and the countryside as well.

Naturally Mob wants to stay with Jesus for the rest of his life, but Jesus won't let him. Mob's family have suffered enough from him being away, and now they will be blessed by him being at home. At home from time to time, anyway – in between his trips to tell others what Jesus has done for him!

✠

Lord Jesus, help us to share your love and peace at home all the time. And may others be able to see a difference in our lives.

✠ ✠ ✠ ✠ ✠

February 25

When Jesus returned to the other side of the lake, the people welcomed him, because they had all been waiting for him. Then a man named Jairus arrived; he was an official in the local synagogue. He threw himself down at Jesus' feet and begged him to go to his home, because his only daughter, who was twelve years old, was dying.

As Jesus went along, the people were crowding him from every side. Among them was a woman who had suffered from severe bleeding for twelve years; she had spent all she had on doctors, but no one had been able to cure her. She came up in the crowd behind Jesus and touched the edge of his cloak, and her bleeding stopped at once. Jesus asked, "Who touched me?"

Everyone denied it, and Peter said, "Master, the people are all round you and crowding in on you."

But Jesus said, "Someone touched me, for I knew it when power went out of me." The woman saw that she had been found out, so she came trembling and threw herself at Jesus' feet. There in front of everybody, she told him why she had touched him and how she had been healed at once. Jesus said to her, "My daughter, your faith has made you well. Go in peace."

Luke 8:40–48

✠

Many people are clamouring to see Jesus, but Jairus' need is by far the most urgent. Jesus goes with him straight away.

But in the crowd is someone who hasn't been out of her house for twelve years. No one has liked to hug her or touch her, or even brush against her, for twelve years. Because all that time she has been bleeding, and the Jewish Law has declared her "unclean". That means she must stay away from other people.

But when she manages to touch Jesus' cloak – like a child asking for attention – she is healed!

✠

Lord Jesus, thank you that you came to help people whom no one else could help or even care for. Help us to be like that with others.

✠ ✠ ✠ ✠ ✠

February 26

While Jesus was saying this, a messenger came from the official's house. "Your daughter has died," he told Jairus; "don't bother the Teacher any longer."

But Jesus heard it and said to Jairus, "Don't be afraid; only believe, and she will be well."

When he arrived at the house, he would not let anyone go in with him except Peter, John, and James, and the child's father and mother. Everyone there was crying and mourning for the child. Jesus said, "Don't cry; the child is not dead – she is only sleeping!"

They all laughed at him, because they knew that she was dead. But Jesus took her by the hand and called out, "Get up, my child!" Her life returned, and she got up at once, and Jesus ordered them to give her something to eat. Her parents were astounded, but Jesus commanded them not to tell anyone what had happened.

Luke 8:49–56

Only Jesus would have the courage to call death "sleep" – to say that the little girl is only sleeping, and to call her to get up. The people outside think he's ridiculous, but they soon have to change their tune!

Everyone will die some day – unless Jesus comes again first. But when we die trusting Jesus, it's only like falling asleep. And the next thing we know, he will be calling us to wake up and enjoy his heaven.

✠

Lord Jesus, even when very sad things happen, help us to turn to you, and find that all is well in the end.

✠ ✠ ✠ ✠ ✠

February 27

Jesus called the twelve disciples together and gave them power and authority to drive out all demons and to cure diseases. Then he sent them out to preach the Kingdom of God and to heal the sick, after saying to them, "Take nothing with you for the journey: no stick, no beggar's bag, no food, no money, not even an extra shirt. Wherever you are welcomed, stay in the same house until you leave that town; wherever people don't welcome you, leave that town and shake the dust off your feet as a warning to them."

The disciples left and travelled through all the villages, preaching the Good News and healing people everywhere.

Luke 9:1–6

Now it's the turn of the disciples to have a go at preaching the Good News by themselves. Jesus gives them power to be just like him – defeating evil spirits and healing illnesses.

And, like Jesus, they must travel very simply – without a lot of baggage to slow them down. That way they will have to rely on God himself for every mouthful they eat and every bed they sleep in. All they have to offer is the Good News – and that is all they will need.

✠

Lord Jesus, may our lives say something true about you.

✠ ✠ ✠ ✠ ✠

February 28

Now King Herod heard about all this, because Jesus' reputation had spread everywhere. Some people were saying, "John the Baptist has come back to life! That is why he has this power to perform miracles."

Others, however, said, "He is Elijah." Others said, "He is a prophet, like one of the prophets of long ago."

When Herod heard it, he said, "He is John the Baptist! I had his head cut off, but he has come back to life!" Herod himself had ordered John's arrest, and he had him chained and put in prison. Herod did this because of Herodias, whom he had married, even though she was the wife of his brother Philip. John the Baptist kept telling Herod, "It isn't right for you to be married to your brother's wife!"

So Herodias held a grudge against John and wanted to kill him, but she could not because of Herod. Herod was afraid of John because he knew that John was a good and holy man, and so he kept him safe. He liked to listen to him, even though he became greatly disturbed every time he heard him.

Mark 6:14–20

✠

Everyone is talking about Jesus and trying to guess who he really is. Certainly he seems to be preaching like one of the old prophets – and performing miracles as they did.

As for King Herod, he is quite convinced that Jesus is John the Baptist come back to life – to haunt him! Herod had arrested John and thrown him in prison, but he had always known in his heart of hearts that John was right – and he was wrong.

✠

Lord Jesus, when we're torn between right and wrong, help us to do what's right – even if it means swallowing our pride.

✠ ✠ ✠ ✠ ✠

February 29

Finally Herodias got her chance. It was on Herod's birthday, when he gave a feast for all the chief government officials, the military commanders, and the leading citizens of Galilee. The daughter of Herodias came in and danced, and pleased Herod and his guests. So the king said to the girl, "What would you like to have? I will give you anything you want." With many vows he said to her, "I swear that I will give you anything you ask for, even as much as half my kingdom!"

So the girl went out and asked her mother, "What shall I ask for?"

"The head of John the Baptist," she answered.

The girl hurried back at once to the king and demanded, "I want you to give me here and now the head of John the Baptist on a dish!"

This made the king very sad, but he could not refuse her because of the vows he had made in front of all his guests.

So he sent off a guard at once with orders to bring John's head. The guard left, went to the prison, and cut John's head off; then he brought it on a dish and gave it to the girl, who gave it to her mother. When John's disciples heard about this, they came and took away his body, and buried it.

Mark 6:21–29

✠

What a fool King Herod was! He so wanted to please a girl that he got trapped into making a silly and tragic promise. And to his foolishness, he added pride – that he couldn't change his mind without losing face. Just think: John was put to death so that Herod could keep his word.

✠

Lord, pride is a killer. It creeps into every family and every friendship. Please release us from its power, and heal us from its effects.

✠ ✠ ✠ ✠ ✠

A Psalm for
March

LORD, who may enter your Temple?
  Who may worship on Zion, your sacred hill?

A person who obeys God in everything
  and always does what is right,
whose words are true and sincere,
  and who does not slander others.
He does no wrong to his friends
  and does not spread rumours about
    his neighbours.
He despises those whom God rejects,
  but honours those who obey the LORD.
He always does what he promises,
  no matter how much it may cost.
He makes loans without charging interest
  and cannot be bribed to testify against
    the innocent.

Whoever does these things will always be secure.

Psalm 15

March 1

After this, Jesus went across Lake Galilee. A large crowd followed him, because they had seen his miracles of healing those who were ill. Jesus went up a hill and sat down with his disciples. The time for the Passover Festival was near. Jesus looked round and saw that a large crowd was coming to him, so he asked Philip, "Where can we buy enough food to feed all these people?" (He said this to test Philip; actually he already knew what he would do.)

Philip answered, "For everyone to have even a little, it would take more than two hundred silver coins to buy enough bread."

Another of his disciples, Andrew, who was Simon Peter's brother, said, "There is a boy here who has five loaves of barley bread and two fish. But they will certainly not be enough for all these people."

John 6:1–9

✠

There's a problem. A huge crowd has followed Jesus, and ended up far from home. If people don't get food soon, then some will be taken ill, and others will start to fight. But as Philip points out, it would take nine months' wages to feed them all – even if there was a large enough food store nearby.

And then Andrew comes forward with a little lad's picnic lunch. As though that could be of any help!

✠

Lord, sometimes we face big problems, and can see only tiny steps forward. But help us to take these small steps in faith – faith in a great God.

✠ ✠ ✠ ✠ ✠

March 2

"Make the people sit down," Jesus told them. (There was a lot of grass there.) So all the people sat down; there were about five thousand men. Jesus took the bread, gave thanks to God, and distributed it to the people who were sitting there. He did the same with the fish, and they all had as much as they wanted. When they were all full, he said to his disciples, "Gather the pieces left over; let us not waste any." So they gathered them all up and filled twelve baskets with the pieces left over from the five barley loaves which the people had eaten.

Seeing this miracle that Jesus had performed, the people there said, "Surely this is the Prophet who was to come into the world!" Jesus knew that they were about to come and seize him in order to make him king by force; so he went off again to the hills by himself.

John 6:10–15

When the little we can offer God is broken and shared, then there's no limit to what God can do through us. Even today, in our overcrowded world, there is enough for everyone – if only we would share what we have.

Meanwhile, the crowds believe that this is a sign that Jesus can raise and feed an army. They want to make him their king to drive out the Romans. But Jesus slips away to the hills. He is not that kind of leader at all.

✠

Lord, all that we have and all that we are comes from you. Please use us for your best advantage.

✠ ✠ ✠ ✠ ✠

March 3

When evening came, Jesus' disciples went down to the lake, got into a boat, and went back across the lake towards Capernaum. Night came on, and Jesus still had not come to them. By then a strong wind was blowing and stirring up the water. The disciples had rowed about five or six kilometres when they saw Jesus walking on the water, coming near the boat, and they were terrified. "Don't be afraid," Jesus told them, "it is I!" Then they willingly took him into the boat, and immediately the boat reached land at the place they were heading for.

John 6:16–21

There are few things more terrifying than being out in an open boat at night in a gale. You feel absolutely exposed and helpless – and you could capsize and drown at any moment.

Sometimes our lives seem like that – dark and stormy, with no hope of rescue.

And then Jesus comes and tells us not to be afraid. And when we invite Jesus into our problems, the storm is no longer so important. Certainly we have his quiet peace in the midst of it.

✠

Lord Jesus, please step into our lives and give us your peace.

✠ ✠ ✠ ✠ ✠

March 4

Then Jesus and his disciples went away to the villages near Caesarea Philippi. On the way he asked them, "Tell me, who do people say I am?"

"Some say that you are John the Baptist," they answered; "others say that you are Elijah, while others say that you are one of the prophets."

"What about you?" he asked them. "Who do you say I am?"

Peter answered, "You are the Messiah."

Then Jesus ordered them, "Do not tell anyone about me."

Mark 8:27–30

For once Jesus is interested in the gossip. What are people saying about him? Who do they think he is?

The rumours persist that he is some great prophet, or John the Baptist back from the dead. But Peter knows better. He says strongly and with full conviction: "You are the Messiah – not a prophet looking forward to God's great King, but the great King himself."

Jesus is thrilled that the truth has dawned on Peter, but he warns his friends not to spread it about. The crowds had already tried to take the law into their own hands.

✠

Lord, help us to know who you really are – not just a good, kind or powerful person, but the Son of God.

✠ ✠ ✠ ✠ ✠

March 5

Then Jesus began to teach his disciples: "The Son of Man must suffer much and be rejected by the elders, the chief priests, and the teachers of the Law. He will be put to death, but three days later he will rise to life." He made this very clear to them. So Peter took him aside and began to rebuke him. But Jesus turned round, looked at his disciples, and rebuked Peter. "Get away from me, Satan," he said. "Your thoughts don't come from God but from man!"

Then Jesus called the crowd and his disciples to him. "If anyone wants to come with me," he told them, "he must forget self, carry his cross, and follow me. For whoever wants to save his own life will lose it; but whoever loses his life for me and for the gospel will save it."

Mark 8:31–35

✠

Jesus calls himself "the Son of Man" – which was a veiled way of saying he was Messiah. (The Messiah was described in the Book of Daniel as "like a human being surrounded by clouds".) But Jesus doesn't promise clouds and glory. He promises suffering and death. The Jewish leaders all plot his death. But three days later he will rise to life.

Peter argues with Jesus to try to get him to see sense. But Jesus has to explain that God's way to victory is not through pride and pomp and show of force. It is quite the opposite. It is a standard of dying – forgetting self for the sake of following Jesus.

✠

Lord, help us to think your thoughts after you and to go your self-giving way.

✠ ✠ ✠ ✠ ✠

March 6

About a week after he had said these things, Jesus took Peter, John, and James with him and went up a hill to pray. While he was praying, his face changed its appearance, and his clothes became dazzling white.

Suddenly two men were there talking with him. They were Moses and Elijah, who appeared in heavenly glory and talked with Jesus about the way in which he would soon fulfil God's purpose by dying in Jerusalem. Peter and his companions were sound asleep, but they woke up and saw Jesus' glory and the two men who were standing with him.

As the men were leaving Jesus, Peter said to him, "Master, how good it is that we are here! We will make three tents, one for you, one for Moses, and one for Elijah." (He did not really know what he was saying.)

While he was still speaking, a cloud appeared and covered them with its shadow; and the disciples were afraid as the cloud came over them. A voice said from the cloud, "This is my Son, whom I have chosen – listen to him!"

Luke 9:28–35

✠

Maybe there is no one on earth who can really understand Jesus, so he talks to Moses and Elijah. It was Moses who had led the Children of Israel out of slavery in Egypt and given them God's Law. It was Elijah who had stood for God's truth in the dark days of King Ahab when Baal worship was at its height.

As the three of them talk, the disciples glimpse Jesus in his heavenly glory. And impetuous Peter wants to stay there for ever. And then God himself speaks!

✠

Lord, thank you for coming to this earth to die for us.

✠ ✠ ✠ ✠ ✠

March 7

The next day Jesus and the three disciples went down from the hill, and a large crowd met Jesus. A man shouted from the crowd, "Teacher! I beg you, look at my son – my only son! A spirit attacks him with a sudden shout and throws him into a fit, so that he foams at the mouth; it keeps on hurting him and will hardly let him go! I begged your disciples to drive it out, but they couldn't."

Jesus answered, "How unbelieving and wrong you people are! How long must I stay with you? How long do I have to put up with you?" Then he said to the man, "Bring your son here."

As the boy was coming, the demon knocked him to the ground and threw him into a fit. Jesus gave a command to the evil spirit, healed the boy, and gave him back to his father. All the people were amazed at the mighty power of God.

Luke 9:37–43

✠

The disciples are just like us. They have their good days and their bad days. Moments of great power and understanding, followed by utter failure and shame. One moment Peter is being praised for recognizing Jesus is the Messiah – and the next he is told that he is Satan's mouthpiece!

And the others – they've enjoyed great success with their healings and exorcisms in the past, but this evil spirit defeats them. The secret is, of course, the power of God. When we forget to depend on God and try to tackle tasks in our own strength, we're on a loser straight away.

✠

Lord, thank you for putting up with us. May we learn to depend on you and you alone in all we do.

✠ ✠ ✠ ✠ ✠

March 8

As they went on their way, a man said to Jesus, "I will follow you wherever you go."

Jesus said to him, "Foxes have holes, and birds have nests, but the Son of Man has nowhere to lie down and rest."

He said to another man, "Follow me." But that man said, "Sir, first let me go back and bury my father."

Jesus answered, "Let the dead bury their own dead. You go and proclaim the Kingdom of God."

Another man said, "I will follow you, sir; but first let me go and say good-bye to my family."

Jesus said to him, "Anyone who starts to plough and then keeps looking back is of no use to the Kingdom of God."

Luke 9:57–62

✠

Jesus sounds very hard to his would-be followers. You would have thought he would have been glad of any volunteers.

But Jesus knows that a hard road lies ahead. Anyone whose heart is really set on home comforts or even family ties will find himself torn in two – trying to look forward and back at the same time. And Jesus needs disciples who will give their whole selves to the work of the Kingdom.

✠

Lord Jesus, help us to put you first in our lives, and to live for your Kingdom before all else.

✠ ✠ ✠ ✠ ✠

March 9

After this the Lord chose another seventy-two men and sent them out two by two, to go ahead of him to every town and place where he himself was about to go. He said to them, "There is a large harvest, but few workers to gather it in. Pray to the owner of the harvest that he will send out workers to gather in his harvest. Go! I am sending you like lambs among wolves. Don't take a purse or a beggar's bag or shoes; don't stop to greet anyone on the road. Whenever you go into a house, first say, 'Peace be with this house.' If a peace-loving man lives there, let your greeting of peace remain on him; if not, take back your greeting of peace."

Jesus said to his disciples, "Whoever listens to you listens to me; whoever rejects you rejects me; and whoever rejects me rejects the one who sent me."

Luke 10:1–6,16

✠

Jesus can only be in one place at a time, and he has many towns and villages to visit. He sends the seventy-two ahead of him, to tell people he is coming. They must live very simply, without any means of defending or providing for themselves. And they mustn't waste time in elaborate eastern greetings. In other words, they are to go for Jesus, stand for Jesus, and speak for Jesus – so that people can accept or reject his Good News.

✠

Lord, fancy trusting your reputation to human messengers – both then and now. May we live and speak faithfully for you, so that we are truly worthy of your trust.

✠ ✠ ✠ ✠ ✠

March 10

The seventy-two men came back in great joy. "Lord," they said, "even the demons obeyed us when we gave them a command in your name!"

Jesus answered them, "I saw Satan fall like lightning from heaven. Listen! I have given you authority, so that you can walk on snakes and scorpions and overcome all the power of the Enemy, and nothing will hurt you. But don't be glad because the evil spirits obey you; rather be glad because your names are written in heaven."

Luke 10:17–20

✠

When the seventy-two return, Jesus tells them that they have been in a successful battle with Satan himself. They are amazed at the powerful things they have been able to do in the name of Jesus.

But Jesus reminds them that following him isn't about having power over evil spirits. It's about having a home in heaven.

✠

Lord Jesus, when we come to you we don't join a powerful clique or a magic circle. We are adopted into your heavenly family as God's own children. Thank you.

✠ ✠ ✠ ✠ ✠

March 11

A man named Lazarus, who lived in Bethany, was ill. Bethany was the town where Mary and her sister Martha lived. (This Mary was the one who poured the perfume on the Lord's feet and wiped them with her hair; it was her brother Lazarus who was ill.) The sisters sent Jesus a message: "Lord, your dear friend is ill."

When Jesus heard it, he said, "The final result of this illness will not be the death of Lazarus: this has happened in order to bring glory to God, and it will be the means by which the Son of God will receive glory."

Jesus loved Martha and her sister and Lazarus. Yet when he received the news that Lazarus was ill, he stayed where he was for two more days. Then he said to the disciples, "Let us go back to Judaea."

John 11:1–7

✠

Sickness and disease are nearly always hard to understand. If God is able to heal, why do so many innocent people suffer? Why do so many people die?

As Jesus puzzles over his friend's illness, he realizes that his heavenly Father is allowing it to happen – so that the power of God will be clearly seen.

✠

Lord, our illnesses and pains are so hard to bear, and maybe we are afraid of death. Help us to know that the final result of the things we go through will be new life for us and more glory for you.

✠ ✠ ✠ ✠ ✠

March 12

When Jesus arrived, he found that Lazarus had been buried four days before. Bethany was less than three kilometres from Jerusalem, and many Judaeans had come to see Martha and Mary to comfort them over their brother's death.

When Martha heard that Jesus was coming, she went out to meet him, but Mary stayed in the house. Martha said to Jesus, "If you had been here, Lord, my brother would not have died! But I know that even now God will give you whatever you ask him for."

"Your brother will rise to life," Jesus told her.

"I know," she replied, "that he will rise to life on the last day."

Jesus said to her, "I am the resurrection and the life. Whoever believes in me will live, even though he dies; and whoever lives and believes in me will never die. Do you believe this?"

"Yes, Lord!" she answered. "I do believe that you are the Messiah, the Son of God, who was to come into the world."

John 11:17–27

✠

Martha and Mary and Jesus are great friends. Even so, Martha has a bone to pick with Jesus: why had he not come sooner? He could have healed her brother so easily! Perhaps Mary is too angry even to face him . . .

But when Martha talks to Jesus, she realizes without a shadow of doubt, that he is the very Lord of life. And her faith paves the way for the greatest of all the signs that Jesus performed.

✠

Lord Jesus, help us to talk straight to you, to tell you the things that make us angry and frustrated. And help us to glimpse afresh your power to do more than we can ask or imagine.

✠ ✠ ✠ ✠ ✠

March 13

Deeply moved once more, Jesus went to the tomb, which was a cave with a stone placed at the entrance. "Take the stone away!" Jesus ordered.

Martha, the dead man's sister, answered, "There will be a bad smell, Lord. He has been buried four days!"

Jesus said to her, "Didn't I tell you that you would see God's glory if you believed?" They took the stone away. Jesus looked up and said, "I thank you, Father, that you listen to me. I know that you always listen to me, but I say this for the sake of the people here, so that they will believe that you sent me." After he had said this, he called out in a loud voice, "Lazarus, come out!" He came out, his hands and feet wrapped in grave clothes, and with a cloth round his face. "Untie him," Jesus told them, "and let him go."

John 11:38–44

✠

Jesus weeps along with everyone else. He grieves at the way sin and death have crept so completely over the world – stealing away even the dearest and best of friends. But he also knows that the power of God can break the stranglehold of Satan. And in seeing Lazarus restored to life, he catches a heartening glimpse of his own resurrection.

And see how ordinary people can work along with God. God alone can give life to Lazarus, but it is his neighbours who must roll the tombstone away and unwind the grave clothes from his body.

✠

Lord God, giver of life, thank you for your promise of eternal life for all who put their trust in you.

March 14

Many of the people who had come to visit Mary saw what Jesus did, and they believed in him. But some of them returned to the Pharisees and told them what Jesus had done. So the Pharisees and the chief priests met with the Council and said, "What shall we do? Look at all the miracles this man is performing! If we let him go on in this way, everyone will believe in him, and the Roman authorities will take action and destroy our Temple and our nation!"

One of them, named Caiaphas, who was High Priest that year, said, "What fools you are! Don't you realize that it is better for you to let one man die for the people, instead of having the whole nation destroyed?"

From that day on the Jewish authorities made plans to kill Jesus.

John 11:45–53

✠

While some people see the mighty works of Jesus and believe in him, others quite wilfully reject him. Some people are guilty of *un*belief. They stubbornly refuse to believe, despite all the evidence in front of them.

The Jewish leaders think Jesus is going to get them all into trouble – that he will start a futile rebellion which will be ruthlessly crushed by the Romans. But then the High Priest has an idea. Why not fix it for Jesus to be arrested and put to death? That way only one person will be killed, and the nation will be spared.

✠

Lord, we believe. Please help our unbelief!

March 15

Six days before the Passover, Jesus went to Bethany, the home of Lazarus, the man he had raised from death. They prepared a dinner for him there, which Martha helped to serve; Lazarus was one of those who were sitting at the table with Jesus. Then Mary took half a litre of a very expensive perfume made of pure nard, poured it on Jesus' feet, and wiped them with her hair. The sweet smell of the perfume filled the whole house. One of Jesus' disciples, Judas Iscariot – the one who was going to betray him – said, "Why wasn't this perfume sold for three hundred silver coins and the money given to the poor?" He said this, not because he cared about the poor, but because he was a thief. He carried the money bag and would help himself from it.

But Jesus said, "Leave her alone! Let her keep what she has for the day of my burial. You will always have poor people with you, but you will not always have me."

John 12:1–8

✠

Jesus is coming to Jerusalem for the Passover festival, as he has done every year since he was old enough to remember. But this year is different, for it will be his last. He stays with Lazarus, Martha and Mary at Bethany – just outside the city.

During supper, Mary does a very beautiful and generous thing for Jesus. She anoints his feet with a most expensive perfume to show how much she cares for him – and perhaps to show that she knows he is going to die.

Judas begins to show where his heart really lies, by complaining that what Mary has done is a wicked waste of money.

✠

Lord Jesus, you gave your very self for us. Help us to give our very best for you.

✠ ✠ ✠ ✠ ✠

March 16

Jesus . . . went on to Jerusalem ahead of them. As he came near Bethphage and Bethany at the Mount of Olives, he sent two disciples ahead with these instructions: "Go to the village there ahead of you; as you go in, you will find a colt tied up that has never been ridden. Untie it and bring it here. If someone asks you why you are untying it, tell him that the Master needs it."

They went on their way and found everything just as Jesus had told them. As they were untying the colt, its owners said to them, "Why are you untying it?"

"The Master needs it," they answered, and they took the colt to Jesus. Then they threw their cloaks over the animal and helped Jesus get on. As he rode on, people spread their cloaks on the road.

Luke 19:28–36

✠

Jesus wants to arrive in Jerusalem in a special way. Not on foot, like many of the pilgrims, but not on a fine horse like a conquering general either. He wants to arrive in a way that will spell peace. So he comes meekly, riding an ass.

But there was an old prophecy which said that one day a king would arrive like this, and that the people would make a royal carpet for him out of their clothes.

✠

Lord Jesus, as you once borrowed Peter's boat, and this man's colt, is there anything of ours you would like to use today?

✠ ✠ ✠ ✠ ✠

March 17

When Jesus came near Jerusalem, at the place where the road went down the Mount of Olives, the large crowd of his disciples began to thank God and praise him in loud voices for all the great things that they had seen: "God bless the king who comes in the name of the Lord! Peace in heaven and glory to God!"

Then some of the Pharisees in the crowd spoke to Jesus. "Teacher," they said, "command your disciples to be quiet!"

Jesus answered, "I tell you that if they keep quiet, the stones themselves will start shouting."

Luke 19:37–40

✠

Jesus comes nearer and nearer to Jerusalem, and everyone is more and more excited. If Jesus is the Messiah – true descendant of the great King David, and Son of God – then who knows what will happen when he comes to the city of Jerusalem? And when the Pharisees try to get Jesus to control his followers, he replies that this is no time for keeping quiet!

✠

Lord Jesus, we rejoice that you are the King of Kings. The whole creation worships you!

✠ ✠ ✠ ✠ ✠

March 18

Jesus came closer to the city, and when he saw it, he wept over it, saying, "If you only knew today what is needed for peace! But now you cannot see it! The time will come when your enemies will surround you with barricades, blockade you, and close in on you from every side. They will completely destroy you and the people within your walls; not a single stone will they leave in its place, because you did not recognize the time when God came to save you!"

Luke 19:41–44

✠

When Jesus comes within sight of Jerusalem, he bursts into tears! He sees so clearly that the welcome will not last, and that he will soon have to suffer and die.

But one day Jerusalem herself will suffer for failing to receive him. With a prophet's insight, Jesus knows that disaster will befall this city. And it happened in AD 70, when she was overrun by the armies of the Roman Emperor Titus.

✠

Lord Jesus, help us all to welcome you while we have the chance.

✠ ✠ ✠ ✠ ✠

March 19

Then Jesus went into the Temple and began to drive out the merchants, saying to them, "It is written in the scriptures that God said, 'My Temple will be called a house of prayer.' But you have turned it into a hideout for thieves!"

Every day Jesus taught in the Temple. The chief priests, the teachers of the Law, and the leaders of the people wanted to kill him, but they could not find a way to do it, because all the people kept listening to him, not wanting to miss a single word.

Luke 19:45–48

✠

The things that went on in the Temple courtyard were a scandal. People had to exchange their money for special coins to put in the collection – and the moneychangers charged them far too much. Then again, all kinds of animals and birds were on sale for people to buy as sacrifices. So instead of being a place of prayer, the Temple was a tourist trap. Everyone knew that it couldn't go on – that one day God's judgement would fall.

✠

Lord, help us to see the things that offend you in our way of life – the outrages we commit or allow – and help us to change our ways.

✠ ✠ ✠ ✠ ✠

March 20

The time was near for the Festival of Unleavened Bread, which is called the Passover. The chief priests and the teachers of the Law were afraid of the people, and so they were trying to find a way of putting Jesus to death secretly.

Then Satan entered Judas, called Iscariot, who was one of the twelve disciples. So Judas went off and spoke with the chief priests and the officers of the temple guard about how he could betray Jesus to them. They were pleased and offered to pay him money. Judas agreed to it and started looking for a good chance to hand Jesus over to them without the people knowing about it.

Luke 22:1–6

✠

The Jewish leaders find it almost impossible to catch Jesus. He is surrounded by friends, and has massive support from all the people. And then they have an unbelievable stroke of good fortune. Judas Iscariot offers to turn traitor . . .

We don't know why Judas did this. Perhaps he felt Jesus was being too slow to proclaim himself as king. Certainly Judas saw a chance to make some money – which he loved. But whatever the reason, we see Satan behind it. The old enemy is at work again.

✠

Lord, even your closest and keenest disciples failed you. Please may we learn from their mistakes and not put our own plans before yours.

March 21

The day came during the Festival of Unleavened Bread when the lambs for the Passover meal were to be killed. Jesus sent off Peter and John with these instructions: "Go and get the Passover meal ready for us to eat."

"Where do you want us to get it ready?" they asked him.

He answered, "As you go into the city, a man carrying a jar of water will meet you. Follow him into the house that he enters, and say to the owner of the house: 'The Teacher says to you, Where is the room where my disciples and I will eat the Passover meal?' He will show you a large furnished room upstairs, where you will get everything ready."

They went off and found everything just as Jesus had told them, and they prepared the Passover meal.

Luke 22:7–13

✠

There is now much more need for secrecy. Jesus knows that all of his movements are watched, but he is determined to have this last Passover meal with his disciples.

And so Peter and John discover the upper room – the room where so much is to happen. This is where Jesus will have his last chance to talk to them before his death, and where the Christian Church is to be born.

✠

Lord, may our homes always be of service to you.

✠ ✠ ✠ ✠ ✠

March 22

When the hour came, Jesus took his place at the table with the apostles. He said to them, "I have wanted so much to eat this Passover meal with you before I suffer! For I tell you, I will never eat it until it is given its full meaning in the Kingdom of God."

Then Jesus took a cup, gave thanks to God, and said, "Take this and share it among yourselves. I tell you that from now on I will not drink this wine until the Kingdom of God comes."

Then he took a piece of bread, gave thanks to God, broke it, and gave it to them, saying, "This is my body, which is given for you. Do this in memory of me." In the same way, he gave them the cup after the supper, saying, "This cup is God's new covenant sealed with my blood, which is poured out for you."

Luke 22:14–20

✠

Normally the Passover meal was a celebration of the Exodus, when the Children of Israel had been rescued by God from slavery in Egypt. But at this particular meal, Jesus is thinking of another exodus – the rescue that is to take place through his death the following day.

And so as he breaks the familiar bread, and passes the wine, he tells the disciples that from now on they must remember his broken body and his shed blood. Today the sharing of broken bread and poured out wine is at the heart of the Church's worship.

✠

May we who share Christ's body live his risen life.

March 23

It was now the day before the Passover Festival. Jesus knew that the hour had come for him to leave this world and go to the Father. He had always loved those in the world who were his own, and he loved them to the very end.

Jesus and his disciples were at supper. The Devil had already put the thought of betraying Jesus into the heart of Judas, the son of Simon Iscariot. Jesus knew that the Father had given him complete power; he knew that he had come from God and was going to God. So he rose from the table, took off his outer garment, and tied a towel round his waist. Then he poured some water into a basin and began to wash the disciples' feet and dry them with the towel round his waist. He came to Simon Peter, who said to him, "Are you going to wash my feet, Lord?"

Jesus answered him, "You do not understand now what I am doing, but you will understand later."

Peter declared, "Never at any time will you wash my feet!"

"If I do not wash your feet," Jesus answered, "you will no longer be my disciple."

John 13:1–8

✠

Washing feet is the work of a slave, and certainly Jesus shouldn't be doing it! It is only because all the others are too proud to get down on their knees and serve the rest . . .

Peter is embarrassed, and indignant. But Jesus insists that he *must* wash his disciples' feet. It's a picture of the forgiveness he came to supply – washing away our sin and guilt – and only he can do it.

Lord, you are the perfect friend. You know the worst about us, and you love us just the same.

✠ ✠ ✠ ✠ ✠

March 24

After Jesus had washed their feet, he put his outer garment back on and returned to his place at the table. "Do you understand what I have just done to you?" he asked. "You call me Teacher and Lord, and it is right that you do so, because that is what I am. I, your Lord and Teacher, have just washed your feet. You, then, should wash one another's feet. I have set an example for you, so that you will do just what I have done for you. I am telling you the truth; no slave is greater than his master, and no messenger is greater than the one who sent him. Now that you know this truth, how happy you will be if you put it into practice!"

John 13:12–17

✠

By washing his disciples' feet, Jesus has acted out all that he came to do for mankind. He laid aside his outer garment just as he had laid aside his heavenly glory to come to earth. And although he is their Teacher and Lord, he stoops to be their slave and even to wash their dusty, smelly feet.

Now Jesus tells them that they will find real happiness if they give their own lives in service to each other. After all, if he has shown his leadership in service, they should show their loyalty to him in the same way.

✠

Lord, help us to serve you in one another and to love as you love us.

✠ ✠ ✠ ✠ ✠

March 25

After Jesus had said this, he was deeply troubled and declared openly, "I am telling you the truth: one of you is going to betray me."

The disciples looked at one another, completely puzzled about whom he meant. One of the disciples, the one whom Jesus loved, was sitting next to Jesus. Simon Peter motioned to him and said, "Ask him whom he is talking about."

So that disciple moved closer to Jesus' side and asked, "Who is it, Lord?"

Jesus answered, "I will dip some bread in the sauce and give it to him; he is the man." So he took a piece of bread, dipped it, and gave it to Judas, the son of Simon Iscariot. As soon as Judas took the bread, Satan entered him. Jesus said to him, "Be quick about what you are doing!" None of the others at the table understood why Jesus said this to him. Since Judas was in charge of the money bag, some of the disciples thought that Jesus had told him to go and buy what they needed for the festival, or to give something to the poor.

Judas accepted the bread and went out at once. It was night.

John 13:21–30

✠

How strange that nobody could guess that it was Judas Iscariot who would betray Jesus. It seems so obvious to us, looking back! But in fact Jesus had just given him a special morsel of food – a sign that he was an honoured friend. How ironic that it was at that very moment that Judas allowed Satan to take control of his life.

✠

Lord, no one is exempt from Satan's attacks. Please keep us safe in the times of testing.

✠ ✠ ✠ ✠ ✠

March 26

After Judas had left, Jesus said, "Now the Son of Man's glory is revealed; now God's glory is revealed through him. And if God's glory is revealed through him, then God will reveal the glory of the Son of Man in himself, and he will do so at once. My children, I shall not be with you very much longer. You will look for me; but I tell you now what I told the Jewish authorities, 'You cannot go where I am going.' And now I give you a new commandment: love one another. As I have loved you, so you must love one another. If you have love for one another, then everyone will know that you are my disciples."

John 13:31–35

✠

The disciples have been itching to see Jesus' glory – but they are in for a surprise. Jesus' glory isn't to be revealed in trumpet fanfares and flashing lights. His glory is that he will go humbly and obediently to the cross – to do the will of his Father in heaven.

Before he leaves the upper room, Jesus gives his disciples a commandment they will never forget – to love one another. Love – putting others first and wanting the best for them – will be the hallmark of Jesus' friends.

✠

Lord Jesus, help us to love one another so that we can show people what you are really like.

✠ ✠ ✠ ✠ ✠

March 27

"Where are you going, Lord?" Simon Peter asked him.

"You cannot follow me now where I am going," answered Jesus; "but later you will follow me."

"Lord, why can't I follow you now?" asked Peter. "I am ready to die for you!"

Jesus answered, "Are you really ready to die for me? I am telling you the truth: before the cock crows you will say three times that you do not know me."

John 13:36–38

Poor Peter. He always wants to be in on the action. He simply can't believe that Jesus will go to meet this crisis without his trusted henchman. After all, he will follow Jesus to the ends of the earth and even die for him. At least, that's the way he feels. But Jesus knows better.

✠

Lord Jesus, you know us through and through. Please forgive us when our support for you is all bluster and froth. Help us to know ourselves better, and to offer our real selves to you.

✠ ✠ ✠ ✠ ✠

March 28

They came to a place called Gethsemane, and Jesus said to his disciples, "Sit here while I pray." He took Peter, James, and John with him. Distress and anguish came over him, and he said to them, "The sorrow in my heart is so great that it almost crushes me. Stay here and keep watch."

He went a little farther on, threw himself on the ground, and prayed that, if possible, he might not have to go through that time of suffering. "Father," he prayed, "my Father! All things are possible for you. Take this cup of suffering away from me. Yet not what I want, but what you want."

Mark 14:32–36

✠

Peter, James and John have shared some wonderful moments with Jesus. They were with him when he raised Jairus' daughter from death. They were with him when he spoke with Moses and Elijah on the mountain. Now they are with him as his deepest suffering begins. And through them we glimpse the agony of Jesus as he prays that the cross might not be necessary after all. Yet the person who taught his disciples to pray "Your will be done" is prepared to say the same to God himself.

✠

Lord God our Father, please have your way in our lives, even if your road for us is a hard one.

✠ ✠ ✠ ✠ ✠

March 29

Then Jesus returned and found the three disciples asleep. He said to Peter, "Simon, are you asleep? Weren't you able to stay awake even for one hour?" And he said to them, "Keep watch, and pray that you will not fall into temptation. The spirit is willing, but the flesh is weak."

He went away once more and prayed, saying the same words. Then he came back to the disciples and found them asleep; they could not keep their eyes open. And they did not know what to say to him.

When he came back the third time, he said to them, "Are you still sleeping and resting? Enough! The hour has come! Look, the Son of Man is now being handed over to the power of sinful men. Get up, let us go. Look, here is the man who is betraying me!"

Mark 14:37–42

✠

Why do the disciples keep falling asleep at the very time Jesus needs them? Perhaps they are exhausted after a long day, or sleepy after the meal. Anyway it reminds us, if we need reminder, that they were only human – realizing very little of what was going on, and too lazy or uninterested to bother much.

✠

Lord, how many times have you wanted us to pray for something, and we have drifted off to sleep instead? May we learn to be alert and urgent about the things which concern you.

✠ ✠ ✠ ✠ ✠

March 30

Jesus was still speaking when Judas, one of the twelve disciples, arrived. With him was a crowd armed with swords and clubs, and sent by the chief priests, the teachers of the Law, and the elders. The traitor had given the crowd a signal: "The man I kiss is the one you want. Arrest him and take him away under guard."

As soon as Judas arrived, he went up to Jesus and said, "Teacher!" and kissed him. So they arrested Jesus and held him tight. But one of those standing there drew his sword and struck at the High Priest's slave, cutting off his ear.

Then Jesus spoke up and said to them, "Did you have to come with swords and clubs to capture me, as though I were an outlaw? Day after day I was with you teaching in the Temple, and you did not arrest me. But the scriptures must come true."

Then all the disciples left him and ran away.

Mark 14:43–50

✠

Jesus goes quietly – despite Peter's attempt to make a fight of it.

Even when he is so roughly grabbed in this cowardly, hole-in-the-corner arrest, Jesus is at peace with himself. It isn't the iron grip of the soldiers that holds him – it is obedience to his Father's will. Nor is it Judas' kiss which betrays him – he freely gives himself up out of love for us.

✠

Lord Jesus, thank you for showing us how to live calmly and trustingly even when life isn't fair, and other people fail us.

✠ ✠ ✠ ✠ ✠

March 31

They arrested Jesus and took him away into the house of the High Priest; and Peter followed at a distance. A fire had been lit in the centre of the courtyard, and Peter joined those who were sitting round it. When one of the servant-girls saw him sitting there at the fire, she looked straight at him and said, "This man too was with Jesus!"

But Peter denied it, "Woman, I don't even know him!"

After a little while a man noticed Peter and said, "You are one of them, too!"

But Peter answered, "Man, I am not!"

And about an hour later another man insisted strongly, "There isn't any doubt that this man was with Jesus, because he also is a Galilean!"

But Peter answered, "Man, I don't know what you are talking about!"

At once, while he was still speaking, a cock crowed. The Lord turned round and looked straight at Peter, and Peter remembered that the Lord had said to him, "Before the cock crows tonight, you will say three times that you do not know me." Peter went out and wept bitterly.

Luke 22:54–62

✠

Peter lurks in the background while Jesus is being questioned. But the big-hearted fisherman, who made such brave promises a few hours earlier, is now afraid for his own life.

When his northern accent gives him away, Peter tries to lie and swear his way out of danger. But when the

Lord turns and looks at him, we can't take any pleasure in Peter's remorse. We know that look too well ourselves.

✠

Lord, please forgive us for the many times we disown you and try to mix with the crowd instead. As you persevered with Peter, we pray that you will be patient with us.

✠ ✠ ✠ ✠ ✠

A Psalm for
April

The law of the LORD is perfect;
  it gives new strength.
The commands of the LORD are
    trustworthy,
  giving wisdom to those who lack it.
The laws of the LORD are right,
  and those who obey them are happy.
The commands of the LORD are just
  and give understanding to the mind.
The worship of the LORD is good;
  it will continue for ever.
The judgements of the LORD are just;
  they are always fair.
They are more desirable than the
    finest gold;
  they are sweeter than the purest honey.
They give knowledge to me, your servant;
  I am rewarded for obeying them.

No one can see his own errors;
  deliver me, LORD, from hidden faults!
Keep me safe, also, from wilful sins;
  don't let them rule over me.
Then I shall be perfect
  and free from the evil of sin.

May my words and my thoughts be
    acceptable to you,
  O LORD, my refuge and my redeemer!

Psalm 19:7–14

April 1

Then some men stood up and told this lie against Jesus: "We heard him say, 'I will tear down this Temple which men have made, and after three days I will build one that is not made by men.'" Not even they, however, could make their stories agree.

The High Priest stood up in front of them all and questioned Jesus, "Have you no answer to the accusation they bring against you?"

But Jesus kept quiet and would not say a word. Again the High Priest questioned him, "Are you the Messiah, the Son of the Blessed God?"

"I am," answered Jesus, "and you will all see the Son of Man seated on the right of the Almighty and coming with the clouds of heaven!"

The High Priest tore his robes and said, "We don't need any more witnesses! You heard his blasphemy. What is your decision?"

They all voted against him; he was guilty and should be put to death.

Some of them began to spit on Jesus, and they blindfolded him and hit him. "Guess who hit you!" they said. And the guards took him and slapped him.

Mark 14:57–65

Jesus has done nothing wrong, and it's impossible to get any evidence against him to stick. The story about him pulling down the Temple might have been some half-remembered saying about the temple of his body which would be raised on the third day after his death.

In the end, the High Priest tries a direct question: "Are you the Messiah?", and gets an unexpectedly direct answer: "I am." So Jesus says in no uncertain terms that he is the Son of God, and the High Priest is appalled at his blasphemy. For those two words he must surely be put to death.

Then the Lord of Glory is subjected to the hatred and mean-minded bullying of his enemies.

✠

Lord, our human nature is so bitter and twisted; yet you ran the gauntlet of all our rage and spite to show your love and bring us back to God. Thank you!

✠ ✠ ✠ ✠ ✠

April 2

The whole group rose up and took Jesus before Pilate, where they began to accuse him: "We caught this man misleading our people, telling them not to pay taxes to the Emperor and claiming that he himself is the Messiah, a king."

Pilate asked him, "Are you the king of the Jews?"

"So you say," answered Jesus.

Then Pilate said to the chief priests and the crowds, "I find no reason to condemn this man."

But they insisted even more strongly, "With his teaching he is starting a riot among the people all through Judaea. He began in Galilee and now has come here."

When Pilate heard this, he asked, "Is this man a Galilean?" When he learnt that Jesus was from the region ruled by Herod, he sent him to Herod, who was also in Jerusalem at that time.

Luke 23:1–7

✠

The Jews have no power to sentence Jesus to death, so they frogmarch him along to the Roman Governor, Pontius Pilate.

As they go, it occurs to them that the Governor won't uphold a sentence for blasphemy. Blasphemy is an insult to God, and Pontius Pilate doesn't believe in the God of the Jews. So they change their story to say that Jesus was encouraging people to rebel against the Romans and make him king.

Pilate is puzzled and plays for time. If Jesus is a Jew from Galilee, then his case should be referred to King Herod.

✠

Lord, you are the King of Kings. Please bless and guide all those in authority – princes, presidents and prime ministers – that they may seek your wisdom and make their decisions in the light of your truth.

✠ ✠ ✠ ✠ ✠

April 3

Herod was very pleased when he saw Jesus, because he had heard about him and had been wanting to see him for a long time. He was hoping to see Jesus perform some miracle. So Herod asked Jesus many questions, but Jesus made no answer.

The chief priests and the teachers of the Law stepped forward and made strong accusations against Jesus. Herod and his soldiers mocked Jesus and treated him with contempt; then they put a fine robe on him and sent him back to Pilate. On that very day Herod and Pilate became friends; before this they had been enemies.

Luke 23:8–12

✠

Herod just loves magicians, conjurers and party tricks. He wants Jesus to amuse him; and when nothing happens, he turns nasty.

In the end he makes his own entertainment by giving Jesus a mock coronation and sending the latest "King of the Jews" back to Pilate.

✠

Lord, everyone has to make up their mind about you. Help us to accept you, not because of what we hope you might do for us, but because of who you are.

✠ ✠ ✠ ✠ ✠

April 4

Pilate called together the chief priests, the leaders, and the people, and said to them, "You brought this man to me and said that he was misleading the people. Now, I have examined him here in your presence, and I have not found him guilty of any of the crimes you accuse him of. Nor did Herod find him guilty, for he sent him back to us. There is nothing this man has done to deserve death. So I will have him whipped and let him go."

The whole crowd cried out, "Kill him! Set Barabbas free for us!" (Barabbas had been put in prison for a riot that had taken place in the city, and for murder.)

Pilate wanted to set Jesus free, so he appealed to the crowd again. But they shouted back, "Crucify him! Crucify him!"

Pilate said to them the third time, "But what crime has he committed? I cannot find he has done anything to deserve death! I will have him whipped and set him free."

But they kept on shouting at the top of their voices that Jesus should be crucified, and finally their shouting succeeded.

So Pilate passed the sentence on Jesus that they were asking for. He set free the man they wanted, the one who had been put in prison for riot and murder, and he handed Jesus over for them to do as they wished.

Luke 23:13–25

✠

The vast crowd is thirsting for blood, and Pilate is unable to resist the mood of the people. The high hopes they had of Jesus and the fervent support they gave him are now turned to hatred. They feel he is powerless, and must be put away. They would even prefer Barabbas. At least he is a man of action, with riot and murder to his credit.

✠

Lord Jesus, please forgive the self-centred anger and violence which was in that crowd and which springs up so easily in us. Thank you for taking all our hatred with you into your death on the cross so that we might find a more loving way.

✠ ✠ ✠ ✠ ✠

April 5

The soldiers led Jesus away, and as they were going, they met a man from Cyrene named Simon who was coming into the city from the country. They seized him, put the cross on him, and made him carry it behind Jesus.

A large crowd of people followed him; among them were some women who were weeping and wailing for him. Jesus turned to them and said, "Women of Jerusalem! Don't cry for me, but for yourselves and your children. For the days are coming when people will say, 'How lucky are the women who never had children, who never bore babies, who never nursed them!' That will be the time when people will say to the mountains, 'Fall on us!' and to the hills, 'Hide us!' For if such things as these are done when the wood is green, what will happen when it is dry?"

Luke 23:26–31

It's as though the whole world is drawn into the death of Jesus. An African called Simon is suddenly drafted into the funeral procession and told to carry the cross. No doubt Jesus was glad of his help – and his company.

As the women set up a funeral lament, Jesus tells them to save their tears for themselves. After all, if this fate can befall him who is the Son of God, what hope can there be for the rest of mankind?

✠

Lord, it was people like us who sent you to the cross, and people like us who watched you die. And yet it was for people like us that you came. Thank you for all your love.

✠ ✠ ✠ ✠ ✠

April 6

Two other men, both of them criminals, were also led out to be put to death with Jesus. When they came to the place called "The Skull", they crucified Jesus there, and the two criminals, one on his right and the other on his left. Jesus said, "Forgive them, Father! They don't know what they are doing."

They divided his clothes among themselves by throwing dice. The people stood there watching while the Jewish leaders jeered at him: "He saved others; let him save himself if he is the Messiah whom God has chosen!"

The soldiers also mocked him: they came up to him and offered him cheap wine, and said, "Save yourself if you are the king of the Jews!"

Above him were written these words: "This is the King of the Jews."

Luke 23:32–38

✠

Crucifixion is one of the most terrible deaths that has ever been devised. Yet Jesus asks God's forgiveness for the soldiers even as they are driving the nails into his hands and feet and dropping the cross into its socket.

But there is far more to the agony of Jesus than the pain of the nails. His trial was unfair and his sentence unjust. Now he is lampooned as "King of the Jews" and must endure the revenge of the Jews and the ridicule of the Romans.

✠

Lord Jesus, you endured every kind of suffering on earth for us, so that we might enjoy every kind of blessing in heaven with you. Thank you.

✠ ✠ ✠ ✠ ✠

April 7

One of the criminals hanging there hurled insults at him: "Aren't you the Messiah? Save yourself and us!"

The other one, however, rebuked him, saying, "Don't you fear God? You received the same sentence he did. Ours, however, is only right, because we are getting what we deserve for what we did; but he has done no wrong." And he said to Jesus, "Remember me, Jesus, when you come as King!"

Jesus said to him, "I promise you that today you will be in Paradise with me."

Luke 23:39–43

✠

Even the criminals being executed with Jesus can't agree about who he is. One insults Jesus and challenges him to prove his power by escaping. The other quietly accepts his own punishment, and asks if he may be a member of Jesus' Kingdom.

Jesus promises him that they will walk together in God's garden that very day.

✠

Lord, thank you that it's never too late to cry to you for help, and that you are always ready and willing to save us, whoever we are and whatever we've done.

✠ ✠ ✠ ✠ ✠

April 8

Standing close to Jesus' cross were his mother, his mother's sister, Mary the wife of Clopas, and Mary Magdalene.

Jesus saw his mother and the disciple he loved standing there; so he said to his mother, "He is your son."

Then he said to the disciple, "She is your mother." From that time the disciple took her to live in his home.

John 19:25–27

✠

As death approaches, Jesus gives his mother into the care of his best friend. He tells Mary that John is to be a son to her now, and that she is to be a mother to him.

It was an ideal choice. Not only did Mary and John share a deep love for Jesus, but they were among the very few who weren't too ashamed of him, or fearful for their own safety, to stand with him while he suffered.

✠

Lord, thank you for those who care for us, and those you have given us to care for. May love and loyalty spread throughout our family, and overflow to those around.

✠ ✠ ✠ ✠ ✠

April 9

It was about twelve o'clock when the sun stopped shining and darkness covered the whole country until three o'clock; and the curtain hanging in the Temple was torn in two. Jesus cried out in a loud voice, "Father! In your hands I place my spirit!" He said this and died.

The army officer saw what had happened, and he praised God, saying, "Certainly he was a good man!"

When the people who had gathered there to watch the spectacle saw what happened, they all went back home, beating their breasts in sorrow. All those who knew Jesus personally, including the women who had followed him from Galilee, stood at a distance to watch.

Luke 23: 44–49

✠

There are dramatic signs in the sky and in the city as Jesus gives up his life. It seems as though the sun wants no part in this dark deed. And yet it is not completely dark, for the Temple curtain that separates God from men is torn apart, to show that Jesus' death has opened the way to God.

And the army officer who has seen the whole affair from start to finish, comes to his own conclusion about Jesus.

✠

Lord Jesus, no one took your life from you. You gave it up for us of your own free will. Thank you for hanging there for us when everything was so dreadful, and you could so easily have escaped.

✠ ✠ ✠ ✠ ✠

April 10

There was a man named Joseph from Arimathea, a town in Judaea. He was a good and honourable man, who was waiting for the coming of the Kingdom of God. Although he was a member of the Council, he had not agreed with their decision and action. He went into the presence of Pilate and asked for the body of Jesus. Then he took the body down, wrapped it in a linen sheet, and placed it in a tomb which had been dug out of solid rock and which had never been used. It was Friday, and the Sabbath was about to begin.

The women who had followed Jesus from Galilee went with Joseph and saw the tomb and how Jesus' body was placed in it. Then they went back home and prepared the spices and perfumes for the body.

On the Sabbath they rested, as the Law commanded.

Luke 23:50–56

✠

Joseph of Arimathea casts caution to the winds. He has been appalled by the events of the last two days, and wants to do all he can to make amends.

Suddenly he doesn't mind defiling himself by going into the Governor's presence, or by handling the dead body of Jesus – both things which would make him "unclean" in the eyes of the Law. Nor does he mind donating his new tomb – perhaps one he had intended for himself.

✠

Lord, you have given your very life for us. Help us to spare no effort in doing right by you and for you.

April 11

Early on Sunday morning, while it was still dark, Mary Magdalene went to the tomb and saw that the stone had been taken away from the entrance. She went running to Simon Peter and the other disciple, whom Jesus loved, and told them, "They have taken the Lord from the tomb, and we don't know where they have put him!"

Then Peter and the other disciple went to the tomb. The two of them were running, but the other disciple ran faster than Peter and reached the tomb first. He bent over and saw the linen wrappings, but he did not go in. Behind him came Simon Peter, and he went straight into the tomb. He saw the linen wrappings lying there and the cloth which had been round Jesus' head. It was not lying with the linen wrappings but was rolled up by itself.

Then the other disciple, who had reached the tomb first, also went in; he saw and believed. (They still did not understand the scripture which said that he must rise from death.) Then the disciples went back home.

John 20:1–10

✠

The first thing that strikes us about the resurrection of Jesus is that it is all so unexpected!

Mary Magdalene immediately assumes that the body has been taken away – perhaps to be thrown on the rubbish tip with the corpses of the criminals.

But when Peter and John see the way the grave clothes have been left behind, they realize that the body hasn't been stolen. If it had, the grave clothes would have gone too – or been thrown in a corner. The fact is that the linen wrappings and the turban have simply collapsed! The body of Jesus has passed through them.

✠

Living Lord, thank you that we have an Easter faith, a victory-over-death faith, a home-with-you-in-heaven faith. Hallelujah!

✠ ✠ ✠ ✠ ✠

April 12

Mary stood crying outside the tomb. While she was still crying, she bent over and looked in the tomb and saw two angels there dressed in white, sitting where the body of Jesus had been, one at the head and the other at the feet. "Woman, why are you crying?" they asked her.

She answered, "They have taken my Lord away, and I do not know where they have put him!"

Then she turned round and saw Jesus standing there; but she did not know that it was Jesus. "Woman, why are you crying?" Jesus asked her. "Who is it that you are looking for?"

She thought he was the gardener, so she said to him, "If you took him away, sir, tell me where you have put him, and I will go and get him."

Jesus said to her, "Mary!"

She turned towards him and said in Hebrew, "Rabboni!" (This means "Teacher".)

"Do not hold on to me," Jesus told her, "because I have not yet gone back up to the Father. But go to my brothers and tell them that I am returning to him who is my Father, and their Father, my God and their God."

So Mary Magdalene went and told the disciples that she had seen the Lord and related to them what he had told her.

John 20:11–18

✠

How very wonderful that Jesus should first appear to Mary Magdalene. Very few people would have chosen her as a witness – and with good reason, if she took him for the gardener! But then her eyes were full of tears, and Jesus was literally the last person she expected to see! But once the truth has dawned, she wastes no time in telling the others the fabulous news.

✠

Risen Lord, thank you that you come to us just where we are, and show yourself to us even through our tears; and call us by our name.

✠ ✠ ✠ ✠ ✠

April 13

On that same day two of Jesus' followers were going to a village named Emmaus, about eleven kilometres from Jerusalem, and they were talking to each other about all the things that had happened. As they talked and discussed, Jesus himself drew near and walked along with them; they saw him, but somehow did not recognize him. Jesus said to them, "What are you talking about to each other, as you walk along?"

They stood still, with sad faces. One of them, named Cleopas, asked him, "Are you the only visitor in Jerusalem who doesn't know the things that have been happening there these last few days?"

Then Jesus said to them, "How foolish you are, how slow you are to believe everything the prophets said!"

Luke 24:13–18,25

We meet two more people who don't expect to see Jesus ever again. Cleopas and his friend are on their way home, thoroughly disheartened by the events of the weekend. So far as they are concerned, Jesus was a flop – and his death the biggest anticlimax of history.

But they are wrong!

✠

Lord, so many people are wrong about you so much of the time. Help us as your people not to be blinkered or handicapped by unbelief.

✠ ✠ ✠ ✠ ✠

April 14

As they came near the village to which they were going, Jesus acted as if he were going farther; but they held him back, saying, "Stay with us; the day is almost over and it is getting dark." So he went in to stay with them. He sat down to eat with them, took the bread, and said the blessing; then he broke the bread and gave it to them. Then their eyes were opened and they recognized him, but he disappeared from their sight.

They said to each other, "Wasn't it like a fire burning in us when he talked to us on the road and explained the scriptures to us?"

They got up at once and went back to Jerusalem, where they found the eleven disciples gathered together with the others and saying, "The Lord is risen indeed! He has appeared to Simon!"

The two then explained to them what had happened on the road, and how they had recognized the Lord when he broke the bread.

Luke 24:28–35

✠

As they invite Jesus to stay with them and share their meal, Cleopas and his friend suddenly realize who it is they have met. Perhaps they catch sight of his wounded hands as he breaks the bread?

Anyway, they suddenly have no doubts at all. This *is* Jesus – Jesus alive after his suffering, as the scriptures had foretold. Just wait till the others hear about this!

✠

Lord, help us to realize that you are alive, and with us today. And give us an infectious enthusiasm in sharing this good news with others.

✠ ✠ ✠ ✠ ✠

April 15

While the two were telling them this, suddenly the Lord himself stood among them and said to them, "Peace be with you."

They were terrified, thinking that they were seeing a ghost. But he said to them, "Why are you alarmed? Why are these doubts coming up in your minds? Look at my hands and my feet, and see that it is I myself.

Feel me, and you will know, for a ghost doesn't have flesh and bones, as you can see I have."

He said this and showed them his hands and his feet. They still could not believe, they were so full of joy and wonder; so he asked them, "Have you anything here to eat?" They gave him a piece of cooked fish, which he took and ate in their presence.

Then he said to them, "These are the very things I told you about while I was still with you: everything written about me in the Law of Moses, the writings of the prophets, and the Psalms had to come true."

Luke 24:36–44

✠

There is so much to get used to. Jesus, who they thought was dead, is alive! But not alive as a ghost to haunt them, or a lovely memory to comfort them. He is *really* alive – as alive as he ever was. More so, in fact, for he has been raised to life the other side of death, and is speaking to them from the firm ground beyond the grave.

✠

Come to us, Lord, and touch our lives with your healing and your peace.

✠ ✠ ✠ ✠ ✠

April 16

One of the twelve disciples, Thomas (called the Twin), was not with them when Jesus came. So the other disciples told him, "We have seen the Lord!"

Thomas said to them, "Unless I see the scars of the nails in his hands and put my finger on those scars and my hand in his side, I will not believe."

A week later the disciples were together again indoors, and Thomas was with them. The doors were locked, but Jesus came and stood among them and said, "Peace be with you." Then he said to Thomas, "Put your finger here, and look at my hands; then stretch out your hand and put it in my side. Stop your doubting, and believe!"

Thomas answered him, "My Lord and my God!"

Jesus said to him, "Do you believe because you see me? How happy are those who believe without seeing me!"

John 20:24–29

✠

It always hurts to be left out when something nice happens to everyone else. It must have been like that for Thomas. He must have wondered what he'd done to miss out so badly on seeing Jesus alive again. He doggedly swears that he won't believe a word of it unless he sees for himself!

But Jesus knows. And Jesus comes to Thomas as well. He doesn't blame any of us for wanting to be sure.

✠

Lord, we can't see you, but we can still be sure you are alive. Thank you for Thomas' honesty – and for using his doubt to strengthen his faith.

April 17

After this, Jesus appeared once more to his disciples at Lake Tiberias. This is how it happened. Simon Peter, Thomas (called the Twin), Nathanael (the one from Cana in Galilee), the sons of Zebedee, and two other disciples of Jesus were all together. Simon Peter said to the others, "I am going fishing."

"We will come with you," they told him. So they went out in a boat, but all that night they did not catch a thing. As the sun was rising, Jesus stood at the water's edge, but the disciples did not know that it was Jesus. Then he asked them, "Young men, haven't you caught anything?"

"Not a thing," they answered.

He said to them, "Throw your net out on the right side of the boat, and you will catch some." So they threw the net out and could not pull it back in, because they had caught so many fish.

The disciple whom Jesus loved said to Peter, "It is the Lord!"

John 21:1–7a

✠

Perhaps Peter feels the only thing he's good at is fishing. He seems to have failed in just about everything else. And then he finds he can't do that either!

In the cold light of dawn, they see a figure on the shore. He tells them to throw the net out on the other side of the boat . . .

Suddenly John realizes they've been here before. The same long cold night – the same unlikely advice – the same miraculous catch – the same Lord Jesus!

✠

Lord, when will we learn to do things in your way and in your strength, rather than charging vainly after our own bright ideas? Help us to look and listen for your direction today.

✠ ✠ ✠ ✠ ✠

April 18

When Peter heard that it was the Lord, he wrapped his outer garment round him (for he had taken his clothes off) and jumped into the water. The other disciples came to shore in the boat, pulling the net full of fish. They were not very far from land, about a hundred metres away. When they stepped ashore, they saw a charcoal fire there with fish on it and some bread. Then Jesus said to them, "Bring some of the fish you have just caught."

Simon Peter went aboard and dragged the net ashore full of big fish, a hundred and fifty-three in all; even though there were so many, still the net did not tear. Jesus said to them, "Come and eat." None of the disciples dared ask him, "Who are you?" because they knew it was the Lord. So Jesus went over, took the bread, and gave it to them; he did the same with the fish.

This, then, was the third time Jesus appeared to the disciples after he was raised from death.

John 21:7b–14

✠

The risen Jesus is new life for all of us. He is the sunrise. He is the morning. He is breakfast!

Despite all their toil, the fire is lit and the food is ready for the disciples. They could have trusted Jesus to provide, and saved themselves a sleepless night.

✠

Lord Jesus, please dispel our dark night of sin and failure; warm us with the sunshine of your love, and feed us with your living bread.

✠ ✠ ✠ ✠ ✠

April 19

After they had eaten, Jesus said to Simon Peter, "Simon son of John, do you love me more than these others do?"

"Yes, Lord," he answered, "you know that I love you."

Jesus said to him, "Take care of my lambs." A second time Jesus said to him, "Simon son of John, do you love me?"

"Yes, Lord," he answered, "you know that I love you."

Jesus said to him, "Take care of my sheep." A third time Jesus said, "Simon son of John, do you love me?"

Peter was sad because Jesus asked him the third time, "Do you love me?" so he said to him, "Lord, you know everything; you know that I love you!"

Jesus said to him, "Take care of my sheep. I am telling you the truth: when you were young, you used to get ready and go anywhere you wanted to; but when you are old, you will stretch out your hands and someone else will bind you and take you where you don't want to go."

(In saying this, Jesus was indicating the way in which Peter would die and bring glory to God.) Then Jesus said to him, "Follow me!"

John 21:15–19

✠

Jesus and Peter need this talk. It's not so long since Peter was seated beside another charcoal fire, swearing three times over that he was nothing to do with Jesus.

Now Jesus asks him three times, "Do you love me? Are you completely committed to me?"

And Peter – older and wiser – can only say, "Lord, you know I'm fond of you." All the same, Jesus accepts his poor love, and goes on to entrust him with the care of his people, both young and old.

✠

Lord, you know we're not as committed to you as we should be, as we would like to be, or as we pretend to be. Thank you that you don't discard us in favour of someone else, but still reach out to forgive us and include us in your loving work.

✠ ✠ ✠ ✠ ✠

April 20

The eleven disciples went to the hill in Galilee where Jesus had told them to go. When they saw him, they worshipped him, even though some of them doubted. Jesus drew near and said to them, "I have been given all authority in heaven and on earth. Go, then, to all peoples everywhere and make them my disciples: baptize them in the name of the Father, the Son, and the Holy Spirit, and teach them to obey everything I have commanded you. And I will be with you always, to the end of the age."

Matthew 28:16–20

✠

The time has come for Jesus to leave his disciples, and these are some of his last words to them. The gospel writers are very honest. They don't try to hide the fact that the disciples were usually slow to understand; or that they were proud and selfish in the way they treated each other.

It is to this group of very ordinary men, with their very mixed feelings, that Jesus commits his life's work. He will be with them in spirit, but they must still set out with faith and courage if the Good News is to travel worldwide.

✠

Lord, take our minds and think through them, take our lips and speak through them, take our hearts and set them on fire with love for you.

✠ ✠ ✠ ✠ ✠

On the night before he died, Jesus said many important things to his disciples. Over the next few days we shall be looking at some of them.

✠

April 21

Jesus said to his disciples, "If you love me, you will obey my commandments. I will ask the Father, and he will give you another Helper, who will stay with you for ever. He is the Spirit who reveals the truth about God. The world cannot receive him, because it cannot see him or know him. But you know him, because he remains with you and is in you.

"When I go, you will not be left all alone; I will come back to you. In a little while the world will see me no more, but you will see me; and because I live, you also will live. When that day comes, you will know that I am in my Father and that you are in me, just as I am in you."

John 14:15–20

✠

Jesus promised his disciples that he wouldn't leave them all alone in the world. He would ask his Father to send the Holy Spirit, who would help them in just the same ways as Jesus had done.

But while Jesus as a man couldn't be in two places at once, the Holy Spirit would be with all of them, everywhere, all the time!

Dear God our Father, thank you for sending us your Holy Spirit, to be like Jesus with us and in us – always.

✠ ✠ ✠ ✠ ✠

April 22

Jesus said to his disciples, "I am the real vine, and my Father is the gardener. He breaks off every branch in me that does not bear fruit, and he prunes every branch that does bear fruit, so that it will be clean and bear more fruit. You have been made clean already by the teaching I have given you. Remain united to me, and I will remain united to you. A branch cannot bear fruit by itself; it can do so only if it remains in the vine. In the same way you cannot bear fruit unless you remain in me."

John 15:1–4

✠

Jesus says he is like a vine.

A vine may look dry and gnarled and twisted, but it produces lovely juicy grapes. The trunk passes on all its life to the branches so that they can bear fruit.

That's how Jesus is with us who are his friends. And God the Gardener patiently prunes and cleans us, so that the fruit of Jesus can grow.

✠

Lord Jesus, help us so to grow in you that we become gorgeous bunches of refreshing love, appetizing joy, and health-giving goodness!

April 23

Jesus said to his disciples, "My commandment is this: love one another, just as I love you. The greatest love a person can have for his friends is to give his life for them. And you are my friends if you do what I command you. I do not call you servants any longer, because a servant does not know what his master is doing. Instead, I call you friends, because I have told you everything I have heard from my Father.

"You did not choose me; I chose you and appointed you to go and bear much fruit, the kind of fruit that endures. And so the Father will give you whatever you ask of him in my name. This, then, is what I command you: love one another."

John 15:12–17

✠

Love means giving our best for other people and counting their lives more important than our own. That has been the secret of Jesus' life, and now he shares it with his friends.

If they keep this one commandment, to love one another, they will never go wrong. Nor will we.

✠

Lord, thank you for loving us and for counting our lives more important than yours. Help us to put others first today, for your sake.

✠ ✠ ✠ ✠ ✠

April 24

Jesus said to his disciples, "I am telling you the truth: it is better for you that I go away, because if I do not go, the Helper will not come to you. But if I do go away, then I will send him to you. And when he comes, he will prove to the people of the world that they are wrong about sin and about what is right and about God's judgement. They are wrong about sin, because they do not believe in me; they are wrong about what is right, because I am going to the Father and you will not see me any more; and they are wrong about judgement, because the ruler of this world has already been judged."

John 16:7–11

✠

Most people think that a little sin here and there doesn't do any harm; that no one can really be sure what's right and what's wrong; and that God will never bother to judge us anyway.

But Jesus says the Holy Spirit will show us the truth. Sin matters so much that Jesus had to give his life to rescue us. All that Jesus said and did was true, and God raised him from death to prove it. And God certainly cares about the way we live. One day he will call us to account for *all* our thoughts and actions.

✠

Lord, may your Holy Spirit lead us into all truth, and change our lives so that we are more and more like you.

✠ ✠ ✠ ✠ ✠

April 25

Today we look back at one of the prophecies of Isaiah. The man who wrote these words never met Jesus or saw him hanging on the cross. He lived nearly eight hundred years before Jesus was born! Yet in this sad and thoughtful song, he sees to the heart of the death of Jesus – God's Servant who was so rejected and who suffered so dreadfully.

✠

The people reply,

"Who would have believed what we now report?
Who could have seen the LORD's hand in this?
It was the will of the LORD that his servant
should grow like a plant taking root
in dry ground.
He had no dignity or beauty
to make us take notice of him.
There was nothing attractive about him,
nothing that would draw us to him.
We despised him and rejected him;
he endured suffering and pain.
No one would even look at him –
we ignored him as if he were nothing.

"But he endured the suffering that
should have been ours,
the pain that we should have borne.
All the while we thought that his suffering
was punishment sent by God.
But because of our sins he was wounded,
beaten because of the evil we did.
We are healed by the punishment he suffered,
made whole by the blows he received.

All of us were like sheep that were lost,
  each of us going his own way.
But the LORD made the punishment fall
    on him,
  the punishment all of us deserved."

Isaiah 53:1–6

✠

The prophet, who sees to the heart of things, tells us why Jesus died. "He endured the suffering that should have been ours . . . the Lord made the punishment fall on him, the punishment all of us deserved." And – very wonderfully – we are healed as a result. Cleansed, forgiven, and set free.

✠

Dear Father, thank you for sending Jesus to rescue us from sin and death. Dear Jesus, thank you for taking our punishment so that we can go free.

✠ ✠ ✠ ✠ ✠

April 26

When the apostles met together with Jesus, they asked him, "Lord, will you at this time give the Kingdom back to Israel?"

Jesus said to them, "The times and occasions are set by my Father's own authority, and it is not for you to know when they will be. But when the Holy Spirit comes upon you, you will be filled with power, and you will be witnesses for me in Jerusalem, in all Judaea and Samaria, and to the ends of the earth."

After saying this, he was taken up to heaven as they watched him, and a cloud hid him from their sight.

They still had their eyes fixed on the sky as he went away, when two men dressed in white suddenly stood beside them and said, "Galileans, why are you standing there looking up at the sky? This Jesus, who was taken from you into heaven, will come back in the same way that you saw him go to heaven."

Acts 1:6–11

✠

The time has come for Jesus to return to his Father. But even up to the last minute, the disciples *still* think he is going to seize power on earth and overthrow the Romans.

Instead, Jesus talks about another power and another Kingdom. They must wait in Jerusalem until the power of the Holy Spirit comes upon them – and then they will take the Good News of Jesus and his Kingdom to the ends of the earth.

Then Jesus is taken into heaven, where he is now – in the place of highest honour. It is from there that he will return, although we don't know when that will be.

✠

Lord Jesus, we worship you in your heavenly glory. Help us to live in such a way that we are ready for you to return at any time.

✠ ✠ ✠ ✠ ✠

April 27

When the day of Pentecost came, all the believers were gathered together in one place. Suddenly there was a noise from the sky which sounded like a strong wind blowing, and it filled the whole house where they were sitting. Then they saw what looked like tongues of fire which spread out and touched each person there. They were all filled with the Holy Spirit and began to talk in other languages, as the Spirit enabled them to speak.

There were Jews living in Jerusalem, religious men who had come from every country in the world. When they heard this noise, a large crowd gathered. They were all excited, because each one of them heard the believers speaking in his own language. In amazement and wonder they exclaimed, "These people who are talking like this are Galileans! How is it, then, that all of us hear them speaking in our own native languages?"

Acts 2:1–8

✠

This is one of the greatest days in the history of the world! The day when God's Holy Spirit was poured out on the believers in Jerusalem.

Doctor Luke describes the symptoms of the Spirit – he is powerful and invisible like wind; he warms and spreads like fire.

The Spirit was given to the disciples so that they could take the Good News of Jesus all over the world. He gave them courage, and equipped them with new languages. The pilgrims who had come to Jerusalem for the festival were the first to hear that Jesus is alive – and they heard the Good News in the languages they spoke back home.

Lord, please fill us with your Holy Spirit, so that we have the courage to speak for you, and the skill to talk about you in ways that other people can understand.

✠ ✠ ✠ ✠ ✠

April 28

Then Peter stood up with the other eleven apostles and in a loud voice began to speak to the crowd: "Fellow-Jews and all of you who live in Jerusalem, listen to me and let me tell you what this means. These people are not drunk, as you suppose; it is only nine o'clock in the morning. Instead, this is what the prophet Joel spoke about:

> 'This is what I will do in the last days,
> God says:
> I will pour out my Spirit on everyone.
> Your sons and daughters will proclaim
> my message;
> your young men will see visions,
> and your old men will have dreams.
> Yes, even on my servants, both men
> and women,
> I will pour out my Spirit in those days,
> and they will proclaim my message.'"

Acts 2:14–18

✠

At first the people in the crowd think the disciples are drunk. They must have been babbling away very happily indeed!

But then Peter speaks. He explains what is going on. It's not the festival wine which has made them so glad, but the Spirit of God within them. He reminds them of the words of the prophet Joel, when God promised to pour out his Spirit on everyone – young and old, men and women, rich and poor – so that all can proclaim his message.

✠

Lord, may we be your glad messengers today. Even if we don't have an opportunity to speak, may our radiant faces be a message in themselves.

✠ ✠ ✠ ✠ ✠

April 29

Peter continued: "All the people of Israel, then, are to know for sure that this Jesus, whom you crucified, is the one that God has made Lord and Messiah!"

When the people heard this, they were deeply troubled and said to Peter and the other apostles, "What shall we do, brothers?"

Peter said to them, "Each one of you must turn away from his sins and be baptized in the name of Jesus Christ, so that your sins will be forgiven; and you will receive God's gift, the Holy Spirit. For God's promise was made to you and your children, and to all who are far away – all whom the Lord our God calls to himself."

Peter made his appeal to them and with many other words he urged them, saying, "Save yourselves from the punishment coming on this wicked people!"

Many of them believed his message and were baptized, and about three thousand people were added to the group that day. They spent their time in learning from the apostles, taking part in the fellowship, and sharing in the fellowship meals and the prayers.

Acts 2:36–42

✠

Peter tells the crowd the plain truth. They crucified God's Messiah!

Outside this very city, just two months previously, they put Jesus of Nazareth to death. But that wasn't the end of Jesus. God raised him from the grave, and in doing so he proved that Jesus of Nazareth is his Son – the Messiah, the Christ.

The people realize they have made a tragic mistake. What can they possibly do to get right with God again? Peter says, "Turn round! Turn back to God!" They must turn away from sin, and come to Jesus instead – be baptized, and receive his Spirit.

That day three thousand people joined the little group of disciples – multiplying it many times over. The Christian Church is born – and growing fast.

✠

Lord, thank you for calling us to belong to you and share your life.

✠ ✠ ✠ ✠ ✠

April 30

One day Peter and John went to the Temple at three o'clock in the afternoon, the hour for prayer. There at the Beautiful Gate, as it was called, was a man who had been lame all his life. Every day he was carried to the gate to beg for money from the people who were going into the Temple. When he saw Peter and John going in, he begged them to give him something. They looked straight at him, and Peter said, "Look at us!" So he looked at them, expecting to get something from them. But Peter said to him, "I have no money at all, but I give you what I have: in the name of Jesus Christ of Nazareth I order you to get up and walk!" Then he took him by his right hand and helped him up. At once the man's feet and ankles became strong; he jumped up, stood on his feet, and started walking around. Then he went into the Temple with them, walking and jumping and praising God. The people there saw him walking and praising God, and when they recognized him as the beggar who had sat at the Beautiful Gate, they were all surprised and amazed at what had happened to him.

Acts 3:1–10

✠

Peter and John had passed the same beggar every day for weeks. But now they "see" him for the first time. Didn't Jesus come to help people like this?

And so they have the courage of their faith, and help the man up in the name of Jesus.

✠

Lord, help us to see those around with your eyes, love them with your heart, and help them for your sake.

A Psalm for
May

I waited patiently for the LORD's help;
  then he listened to me and heard my cry.
He pulled me out of a dangerous pit,
  out of the deadly quicksand.
He set me safely on a rock
  and made me secure.
He taught me to sing a new song,
  a song of praise to our God.
Many who see this will take warning
  and will put their trust in the LORD.

Happy are those who trust the LORD,
  who do not turn to idols
  or join those who worship false gods.
You have done many things for us, O
    LORD our God;
  there is no one like you!
  You have made many wonderful
    plans for us.
I could never speak of them all –
  their number is so great!

Psalm 40:1–5

A Psalm for

Mary

waited patiently for the Lord's help;
then he listened to me and heard my cry.
He pulled me out of a dangerous pit,
out of the deadly quicksand.
He set me safely on a rock
and made me secure.
He taught me to sing a new song,
a song of praise to our God.
Many who see this will take warning
and will put their trust in the Lord.

Happy are those who trust the Lord,
who do not turn to idols
or join those who worship false gods.
You have done many things for us, O
Lord our God;
there is no one like you!
You have made many wonderful
plans for us.
I could never speak of them all—
their number is so great.

Psalm 40:1-5

May 1

Stephen, a man richly blessed by God and full of power, performed great miracles and wonders among the people. But he was opposed by some men who were members of the synagogue of the Freedmen (as it was called), which included Jews from Cyrene and Alexandria. They and other Jews from the provinces of Cilicia and Asia started arguing with Stephen. But the Spirit gave Stephen such wisdom that when he spoke, they could not refute him. So they bribed some men to say, "We heard him speaking against Moses and against God!" In this way they stirred up the people, the elders, and the teachers of the Law. They seized Stephen and took him before the Council. Then they brought in some men to tell lies about him. "This man," they said, "is always talking against our sacred Temple and the Law of Moses. We heard him say that this Jesus of Nazareth will tear down the Temple and change all the customs which have come down to us from Moses!" All those sitting in the Council fixed their eyes on Stephen and saw that his face looked like the face of an angel.

Acts 6:8–15

Stephen is only one of the helpers, but he is full of the Holy Spirit – and he has a brilliant brain!

He realizes that since the coming of Jesus, the Jewish religion will have to change. The sacrifices in the Temple aren't needed any more, and all the rules and regulations of the old days are things of the past. We don't get right with God by keeping rules, but by turning to Jesus and trusting him. Not surprisingly, Stephen is soon in trouble for his views, but even his judges can see what a fine man he is.

✠

Lord Jesus, you came to change our lives in so many ways. Help us to worship you with our minds and with our understanding, just as Stephen did. And to stand up for what we believe is true.

✠ ✠ ✠ ✠ ✠

May 2

As the members of the Council listened to Stephen, they became furious and ground their teeth at him in anger. But Stephen, full of the Holy Spirit, looked up to heaven and saw God's glory and Jesus standing at the right-hand side of God. "Look!" he said. "I see heaven opened and the Son of Man standing at the right-hand side of God!"

With a loud cry the members of the Council covered their ears with their hands. Then they all rushed at him at once, threw him out of the city, and stoned him. The witnesses left their cloaks in the care of a young man named Saul.

They kept on stoning Stephen as he called out to the Lord, "Lord Jesus, receive my spirit!" He knelt down and cried out in a loud voice, "Lord! Do not remember this sin against them!" He said this and died.

And Saul approved of his murder.

Acts 7:54–60

✠

Stephen is the first follower of Jesus to die for his faith.

Jesus had warned his disciples that suffering lay ahead for some of them, but he promised to be with them whatever happened. Even as Stephen is dying, he knows that he is going to be with Jesus in heaven. And do you notice that a young man called Saul is watching when Stephen is stoned – Saul who will one day become the apostle Paul? In some strange way, God can even use the suffering of his people to draw others to his love.

✠

Lord Jesus, we're not very brave and we don't want to suffer. But if that's your way for us, help us to know that you are always with us, and that not even death can separate us from you.

✠ ✠ ✠ ✠ ✠

May 3

An angel of the Lord said to Philip, "Get ready and go south to the road that goes from Jerusalem to Gaza." (This road is not used nowadays.) So Philip got ready and went. Now an Ethiopian eunuch, who was an important official in charge of the treasury of the queen of Ethiopia, was on his way home. He had been to Jerusalem to worship God and was going back home in his carriage. As he rode along, he was reading from the book of the prophet Isaiah. The Holy Spirit said to Philip, "Go over to that carriage and stay close to it." Philip ran over and heard him reading from the book of the prophet Isaiah. He asked him, "Do you understand what you are reading?"

The official replied, "How can I understand unless someone explains it to me?" And he invited Philip to climb up and sit in the carriage with him. Then Philip began to speak; starting from this passage of scripture, he told him the Good News about Jesus. As they travelled down the road, they came to a place where there was some water, and the official said, "Here is some water. What is to keep me from being baptized?"

The official ordered the carriage to stop, and both Philip and the official went down into the water, and Philip baptized him. When they came up out of the water, the Spirit of the Lord took Philip away. The official did not see him again, but continued on his way, full of joy.

Acts 8:26–31,35–39

✠

An African pilgrim is going home to Ethiopia. And very splendid he is, being Chancellor of the Exchequer. But he is badly disappointed. He has been all the way to Jerusalem, but the Jews wouldn't let him into their Temple. All he could do was buy a book – the Prophecy of Isaiah – and he can't understand a word of it!

But then he gives a lift to Philip, who is able to explain the meaning of the words and tell him the Good News of Jesus.

When they come to some water, the African asks to be baptized. And there is a Christian church in his country to this very day!

✠

Lord, thank you for prompting Philip to share his Good News. May we be the kind of people who welcome strangers and make friends with those who are lonely.

May 4

In the meantime Saul kept up his violent threats of murder against the followers of the Lord. He went to the High Priest and asked for letters of introduction to the synagogues in Damascus, so that if he should find there any followers of the Way of the Lord, he would be able to arrest them, both men and women, and bring them back to Jerusalem.

As Saul was coming near the city of Damascus, suddenly a light from the sky flashed round him. He fell to the ground and heard a voice saying to him, "Saul, Saul! Why do you persecute me?"

"Who are you, Lord?" he asked.

"I am Jesus, whom you persecute," the voice said. "But get up and go into the city, where you will be told what you must do."

The men who were travelling with Saul had stopped, not saying a word; they heard the voice but could not see anyone.

Acts 9:1–7

✠

Saul is a bright young man – very bright. And very angry. He is angry with the followers of Jesus for talking such nonsense and doing such damage to the Jewish religion. He decides to stamp out this Jesus business once and for all – and gets special permission to arrest the Christians in Damascus.

But just as he is approaching the city, Jesus meets him! In a moment, Saul realizes that Jesus *is* the Christ and that he is alive in heaven. He also realizes that when he hurts Jesus' followers, he is persecuting Jesus himself.

Lord, thank you that you even love your enemies and want them to know you for themselves.

✠ ✠ ✠ ✠ ✠

May 5

Saul got up from the ground and opened his eyes, but could not see a thing. So they took him by the hand and led him into Damascus. For three days he was not able to see, and during that time he did not eat or drink anything.

There was a Christian in Damascus named Ananias. He had a vision, in which the Lord said to him, "Ananias!"

"Here I am, Lord," he answered.

The Lord said to him, "Get ready and go to Straight Street, and at the house of Judas ask for a man from Tarsus named Saul. He is praying, and in a vision he has seen a man named Ananias come in and place his hands on him so that he might see again."

So Ananias went, entered the house where Saul was, and placed his hands on him. "Brother Saul," he said, "the Lord has sent me – Jesus himself, who appeared to you on the road as you were coming here. He sent me so that you might see again and be filled with the Holy Spirit." At once something like fish scales fell from Saul's eyes, and he was able to see again. He stood up and was baptized; and after he had eaten, his strength came back.

Acts 9:8–12,17–19

✠

Saul is blind and helpless. The powerful young man who had come storming towards Damascus now has to be led by the hand. His pride and strength have collapsed. But God knows where Saul is, and has a plan for him. He sends Ananias to befriend him and heal him – Ananias, whom Saul would surely have arrested and imprisoned given half a chance.

✠

Lord, your love is very wonderful. You bless your enemies, and turn them into friends. And you break down the barriers between ourselves and those who hate us.

✠ ✠ ✠ ✠ ✠

May 6

Saul stayed for a few days with the believers in Damascus. He went straight to the synagogues and began to preach that Jesus was the Son of God.

All who heard him were amazed and asked, "Isn't he the one who in Jerusalem was killing those who worship that man Jesus? And didn't he come here for the very purpose of arresting those people and taking them back to the chief priests?"

But Saul's preaching became even more powerful, and his proofs that Jesus was the Messiah were so convincing that the Jews who lived in Damascus could not answer him.

After many days had gone by, the Jews met together and made plans to kill Saul, but he was told of their plan. Day and night they watched the city gates in order to kill him. But one night Saul's followers took him and let him down through an opening in the wall, lowering him in a basket.

Acts 9:19–25

✠

Saul the Persecutor is now the star preacher of the Jesus Way. Those who hear him can hardly believe their ears.

Before long, the Jews who had looked forward to his arrival are planning to kill him. It seems the only way to stop his talk of Jesus being the Messiah, God's chosen King.

Soon Saul has to escape from Damascus, hidden in a laundry basket. Not a very dignified exit for someone as proud as Saul – but he is learning fast.

✠

Lord, thank you for calling Saul to be your apostle, and for the people who welcomed him, trusted him, and protected him in those early days. Help us in our turn to be alert to your plans, and to help in any way we can.

✠ ✠ ✠ ✠ ✠

May 7

There was a man in Caesarea named Cornelius, who was a captain in the Roman regiment called "The

Italian Regiment". He was a religious man; he and his whole family worshipped God. He also did much to help the Jewish poor people and was constantly praying to God. It was about three o'clock one afternoon when he had a vision, in which he clearly saw an angel of God come in and say to him, "Cornelius!"

He stared at the angel in fear and said, "What is it, sir?"

The angel answered, "God is pleased with your prayers and works of charity, and is ready to answer you. And now send some men to Joppa for a certain man whose full name is Simon Peter. He is a guest in the home of a leather-worker named Simon, who lives by the sea." Then the angel went away, and Cornelius called two of his house servants and a soldier, a religious man who was one of his personal attendants. He told them what had happened and sent them off to Joppa.

Acts 10:1–8

✠

Cornelius is a great man – "an officer and a gentleman". He is strong enough to be open to the beliefs and ways of the Jews around him, and humble enough to pray to their God.

But that is as far as Cornelius can go. Like the African we met a few days ago, Cornelius is an outsider. He keeps running into the "Keep Out" sign.

But it isn't God who is keeping him out. God's plan is to introduce Cornelius to Simon Peter – and he does so by giving each of them a vision.

✠

Lord, thank you that nothing is impossible for you. You can break down the mighty barriers we erect between ourselves and others. Help us to play our part in deflating pride and demolishing prejudice.

✠ ✠ ✠ ✠ ✠

May 8

The next day, as they were on their way and coming near Joppa, Peter went up on the roof of the house about noon in order to pray. He became hungry and wanted something to eat; while the food was being prepared, he had a vision. He saw heaven opened and something coming down that looked like a large sheet being lowered by its four corners to the earth. In it were all kinds of animals, reptiles, and wild birds. A voice said to him, "Get up, Peter; kill and eat!"

But Peter said, "Certainly not, Lord! I have never eaten anything ritually unclean or defiled."

The voice spoke to him again, "Do not consider anything unclean that God has declared clean." This happened three times, and then the thing was taken back up into heaven.

While Peter was wondering about the meaning of this vision, the men sent by Cornelius had learnt where Simon's house was, and they were now standing in front of the gate. They called out and asked, "Is there a guest here by the name of Simon Peter?"

Peter was still trying to understand what the vision meant, when the Spirit said, "Listen! Three men are here looking for you. So get ready and go down, and do not hesitate to go with them, for I have sent them."

Acts 10:9–20

✠

Just think. Peter has never set foot in the house of a Gentile – a non-Jew. But he has at least learnt to stay at the home of Simon the Tanner – another person who was an outsider. A tanner had to handle the dead bodies of animals, and this made him "unclean" – unfit to worship God (or so the Jews thought).

Now Peter has a dream about all the unclean creatures in the world – and God is calling them clean! And just as Peter is wondering what it means, there is a knock at the door, and three "unclean" (Gentile) men come calling for him.

✠

Lord, we live in such neat compartments. There are those we allow in, and those we keep out. Please show us your different way – your way of love and trust – so that the whole world can share your life.

✠ ✠ ✠ ✠ ✠

May 9

Peter went with the messengers and met Cornelius. He still surprised himself mightily by going into the house of a Gentile! But once he was there, he had no doubt that God had sent him to tell this Roman family about Jesus. And tell them he did.

✠

While Peter was still speaking, the Holy Spirit came down on all those who were listening to his message. The Jewish believers who had come from Joppa with Peter were amazed that God had poured out his gift of the Holy Spirit on the Gentiles also. For they heard them speaking in strange tongues and praising God's greatness. Peter spoke up: "These people have received the Holy Spirit, just as we also did. Can anyone, then, stop them from being baptized with water?" So he ordered them to be baptized in the name of Jesus Christ. Then they asked him to stay with them for a few days.

Acts 10:44–48

✠

Peter and his companions are amazed that the Holy Spirit is being poured out on Romans. Fancy Romans speaking in strange languages and praising God! Whatever next?

✠

Lord, why are we always so surprised when you do something new? Help us to see that you want to draw everyone *to yourself – not just the people we happen to like.*

May 10

About this time King Herod began to persecute some members of the church. He had James, the brother of John, put to death by the sword. When he saw that this pleased the Jews, he went on to arrest Peter. (This happened during the time of the Festival of Unleavened Bread.) After his arrest Peter was put in jail, where he was handed over to be guarded by four groups of four soldiers each. Herod planned to put him on trial in public after Passover. So Peter was kept in jail, but the people of the church were praying earnestly to God for him.

Acts 12:1–5

✠

Now King Herod starts to lash out at the followers of Jesus. Like his grandfather (who had the Bethlehem babies put to death) this king, Herod Agrippa I, is a vicious man.

James, the fisherman Jesus called to follow him from the shores of Galilee, is executed. And his death is so well received by the Jews that Herod Agrippa plans to put on an even better show with the arrest, trial and death of Peter. But the believers *pray*!

✠

Lord, you said that your disciples would have to suffer – and suffering may befall us as well. Please be close to all your people who are going through testing times, wherever they are around the world.

✠ ✠ ✠ ✠ ✠

May 11

The night before Herod was going to bring him out to the people, Peter was sleeping between two guards. He was tied with two chains, and there were guards on duty at the prison gate. Suddenly an angel of the Lord stood there, and a light shone in the cell. The angel shook Peter by the shoulder, woke him up, and said, "Hurry! Get up!" At once the chains fell off Peter's hands. Then the angel said, "Fasten your belt and put on your sandals." Peter did so, and the angel said, "Put your cloak round you and come with me." Peter followed him out of the prison, not knowing, however, if what the angel was doing was real; he thought he was seeing a vision. They passed by the first guard post and then the second, and came at last to the iron gate leading into the city. The gate opened for them by itself, and they went out. They walked down a street, and suddenly the angel left Peter.

Acts 12:6–10

✠

However does Peter manage to escape? Is it an "inside job", with one of the prison staff unlocking the chains and doors? It can't be the soldiers, for they would be put to death for allowing a prisoner to get out.

Luke tells us that it is none other than one of God's angels who sets Peter free. But if this is possible, why didn't an angel rescue James as well? We don't know the answer. Sometimes God allows people to be killed because he is ready for them to come to him. Sometimes he rescues them because there is still more work for them to do here on earth. Either way, our lives are always safe in his hands.

Lord, thank you that you have a purpose for each of us while we live on earth – and that we can't possibly die before our work for you is finished.

✠ ✠ ✠ ✠ ✠

May 12

Then Peter realized what had happened to him, and said, "Now I know that it is really true! The Lord sent his angel to rescue me from Herod's power and from everything the Jewish people expected to happen."

Aware of his situation, he went to the home of Mary, the mother of John Mark, where many people had gathered and were praying. Peter knocked at the outside door, and a servant-girl named Rhoda came to answer it. She recognized Peter's voice and was so happy that she ran back in without opening the door, and announced that Peter was standing outside. "You are mad!" they told her. But she insisted that it was true. So they answered, "It is his angel."

Meanwhile Peter kept on knocking. At last they opened the door, and when they saw him, they were amazed. He motioned with his hand for them to be quiet, and he explained to them how the Lord had brought him out of prison. "Tell this to James and the rest of the believers," he said; then he left and went somewhere else.

Acts 12:11–17

✠

Although the house of John Mark's mother is packed with people praying for Peter, no one believes for a moment that he's standing outside the front door!

✠

Lord, help us to pray bold prayers – to ask you for great things – and to pray expecting that you will answer.

✠ ✠ ✠ ✠ ✠

May 13

In the church at Antioch there were some prophets and teachers: Barnabas, Simeon (called the Black), Lucius (from Cyrene), Manaen (who had been brought up with Herod the governor), and Saul. While they were serving the Lord and fasting, the Holy Spirit said to them, "Set apart for me Barnabas and Saul, to do the work to which I have called them."

They fasted and prayed, placed their hands on them, and sent them off.

Acts 13:1–3

✠

The believers at Antioch are a real mixture. They come from different races, and different classes of society. But they are united in loving the Lord and serving him.

One day, while they are praying, the Holy Spirit gives them an idea which is to affect the lives of millions of people in many parts of the world and in all the ages to come. The idea is that Barnabas and Saul shall be specially commissioned to take the Good News to other cities. They are to become missionaries.

✠

Lord, thank you for every way in which the message of Jesus is carried around the world. And thank you for all those people who have passed on the Good News so carefully and courageously, so that it has reached us as well.

✠ ✠ ✠ ✠ ✠

May 14

They went all the way across the island to Paphos, where they met a certain magician named Bar-Jesus, a Jew who claimed to be a prophet. He was a friend of the governor of the island, Sergius Paulus, who was an intelligent man. The governor called Barnabas and Saul before him because he wanted to hear the word of God. But they were opposed by the magician Elymas (that is his name in Greek), who tried to turn the governor away from the faith. Then Saul – also known as Paul – was filled with the Holy Spirit; he looked straight at the magician and said, "You son of the Devil! You are the enemy of everything that is good. You are full of all kinds of evil tricks, and you always keep trying to turn the Lord's truths into lies! The Lord's hand will come down on you now; you will be blind and will not see the light of day for a time."

At once Elymas felt a dark mist cover his eyes, and he walked about trying to find someone to lead him by the hand.

When the governor saw what had happened, he believed; for he was greatly amazed at the teaching about the Lord.

Acts 13:6–12

✠

Wherever the Good News is preached, there is a fight with the forces of evil. At Paphos there is even a magician calling himself "Son of Jesus" – and he wants to stop his friend the governor hearing the truth.

Saul challenges the magician, taking him head-on. He tells him he isn't a Son of Jesus at all, but a Son of the Devil! And it is soon clear to everyone that Elymas has met his match.

✠

Lord, you are the only true God, but your enemies are still too strong for us unless you help us. Thank you that the presence of your Spirit with us means that we need never be afraid of anything or anyone.

✠ ✠ ✠ ✠ ✠

May 15

They travelled through the region of Phrygia and Galatia because the Holy Spirit did not let them preach the message in the province of Asia. When they reached the border of Mysia, they tried to go into the province of Bithynia, but the Spirit of Jesus did not allow them. So they travelled right on through Mysia and went to Troas. That night Paul had a vision in which he saw a Macedonian standing and begging him, "Come over to Macedonia and help us!" As soon as Paul had this vision, we got ready to leave for Macedonia, because we decided that God had called us to preach the Good News to the people there.

Acts 16:6–10

✠

Paul is puzzled. He keeps trying to go south to the towns of Asia, but somehow he is always prevented. In the end he and Silas keep travelling on until they come to the sea.

And then Paul has a dream. He sees a man from Macedonia – across the water – calling for help. (It may be that the man was Luke, who later wrote one of the gospels, as well as this Book of Acts.)

Suddenly Paul realizes what God is doing. The Holy Spirit hasn't allowed them to preach in Asia, because he was all the time leading them to another continent altogether – Europe!

✠

Lord, however frustrating things may seem, we need never be out of your plan. Help us to see that when you are blocking one way, it's because you are gently showing us another.

✠ ✠ ✠ ✠ ✠

May 16

We left by ship from Troas and sailed straight across to Samothrace, and the next day to Neapolis. From there we went inland to Philippi, a city of the first district of Macedonia; it is also a Roman colony. We spent several days there. On the Sabbath we went out of the city to the river-side, where we thought there would be a place where Jews gathered for prayer. We sat down and talked to the women who gathered there. One of those who heard us was Lydia from Thyatira, who was a dealer in purple cloth. She was a woman who worshipped God, and the Lord opened her mind to pay attention to what Paul was saying. After she and the people of her house had been baptized, she invited us, "Come and stay in my house if you have decided that I am a true believer in the Lord." And she persuaded us to go.

Acts 16:11–15

✠

Paul has to use his wits. He decides to start his mission in Philippi, the capital of Macedonia. Normally there would be a synagogue in each city, but in Philippi there aren't enough Jewish men to form a church.

So Paul waits for the Sabbath day, and then goes down to the river-side to see if anyone is meeting for prayer. Sure enough, there is a group of women there, and Paul tells them about Jesus.

One of the ladies, a wealthy businesswoman called Lydia, invites them to her home. And Lydia turns out to be from Thyatira – one of the cities of Asia. So the Good News will be travelling into Asia after all! How God must have smiled when Paul realized what was going on.

✠

Lord, please use every part of our lives – our home, our work, and our friendships – to introduce more and more people to the life and love of Jesus.

✠ ✠ ✠ ✠ ✠

May 17

One day as we were going to the place of prayer, we were met by a slave-girl who had an evil spirit that enabled her to predict the future. She earned a lot of money for her owners by telling fortunes. She followed Paul and us, shouting, "These men are servants of the Most High God! They announce to you how you can be saved!" She did this for many days, until Paul became so upset that he turned round and said to the spirit, "In the name of Jesus Christ I order you to come out of her!" The spirit went out of her that very moment.

When her owners realized that their chance of making money was gone, they seized Paul and Silas and dragged them to the authorities in the public square. They brought them before the Roman officials, and said, "These men are Jews, and they are causing trouble in our city. They are teaching customs that are against our law; we are Roman citizens, and we cannot accept these customs or practise them." And the crowd joined in the attack against Paul and Silas.

Then the officials tore the clothes off Paul and Silas and ordered them to be whipped. After a severe beating, they were thrown into jail, and the jailer was ordered to lock them up tight.

Acts 16:16–23

Once again, the message of Jesus plunges Paul and Silas into a battle. This time they are at odds with the owners of a slave girl who tells fortunes. There is no doubt that she can see into the future – but the power that enables her to do so is evil.

Evil spirits recognized Jesus during his life on earth, and now they recognize his followers. When Paul casts out the evil spirit from the girl, she becomes useless to her owners, because she is no longer "clairvoyant". So the owners drag Paul and Silas before the authorities, who have them beaten and thrown into jail.

✠

Lord, may we not be afraid to take our stand for you, even when it gets us into trouble.

✠ ✠ ✠ ✠ ✠

May 18

About midnight Paul and Silas were praying and singing hymns to God, and the other prisoners were listening to them. Suddenly there was a violent earthquake, which shook the prison to its foundations. At once all the doors opened, and the chains fell off all the prisoners. The jailer woke up, and when he saw the prison doors open, he thought that the prisoners had escaped; so he pulled out his sword and was about to kill himself. But Paul shouted at the top of his voice, "Don't harm yourself! We are all here!"

The jailer called for a light, rushed in, and fell trembling at the feet of Paul and Silas. Then he led them out and asked, "Sirs, what must I do to be saved?"

They answered, "Believe in the Lord Jesus, and you will be saved – you and your family." Then they preached the word of the Lord to him and to all the others in his house. At that very hour of the night the jailer took them and washed their wounds; and he and all his family were baptized at once. Then he took Paul and Silas up into his house and gave them some food to eat. He and his family were filled with joy, because they now believed in God.

Acts 16:25–34

✠

There's no stopping Paul and Silas. They have been ill-treated, flogged, and thrown into a dark and dirty Roman prison – but we find them singing!

And then, at midnight, the whole place is rocked by an earthquake, and all the locks and bars are shaken free, so that they can simply walk out.

But they don't. Instead, they call to the jailer, spare his life, and share the Good News about Jesus with him and his family. And the next thing we see is the tough old Roman veteran gently washing the cut and bleeding backs of his prisoners. What a difference Jesus makes!

✠

Lord, thank you that by your mighty power you give freedom, forgiveness and joy.

✠ ✠ ✠ ✠ ✠

May 19

Sometimes Paul was in prison for months or years at a time. When this happened, he would write letters to the people at the churches he had started. He even wrote to Christians he had never met, but hoped to see one day. This is part of his letter to the Christians in Rome.

✠

When we were still helpless, Christ died for the wicked at the time that God chose. It is a difficult thing for someone to die for a righteous person. It may even be that someone might dare to die for a good person. But God has shown us how much he loves us – it was while we were still sinners that Christ died for us! By his death we are now put right with God; how much more, then, will we be saved by him from God's anger! We were God's enemies, but he made us his friends through the death of his Son.

Romans 5:6–10

✠

Paul explains that Jesus didn't deserve to die. And certainly we weren't worth dying for. The human race was far-gone in sin, and full of anger and hostility towards God.

Even so, God sent Jesus into the world to make friends with us again. Not because we deserved in any way to be saved – but because he loves us so much.

✠

Thank you, Lord, for your saving love.

May 20

I find that this law is at work: when I want to do what is good, what is evil is the only choice I have. My inner being delights in the law of God. But I see a different law at work in my body – a law that fights against the law which my mind approves of. It makes me a prisoner to the law of sin which is at work in my body. What an unhappy man I am! Who will rescue me from this body that is taking me to death? Thanks be to God, who does this through our Lord Jesus Christ!

Romans 7:21–25

✠

Even though Paul is a Christian, he still knows there is a struggle going on inside him. And we can all echo his words.

There are always things we ought to do that are good. Yet we often end up doing the things we hate or regret.

But there is a way out! Jesus is the one who gives us forgiveness when we are sorry for the past, and offers us his own friendship and strength in the present. It's when we are really helpless that Jesus is at last able to do everything for us.

✠

Lord Jesus, help us to die to our old selfish ways and come alive to you instead – every day.

✠ ✠ ✠ ✠ ✠

May 21

I am certain that nothing can separate us from his love: neither death nor life, neither angels nor other heavenly rulers or powers, neither the present nor the future, neither the world above nor the world below – there is nothing in all creation that will ever be able to separate us from the love of God which is ours through Christ Jesus our Lord.

Romans 8:38–39

✠

The greatest thing in the universe is God's love. God *is* love – that's what he's like. And that means that wherever we go, and whatever happens to us, he will always be with us.

✠

Lord God our Father, thank you for your great and everlasting love.

✠ ✠ ✠ ✠ ✠

May 22

So then, my brothers, because of God's great mercy to us I appeal to you: Offer yourselves as a living sacrifice to God, dedicated to his service and pleasing to him. This is the true worship that you should offer. Do not conform yourselves to the standards of this world, but let God transform you inwardly by a complete change of your mind. Then you will be able to know the will of God – what is good and is pleasing to him and is perfect.

Romans 12:1–2

✠

Paul says that God has done everything for us – given us this life and offered us eternal life. So surely the very best thing we can do is to give ourselves back to him. Then he can give us new hearts and minds, and show us his good and perfect will for our lives.

Without God at work within us, we'll just be squeezed by the pressures of the world around. That means we will be shaped by selfishness and greed, which leaves us lonely and bitter inside. We will also be left without any clues about the meaning of our lives, or how to find true happiness.

✠

Lord, you gave yourself for us. Please accept our offering of our lives back to you.

✠ ✠ ✠ ✠ ✠

May 23

Paul knew the Christians at Corinth very well. They tended to be jealous of each other – wondering which of them was most important. But Paul told them that they were *all* important – like parts of a body.

✠

Christ is like a single body, which has many parts; it is still one body, even though it is made up of different parts. In the same way, all of us, whether Jews or Gentiles, whether slaves or free, have been baptized into the one body by the same Spirit, and we have all been given the one Spirit to drink.

For the body itself is not made up of only one part, but of many parts. If the foot were to say, "Because I am not a hand, I don't belong to the body", that would not keep it from being a part of the body. And if the ear were to say, "Because I am not an eye, I don't belong to the body", that would not keep it from being a part of the body. If the whole body were just an eye, how could it hear? And if it were only an ear, how could it smell? As it is, however, God put every different part in the body just as he wanted it to be. There would not be a body if it were all only one part! As it is, there are many parts but one body.

1 Corinthians 12:12–20

✠

Lord, you have made us all different in your church – but we all belong together. Help us to see that we can't get on without other people – and show us the special place you have for us to be, and the work you have for us to do.

✠ ✠ ✠ ✠ ✠

May 24

I may be able to speak the languages of men and even of angels, but if I have no love, my speech is no more than a noisy gong or a clanging bell. I may have the gift of inspired preaching; I may have all knowledge and understand all secrets; I may have all the faith needed to move mountains – but if I have no love, I am nothing. I may give away everything I have, and even give up my body to be burnt – but if I have no love, this does me no good.

Love is patient and kind; it is not jealous or conceited or proud; love is not ill-mannered or selfish or irritable; love does not keep a record of wrongs; love is not happy with evil, but is happy with the truth. Love never gives up; and its faith, hope, and patience never fail.

1 Corinthians 13:1–7

✠

The Christians at Corinth have been squabbling. They are jealous of each other's gifts. But Paul says that all gifts are pointless without love. It's love that counts, because love is the most important way in which we are like God. And, in the end, love is the only thing that will last.

✠

Lord, help us to live truly loving lives today.

✠ ✠ ✠ ✠ ✠

May 25

The Spirit produces love, joy, peace, patience, kindness, goodness, faithfulness, humility, and self-control. There is no law against such things as these.

And those who belong to Christ Jesus have put to death their human nature with all its passions and desires. The Spirit has given us life; he must also control our lives. We must not be proud or irritate one another or be jealous of one another.

Galatians 5:22–26

✠

Paul writes to the Christians in Galatia about the "fruit" that the Holy Spirit produces in every Christian life. Love, joy, peace and the others aren't different fruits, like apples, pears and bananas. Rather, they are different aspects of the *same* fruit – like segments in an orange. If the Holy Spirit is at work in our lives, then *all* these qualities will be steadily growing.

✠

Lord, may we gently, steadily, grow more and more like you.

✠ ✠ ✠ ✠ ✠

May 26

Paul writes to the Christians at Ephesus and talks about the way husbands and wives should treat each other when they are both Christians.

✠

Submit yourselves to one another because of your reverence for Christ.

Wives, submit to your husbands as to the Lord. For a husband has authority over his wife just as Christ has authority over the church; and Christ is himself the Saviour of the church, his body. And so wives must submit completely to their husbands just as the church submits itself to Christ.

Husbands, love your wives just as Christ loved the church and gave his life for it.

Ephesians 5:21–25

✠

In Christian marriage, the keynote is Jesus. Wives must put their husbands first, just as they put Jesus first. But then, says Paul, the husbands must put their wives first – loving them, and giving their lives for them. Just as Jesus gave his life for all of us.

✠

Lord, thank you for your gift of marriage. Help us to put one another first and want the very best for each other.

✠ ✠ ✠ ✠ ✠

May 27

Children, it is your Christian duty to obey your parents, for this is the right thing to do. "Respect your father and mother" is the first commandment that has a promise added: "so that all may go well with you, and you may live a long time in the land."

Parents, do not treat your children in such a way as to make them angry. Instead, bring them up with Christian discipline and instruction.

Ephesians 6:1–4

✠

When Paul writes about parents and children, we find the same theme of "one-anotherness" that he spoke of in marriage.

Children should obey their parents, because the family is the basic building block out of which the whole of society is made. If families fall apart, then communities disintegrate, and the nation will collapse.

That's why God promises that a nation will be stable if children honour their parents. But, says Paul, although parents should be obeyed, they must always be loving and considerate in the demands they make.

✠

Lord, please help us to grow into a strong and loving family.

✠ ✠ ✠ ✠ ✠

May 28

Finally, build up your strength in union with the Lord and by means of his mighty power. Put on all the armour that God gives you, so that you will be able to stand up against the Devil's evil tricks. For we are not fighting against human beings but against the wicked spiritual forces in the heavenly world, the rulers, authorities, and cosmic powers of this dark age. So put on God's armour now! Then when the evil day comes, you will be able to resist the enemy's attacks; and after fighting to the end, you will still hold your ground.

So stand ready, with truth as a belt tight round your waist, with righteousness as your breastplate, and as your shoes the readiness to announce the Good News of peace. At all times carry faith as a shield; for with it you will be able to put out all the burning arrows shot by the Evil One. And accept salvation as a helmet, and the word of God as the sword which the Spirit gives you.

Ephesians 6:10–17

✠

Paul tells the Christians at Ephesus that they are caught up in a spiritual war against invisible powers. And for a spiritual war, they need spiritual armour – the protection of faith and the weapons of truth.

This spiritual war continues to this day – and will go on until Jesus comes again. So we must be ready to defend ourselves at all times, and to take the fight to the enemy on occasions as well.

✠

Lord, thank you that we have spiritual armour for the spiritual battle. Thank you that you are the Captain and that you have called us to fight with you on your winning side.

✠ ✠ ✠ ✠ ✠

May 29

Paul is writing to the Christians at Philippi. We've met some of them – remember Lydia, the old jailer, and the little slave girl? In his letter, Paul includes part of a beautiful hymn about Jesus.

✠

The attitude you should have is the one that Christ Jesus had:

He always had the nature of God,
  but he did not think that by force
    he should try to become equal with God.
Instead of this, of his own free will he
    gave up all he had,
  and took the nature of a servant.
He became like man
  and appeared in human likeness.
He was humble and walked the path
    of obedience all the way to death –
  his death on the cross.
For this reason God raised him to the
    highest place above
  and gave him the name that is greater
    than any other name.

And so, in honour of the name of Jesus
all beings in heaven, on earth, and
in the world below
will fall on their knees,
and all will openly proclaim that Jesus
Christ is Lord,
to the glory of God the Father.

Philippians 2:5–11

✠

Jesus showed us how to live – not standing on his rights or putting on airs, but humbly making himself the servant of all – even to the extent of laying down his life.

The only opinion that matters is what God thinks of us. Nobody else knows all the facts, and nobody else knows what goes on in our hearts. God was pleased with the way his Son behaved, and has given him the highest place in heaven.

✠

Loving Lord, please give us humble hearts in this life, so that we may share your glory in the life to come.

✠ ✠ ✠ ✠ ✠

May 30

Christ is the visible likeness of the invisible God. He is the first-born Son, superior to all created things. For through him God created everything in heaven and on earth, the seen and the unseen things, including spiritual powers, lords, rulers, and authorities. God created the whole universe through him and for him. Christ existed before all things, and in union with him all things have their proper place. He is the head of his body, the church; he is the source of the body's life. He is the first-born Son, who was raised from death, in order that he alone might have the first place in all things.

Colossians 1:15–18

✠

The more we study the universe around us, the more amazed we are. It is breathtaking in size, complexity, beauty and harmony.

Paul says to the Christians at Colossae, "It's because of Jesus that everything is so wonderful." It was through Jesus and for Jesus that everything was made. It is because of Jesus that everything holds together.

✠

Living Lord, you are so much greater than we can ever imagine. We praise you for your greatness, and thank you for your love.

✠ ✠ ✠ ✠ ✠

May 31

This is the last time we look over Paul's shoulder as he writes his letters. Today we have a glimpse of something he has to say to the Christians at Colossae.

✠

You are the people of God; he loved you and chose you for his own. So then, you must clothe yourselves with compassion, kindness, humility, gentleness, and patience. Be tolerant with one another and forgive one another whenever any of you has a complaint against someone else. You must forgive one another just as the Lord has forgiven you. And to all these qualities add love, which binds all things together in perfect unity. The peace that Christ gives is to guide you in the decisions you make; for it is to this peace that God has called you together in the one body. And be thankful.

Colossians 3:12–15

✠

Paul is telling his friends that they must sometimes "put on" attitudes which don't come naturally. They must remember God's forgiveness to them and in turn be forgiving to others. He reminds them that everything is summed up and held together in love. And love makes way for peace, harmony and thanksgiving.

What a beautiful lifestyle for the people of God in every place and every age!

✠

Lord, may we know more and more what it is to be different – *to live the Jesus life together, for your glory.*

✠ ✠ ✠ ✠ ✠

A Psalm for

June

Be merciful to me, O God,
  because of your constant love.
Because of your great mercy
  wipe away my sins!
Wash away all my evil
  and make me clean from my sin!

I recognize my faults;
  I am always conscious of my sins.
I have sinned against you – only against you –
  and done what you consider evil.
So you are right in judging me;
  you are justified in condemning me.
I have been evil from the time I was born;
  from the day of my birth I have been sinful.

Sincerity and truth are what you require;
  fill my mind with your wisdom.
Remove my sin, and I will be clean;
  wash me, and I will be whiter than snow.
Let me hear the sounds of joy and gladness;
  and though you have crushed me and broken me,
  I will be happy once again.
Close your eyes to my sins
  and wipe out all my evil.

Create a pure heart in me, O God,
  and put a new and loyal spirit in me.

Psalm 51:1–10

June 1

In the beginning, when God created the universe, the earth was formless and desolate. The raging ocean that covered everything was engulfed in total darkness, and the power of God was moving over the water. Then God commanded, "Let there be light" – and light appeared. God was pleased with what he saw. Then he separated the light from the darkness, and he named the light "Day" and the darkness "Night". Evening passed and morning came – that was the first day.

Genesis 1:1–5

✠

The Bible doesn't tell us how the world was made – not in the way that a scientist would.

But what the Bible tells us is that God is behind it all. It was his Spirit that was at work in the earliest stages of darkness and chaos. It was he who said, "Let there be light!", and light appeared.

✠

Lord God, by your mighty power you made the universe and gave us life and light. Thank you for your wonderful creation.

✠ ✠ ✠ ✠ ✠

June 2

Then God commanded, "Let there be a dome to divide the water and to keep it in two separate places" – and it was done. So God made a dome, and it separated the water under it from the water above it. He named the dome "Sky". Evening passed and morning came – that was the second day.

Then God commanded, "Let the water below the sky come together in one place, so that the land will appear" – and it was done. He named the land "Earth", and the water which had come together he named "Sea". And God was pleased with what he saw. Then he commanded, "Let the earth produce all kinds of plants, those that bear grain and those that bear fruit" – and it was done. So the earth produced all kinds of plants, and God was pleased with what he saw. Evening passed and morning came – that was the third day.

Genesis 1:6–13

✠

In the old days people thought that the sky was a vast dome overhead, with water above it. The water came through tiny holes (the stars) and gave rain.

Today we know so much more about the way the world works – and the more we discover and explore, the more amazed we are by what we find.

Whether we gaze through a telescope or peer through a microscope – or simply watch the nature films on television – the universe around us is fabulous and fascinating.

✠

Lord God, by your mighty power you made the universe and gave us everything to enjoy. Thank you for your wonderful creation.

✠ ✠ ✠ ✠ ✠

June 3

Then God commanded, "Let lights appear in the sky to separate day from night and to show the time when days, years, and religious festivals begin; they will shine in the sky to give light to the earth" – and it was done. So God made the two larger lights, the sun to rule over the day and the moon to rule over the night; he also made the stars. He placed the lights in the sky to shine on the earth, to rule over the day and the night, and to separate light from darkness. And God was pleased with what he saw. Evening passed and morning came – that was the fourth day.

Genesis 1:14–19

✠

The universe hangs together with a beautiful order and symmetry. There are times and seasons, cycles and phases. We can *rely* on dawn breaking after a dark night, and on spring following winter. And just think – God made *time*! However did he do that?

✠

Lord God, by your mighty power you made the universe, and gave us times and seasons. We thank you for this new day – a day that has never been before. Thank you for each hour, each moment. Help us to use them well.

✠ ✠ ✠ ✠ ✠

June 4

Then God commanded, "Let the water be filled with many kinds of living beings, and let the air be filled with birds." So God created the great sea-monsters, all kinds of creatures that live in the water, and all kinds of birds. And God was pleased with what he saw. He blessed them all and told the creatures that live in the water to reproduce, and to fill the sea, and he told the birds to increase in number. Evening passed and morning came – that was the fifth day.

Then God commanded, "Let the earth produce all kinds of animal life: domestic and wild, large and small" – and it was done. So God made them all, and he was pleased with what he saw.

Genesis 1:20–25

God has made animals and birds, reptiles and insects, in astonishing variety – each species able faithfully to reproduce itself.

How important it is that we should treasure God's creation and care for our fellow creatures. And what a tragedy that many hundreds of species have been wiped out by our carelessness or greed.

✠

Lord God, by your mighty power you made the universe, and filled the earth with life. Help us to value every aspect of your creation, and care for this world as your treasured gift to us.

✠ ✠ ✠ ✠ ✠

June 5

Then God said, "And now we will make human beings; they will be like us and resemble us. They will have power over the fish, the birds, and all animals, domestic and wild, large and small." So God created human beings, making them to be like himself. He created them male and female, blessed them, and said, "Have many children, so that your descendants will live all over the earth and bring it under their control. I am putting you in charge of the fish, the birds, and all the wild animals. I have provided all kinds of grain and all kinds of fruit for you to eat; but for all the wild animals and for all the birds I have provided grass and leafy plants for food" – and it was done. God looked at everything he had made, and he was very pleased.

Evening passed and morning came – that was the sixth day.

Genesis 1:26–31

✠

The Bible tells us that man is the last and most precious piece of God's creation. Of all creatures, mankind – men, women and children – are the most special.

We are special, because man is like God. We are in a class of our own! We can laugh, love, make things, go shopping, play chess – and cook. We are the only creatures that can observe and appreciate the world around us, the only creatures that know the difference between right and wrong, and the only creatures that can worship God.

✠

Lord God, by your mighty power you made the universe, and gave the world into our care. Help us to be worthy of your trust, and to do everything in ways that please you.

✠ ✠ ✠ ✠ ✠

June 6

Then the LORD God planted a garden in Eden, in the East, and there he put the man he had formed. He made all kinds of beautiful trees grow there and produce good fruit. In the middle of the garden stood the tree that gives life and the tree that gives knowledge of what is good and what is bad.

Then the LORD God placed the man in the Garden of Eden to cultivate it and guard it. He said to him, "You may eat the fruit of any tree in the garden, except the tree that gives knowledge of what is good and what is bad. You must not eat the fruit of that tree; if you do, you will die the same day."

Genesis 2:8–9,15–16

✠

This is another story about creation, and this time we learn about the choices men and women have to make.

In the beginning, life was perfect – the trees were beautiful and the fruit was good. But God said that the fruit of one tree was "out of bounds" – the tree that gave the knowledge of what was good and what was bad.

Along with all his other blessings, God gave us free will – the ability to choose whether to do as we are told, or not! But the choice we make is the difference between a way of life and a way of death.

✠

Lord God, in all our decisions today, help us to "choose life" – to go your way.

✠ ✠ ✠ ✠ ✠

June 7

Then the LORD God said, "It is not good for the man to live alone. I will make a suitable companion to help him." So he took some soil from the ground and formed all the animals and all the birds. Then he brought them to the man to see what he would name them; and that is how they all got their names. So the man named all the birds and all the animals; but not one of them was a suitable companion to help him.

Then the LORD God made the man fall into a deep sleep, and while he was sleeping, he took out one of the man's ribs and closed up the flesh. He formed a woman out of the rib and brought her to him. Then the man said,

"At last, here is one of my own kind –
Bone taken from my bone, and flesh
from my flesh.
'Woman' is her name because she was
taken out of man."

That is why a man leaves his father and mother and is united with his wife, and they become one.

The man and the woman were both naked, but they were not embarrassed.

Genesis 2:18–25

✠

The story tells how God made the first man and woman for each other. Deep within us is the longing to be accepted and loved by someone else. When the first man saw the first woman, he knew straight away that this was the companion who would make him complete.

✠

Lord, thank you for your very precious gift of married life and married love.

✠ ✠ ✠ ✠ ✠

June 8

Now the snake was the most cunning animal that the LORD God had made. The snake asked the woman, "Did God really tell you not to eat fruit from any tree in the garden?"

"We may eat the fruit of any tree in the garden," the woman answered, "except the tree in the middle of it. God told us not to eat the fruit of that tree or even touch it; if we do, we will die."

The snake replied, "That's not true; you will not die. God said that, because he knows that when you eat it you will be like God and know what is good and what is bad."

The woman saw how beautiful the tree was and how good its fruit would be to eat, and she thought how wonderful it would be to become wise. So she took some of the fruit and ate it. Then she gave some to her husband, and he also ate it. As soon as they had eaten it, they were given understanding and realized that they were naked; so they sewed fig leaves together and covered themselves.

Genesis 3:1–7

✠

In the snake, we see Satan. Satan is God's enemy – one of God's angels who became proud, and set out to prove that mankind is a failure.

Satan begins by planting a doubt in the woman's mind: "Did God *really* tell you not to eat that? Do you *really* suppose you'll die if you do?"

And so Satan awakens pride and greed in the human heart – and it quickly spreads, bringing with it fear and guilt and shame.

✠

Lord God, this is the way we are. We often think and say and do things that are wrong. Please forgive us and set us free from our burden of guilt.

✠ ✠ ✠ ✠ ✠

June 9

That evening they heard the LORD God walking in the garden, and they hid from him among the trees. But the LORD God called out to the man, "Where are you?"

He answered, "I heard you in the garden; I was afraid and hid from you, because I was naked."

"Who told you that you were naked?" God asked. "Did you eat the fruit that I told you not to eat?"

The man answered, "The woman you put here with me gave me the fruit, and I ate it."

And he said to the man, "You listened to your wife and ate the fruit which I told you not to eat. Because of what you have done, the ground will be under a curse. You will have to work hard all your life to make it produce enough food for you. It will produce weeds and thorns, and you will have to eat wild plants. You will have to work hard and sweat to make the soil produce anything, until you go back to the soil from which you were formed. You were made from soil, and you will become soil again."

Genesis 3:8–12,17–19

✠

God's perfect world is tragically spoilt. His friends, man and woman, are hiding from him because they know they've done wrong.

Then the man blames the woman for what has happened – and tomorrow we'll see that the woman blames the snake.

Because of their disobedience, life on earth can never be the same again. The perfect world of the garden will give way to the hard life of the farm, where they will have to scratch a living from the soil. And at the end of their time they will die.

✠

Lord God, the whole of creation is spoilt because of our sin. Forgive us for our part in this dreadful situation. And thank you for Jesus, who came to rescue us and "make all things new".

✠ ✠ ✠ ✠ ✠

June 10

The LORD God asked the woman, "Why did you do this?"

She replied, "The snake tricked me into eating it."

Then the LORD God said to the snake, "You will be punished for this; you alone of all the animals must bear this curse: From now on you will crawl on your belly, and you will have to eat dust as long as you live. I will make you and the woman hate each other; her offspring and yours will always be enemies. Her offspring will crush your head, and you will bite their heel."

And he said to the woman, "I will increase your trouble in pregnancy and your pain in giving birth. In spite of this, you will still have desire for your husband, yet you will be subject to him."

Adam named his wife Eve, because she was the mother of all human beings. And the LORD God made clothes out of animal skins for Adam and his wife, and he clothed them.

Genesis 3:13–16,20–21

✠

God is the perfect judge. The man and woman have done wrong, and they must live with the consequences. There will be enmity between Satan and the human race, and many difficulties in birth and marriage.

Yet, in it all, we glimpse God's mercy. He loves mankind, although he is heartbroken at what has happened. See how God tenderly makes clothes for Adam and Eve to cover their nakedness and to keep them warm.

✠

Lord, thank you that you go on loving us, and show your love in so many practical ways.

June 11

Then the LORD God said, "Now the man has become like one of us and has knowledge of what is good and what is bad. He must not be allowed to eat fruit from the tree of life, and live for ever." So the LORD God sent him out of the Garden of Eden and made him cultivate the soil from which he had been formed. Then at the east side of the garden he put living creatures and a flaming sword which turned in all directions. This was to keep anyone from coming near the tree of life.

Genesis 3:22–24

✠

And so the story of creation ends sadly, with the first man and woman shut out of the Garden of Eden – shut out of heaven on earth.

To this day, we know the difference between good and evil, right and wrong. But we haven't at all solved the problem of where life comes from or why we all die. Yet the God who gives us life wants us to know him – and to live with him for ever.

✠

Lord God, thank you that through Jesus we can be friends with you again, and share your heaven.

✠ ✠ ✠ ✠ ✠

June 12

Then Adam had intercourse with his wife, and she became pregnant. She bore a son and said, "By the LORD's help I have acquired a son." So she named him Cain. Later she gave birth to another son, Abel. Abel became a shepherd, but Cain was a farmer. After some time, Cain brought some of his harvest and gave it as an offering to the LORD. Then Abel brought the first lamb born to one of his sheep, killed it, and gave the best parts of it as an offering. The LORD was pleased with Abel and his offering, but he rejected Cain and his offering. Cain became furious, and he scowled in anger. Then the LORD said to Cain, "Why are you angry? Why that scowl on your face? If you had done the right thing, you would be smiling; but because you have done evil, sin is crouching at your door. It wants to rule you, but you must overcome it."

Then Cain said to his brother Abel, "Let's go out in the fields." When they were out in the fields, Cain turned on his brother and killed him.

Genesis 4:1–8

✠

Isn't it dreadful to read of the very first brothers that there is jealousy between them, and that one kills the other? And it's the one who does right – Abel, who gives his first and best lamb to God – who gets killed.

Serving God doesn't mean that we "live happily ever after". Sometimes it means that we are on the receiving end of other people's frustration and anger – including the anger they feel against God.

✠

Lord, you have given us everything. When we give you something in return, may it be a thoughtful, generous and wholehearted offering.

✠ ✠ ✠ ✠ ✠

June 13

The LORD asked Cain, "Where is your brother Abel?"

He answered, "I don't know. Am I supposed to take care of my brother?"

Then the LORD said, "Why have you done this terrible thing? Your brother's blood is crying out to me from the ground, like a voice calling for revenge. You are placed under a curse and can no longer farm the soil. It has soaked up your brother's blood as if it had opened its mouth to receive it when you killed him. If you try to grow crops, the soil will not produce anything; you will be a homeless wanderer on the earth."

And Cain said to the LORD, "This punishment is too hard for me to bear. You are driving me off the land and away from your presence. I will be a homeless wanderer on the earth, and anyone who finds me will kill me."

But the LORD answered, "No. If anyone kills you, seven lives will be taken in revenge." So the LORD put a mark on Cain to warn anyone who met him not to kill him. And Cain went away from the LORD's presence and lived in a land called "Wandering", which is east of Eden.

Genesis 4:9–16

✠

Cain thinks that no one has seen him kill his brother. But he is wrong. God sees all that we do, and knows all the secrets of our hearts. And he who sees and knows everything is also our judge.

Cain has murdered his brother, and now he is at odds with everything – with the farmland, with God, and with other people. But that doesn't mean that anyone else can kill him – it is God alone who has the right to punish.

✠

Lord, please give us your love and peace in our family, so that our home may be a taste of heaven, and not a glimpse of hell.

✠ ✠ ✠ ✠ ✠

June 14

This is the story of Noah. He had three sons, Shem, Ham, and Japheth. Noah had no faults and was the only good man of his time. He lived in fellowship with God, but everyone else was evil in God's sight, and violence had spread everywhere. God looked at the world and saw that it was evil, for the people were all living evil lives.

God said to Noah, "I have decided to put an end to all mankind. I will destroy them completely, because the world is full of their violent deeds. Build a boat for yourself out of good timber; make rooms in it and cover it with tar inside and out. Make it 133 metres long, 22 metres wide, and 13 metres high. Make a roof for the boat and leave a space of 44 centimetres between the roof and the sides. Build it with three decks and put a door in the side. I am going to send a flood on the earth to destroy every living being. Everything on the earth will die, but I will make a covenant with you. Go into the boat with your wife, your sons, and their wives. Take into the boat with you a male and a female of every kind of animal and of every kind of bird, in order to keep them alive. Take along all kinds of food for you and for them." Noah did everything that God commanded.

Genesis 6:9–22

✠

What astonishing faith Noah has, to build a boat when he doesn't live anywhere near water, in a place which has never had any rain! But build it he does, and it proves to be the saving of himself and his family, as well as many species of animals and birds.

Not many of us have such clear instructions as Noah, but we usually know very well what God is prompting us to do. So let's do it – and be life and health to our families in the process.

✠

Lord, thank you that your way is good, and that you honour those who do your will.

✠ ✠ ✠ ✠ ✠

June 15

When Noah was six hundred years old, on the seventeenth day of the second month all the outlets of the vast body of water beneath the earth burst open, all the floodgates of the sky were opened, and rain fell on the earth for forty days and nights. On that same day Noah and his wife went into the boat with their three sons, Shem, Ham, and Japheth, and their wives. With them went every kind of animal, domestic and wild, large and small, and every kind of bird. A male and a female of each kind of living being went into the boat with Noah, as God had commanded. Then the LORD shut the door behind Noah.

The flood continued for forty days, and the water became deep enough for the boat to float. The water became deeper, and the boat drifted on the surface. It became so deep that it covered the highest mountains; it went on rising until it was seven metres above the tops of the mountains. Every living being on the earth died – every bird, every animal, and every person. Everything on earth that breathed died. The LORD destroyed all living beings on the earth – human beings, animals and birds. The only ones left were Noah and those who were with him in the boat. The water did not start going down for a hundred and fifty days.

Genesis 7:11–24

✠

How terrible! We get so used to the fun of Noah's ark, and the animals going in two by two, that we forget that it was the most dreadful judgement the world has ever seen.

✠

Lord, you are a righteous judge and you hate sin. Thank you that you love us although you hate our sin. And thank you that you are so patient, and give us time to love you in return.

✠ ✠ ✠ ✠ ✠

June 16

After forty days Noah opened a window and sent out a raven. It did not come back, but kept flying around until the water was completely gone. Meanwhile, Noah sent out a dove to see if the water had gone down, but since the water still covered all the land, the dove did not find a place to alight. It flew back to the boat, and Noah reached out and took it in. He waited another seven days and sent out the dove again. It returned to him in the evening with a fresh olive leaf in its beak. So Noah knew that the water had gone down. Then he waited another seven days and sent out the dove once more; this time it did not come back.

When Noah was 601 years old, on the first day of the first month, the water was gone. Noah removed the covering of the boat, looked round, and saw that the ground was getting dry. By the twenty-seventh day of the second month the earth was completely dry.

God said to Noah, "Go out of the boat with your wife, your sons, and their wives. Take all the birds and animals out with you, so that they may reproduce and spread over all the earth." So Noah went out of the boat with his wife, his sons, and their wives. All the animals and birds went out of the boat in groups of their own kind.

Genesis 8:6–19

✠

So God starts again, with Noah and his family. And the olive branch in the beak of a dove is, to this day, a sign of peace. God is reaching out to make peace with us, and inviting us to start all over again with him.

✠

Thank you, Lord, for the new beginnings you give us – every new day is a sign of your constant love.

✠ ✠ ✠ ✠ ✠

June 17

Noah built an altar to the LORD; he took one of each kind of ritually clean animal and bird, and burnt them whole as a sacrifice on the altar. The odour of the sacrifice pleased the LORD, and he said to himself, "Never again will I put the earth under a curse because of what man does; I know that from the time he is young his thoughts are evil. Never again will I destroy all living beings, as I have done this time. As long as the world exists, there will be a time for planting and a time for harvest. There will always be cold and heat, summer and winter, day and night."

Genesis 8:20–22

✠

How strange to listen in on God talking to himself! He's not under any illusions about human nature. He knows that we think wrong things from a very early age, and that wrong actions are always bound to follow. But he decides that the world shall be a reliable place to live in. The seasons will come round in their turn each year, and the crops will grow. The reliability of the good earth is one of our greatest blessings – and one that we most take for granted.

✠

Lord, you quietly, lovingly provide for us in this majestic and beautiful world. Every gift is a token of your great goodness and your love.

✠ ✠ ✠ ✠ ✠

June 18

God blessed Noah and his sons and said, "Have many children, so that your descendants will live all over the earth. All the animals, birds, and fish will live in fear of you. They are all placed under your power. Now you can eat them, as well as green plants; I give them all to you for food."

God said to Noah and his sons, "I am now making my covenant with you and with your descendants, and with all living beings – all birds and all animals – everything that came out of the boat with you. With these words I make my covenant with you: I promise that never again will all living beings be destroyed by a flood; never again will a flood destroy the earth. As a sign of this everlasting covenant which I am making with you and with all living beings, I am putting my bow in the clouds. It will be the sign of my covenant with the world."

Genesis 9:1–3,8–13

✠

God is the Creator and Lord of the universe. Why should he trouble to make promises to the selfish little people on planet earth? Surely he doesn't have to! He doesn't need us at all.

But in his love, God perseveres with mankind. He enters into a covenant with Noah, and with all of us, that there will never again be a worldwide flood. That's God's free promise – there's nothing we have to do to deserve it. And when we see the rainbow, we are reminded of the God who makes promises – and keeps them.

✠

Lord, thank you for talking to us – through the wonders of creation, through your word in the Bible, and through your Spirit today.

✠ ✠ ✠ ✠ ✠

June 19

At first, the people of the whole world had only one language and used the same words. As they wandered about in the East, they came to a plain in Babylonia and settled there. They said to one another, "Come on! Let's make bricks and bake them hard." So they had bricks to build with and tar to hold them together. They said, "Now let's build a city with a tower that reaches the sky, so that we can make a name for ourselves and not be scattered all over the earth."

Then the LORD came down to see the city and the tower which those men had built, and he said, "Now then, these are all one people and they speak one language; this is just the beginning of what they are going to do. Soon they will be able to do anything they want! Let us go down and mix up their language so that they will not understand one another." So the LORD scattered them all over the earth, and they stopped building the city. The city was called Babylon, because there the LORD mixed up the language of all the people, and from there he scattered them all over the earth.

Genesis 11:1–9

✠

This is an old story about how we got so many languages in the world. But underneath, it is a story about our human pride.

The men who build the city and the tower are getting above themselves – literally! They are putting themselves at the centre of the world, hoping that they will be recognized and admired. But they are also putting themselves in the place of God.

So God confounds them, and their proud speeches become a babble.

✠

Lord, help us always to give you your rightful place in our lives and in our world.

✠ ✠ ✠ ✠ ✠

June 20

Today we turn again to the story of Jesus, and look at some of the marvellous things he did.

✠

There was a wedding in the town of Cana in Galilee. Jesus' mother was there, and Jesus and his disciples had also been invited to the wedding. When the wine had given out, Jesus' mother said to him, "They have no wine left."

"You must not tell me what to do," Jesus replied. "My time has not yet come."

Jesus' mother then told the servants, "Do whatever he tells you."

The Jews have rules about ritual washing, and for

this purpose six stone water jars were there, each one large enough to hold about a hundred litres. Jesus said to the servants, "Fill these jars with water." They filled them to the brim, and then he told them, "Now draw some water out and take it to the man in charge of the feast." They took him the water, which now had turned into wine, and he tasted it. He did not know where this wine had come from (but, of course, the servants who had drawn out the water knew); so he called the bridegroom and said to him, "Everyone else serves the best wine first, and after the guests have had plenty to drink, he serves the ordinary wine. But you have kept the best wine until now!"

Jesus performed this first miracle in Cana in Galilee; there he revealed his glory, and his disciples believed in him.

John 2:1–11

✠

When Jesus turns the water into wine, it is a sign of the difference he has come to make. The Jews (the strict ones, anyway) are endlessly trying to keep clean. They carefully wash everything – hands and feet, pots and basins.

But when Jesus comes, he turns the washing water to wine. And it's the best wine anyone has ever tasted. The days of trying to get on the right side of God by keeping clean are past. The glad wedding party of God's love has begun!

✠

Lord, help us to do whatever you tell us, as the servants did, so that everyday duties may be filled with heavenly blessings.

June 21

There was a Jewish leader named Nicodemus, who belonged to the party of the Pharisees. One night he went to Jesus and said to him, "Rabbi, we know that you are a teacher sent by God. No one could perform the miracles you are doing unless God were with him."

Jesus answered, "I am telling you the truth: no one can see the Kingdom of God unless he is born again."

"How can a grown man be born again?" Nicodemus asked. "He certainly cannot enter his mother's womb and be born a second time!"

"I am telling you the truth," replied Jesus. "No one can enter the Kingdom of God unless he is born of water and the Spirit. A person is born physically of human parents, but he is born spiritually of the Spirit. Do not be surprised because I tell you that you must all be born again. The wind blows wherever it wishes; you hear the sound it makes, but you do not know where it comes from or where it is going. It is like that with everyone who is born of the Spirit."

John 3:1–8

✠

Nicodemus is an important man – a leader of the Jews, and a member of the Jewish Council. But he doesn't know how to enter the Kingdom of God.

Jesus says, "Nicodemus – you must be born again! Not by climbing back inside your mother, but by starting a whole new life with God's Spirit inside you."

When we are born again, the Holy Spirit is our mother, and the sign that we are coming alive to God is baptism. Of course, the Spirit of God is invisible, so how do we know when he is around? Jesus says that the Spirit is like the wind. Just as we can see the wind when it moves trees or yachts or windmills, so we can see the Holy Spirit wherever there is love and joy, healing and peace.

✠

Lord, help us to live and grow in the freedom and power of your Holy Spirit today.

✠ ✠ ✠ ✠ ✠

June 22

In Samaria Jesus came to a town named Sychar, which was not far from the field that Jacob had given to his son Joseph. Jacob's well was there, and Jesus, tired out by the journey, sat down by the well. It was about noon.

A Samaritan woman came to draw some water, and Jesus said to her, "Give me a drink of water." (His disciples had gone into town to buy food.)

The woman answered, "You are a Jew, and I am a Samaritan – so how can you ask me for a drink?" (Jews will not use the same cups and bowls that Samaritans use.)

Jesus answered, "If only you knew what God gives and who it is that is asking you for a drink, you would ask him, and he would give you life-giving water."

"Sir," the woman said, "you haven't got a bucket, and the well is deep. Where would you get that life-giving water? It was our ancestor Jacob who gave us this well; he and his sons and his flocks all drank from it. You don't claim to be greater than Jacob, do you?"

Jesus answered, "Whoever drinks this water will be thirsty again, but whoever drinks the water that I will give him will never be thirsty again. The water that I will give him will become in him a spring which will provide him with life-giving water and give him eternal life."

"Sir," the woman said, "give me that water! Then I will never be thirsty again."

John 4:5–15

✠

Jesus breaks down all the barriers between people. The Samaritan woman comes to the well in the heat of the day, because she has no friends. The other women have rejected her because of the kind of life she leads. How she wishes she had a water supply at home so that she needn't come out at all!

Jesus shouldn't really be seen with her, because he's a Jew, and Jews and Samaritans hate each other. But Jesus doesn't care about that. He finds a way of talking to her, and tells her that there is a life-giving water which will meet every need of her thirsty, lonely life.

✠

Lord Jesus, you are the living water. You came to share with us the life of God. Thank you.

✠ ✠ ✠ ✠ ✠

June 23

Then Jesus went back to Cana in Galilee, where he had turned the water into wine. A government official was there whose son was ill in Capernaum. When he heard that Jesus had come from Judaea to Galilee, he went to him and asked him to go to Capernaum and heal his son, who was about to die. Jesus said to him, "None of you will ever believe unless you see miracles and wonders."

"Sir," replied the official, "come with me before my child dies."

Jesus said to him, "Go, your son will live!"

The man believed Jesus' words and went. On his way home his servants met him with the news, "Your boy is going to live!"

He asked them what time it was when his son got better, and they answered, "It was one o'clock yesterday afternoon when the fever left him." Then the father remembered that it was at that very hour when Jesus had told him, "Your son will live." So he and all his family believed.

John 4:46–53

✠

The poor father has trekked all the way from Capernaum to Cana in search of Jesus, hoping against hope that Jesus will go back with him to heal his son.

But Jesus doesn't need to go with him at all. He can heal at a distance, thanks to the power of God and the faith of the father.

So the man travels home with the words of Jesus ringing in his ears – and finds that his son is indeed alive and well.

Lord, thank you that in all our needs we can cry to you for help, and that there is nowhere that your love cannot reach when we turn to you.

✠ ✠ ✠ ✠ ✠

June 24

Once Jesus was in a town where there was a man who was suffering from a dreaded skin-disease. When he saw Jesus, he threw himself down and begged him, "Sir, if you want to, you can make me clean!"

Jesus stretched out his hand and touched him. "I do want to," he answered. "Be clean!" At once the disease left the man. Jesus ordered him, "Don't tell anyone, but go straight to the priest and let him examine you; then to prove to everyone that you are cured, offer the sacrifice as Moses ordered."

But the news about Jesus spread all the more widely, and crowds of people came to hear him and be healed from their diseases. But he would go away to lonely places, where he prayed.

Luke 5:12–16

✠

The golden rule with skin disease is "Don't touch!" So people with leprosy had to ring a bell and shout "Unclean!" to warn other folk to stay clear.

But when Jesus meets this leper, he dares to reach out and touch him, and says, "Be clean!"

It's as though the health in Jesus can somehow be caught. God's power in Jesus is stronger than the skin disease of the leper. So instead of Jesus catching death, the leper catches life.

✠

Lord, thank you for reaching out to all the needy people of the world, including ourselves. Thank you for offering us new life, new health and new hope.

✠ ✠ ✠ ✠ ✠

June 25

One day when Jesus was teaching, some Pharisees and teachers of the Law were sitting there who had come from every town in Galilee and Judaea and from Jerusalem. The power of the Lord was present for Jesus to heal the sick. Some men came carrying a paralysed man on a bed, and they tried to take him into the house and put him in front of Jesus.

Because of the crowd, however, they could find no way to take him in. So they carried him up on the roof, made an opening in the tiles, and let him down on his bed into the middle of the group in front of Jesus. When Jesus saw how much faith they had, he said to the man, "Your sins are forgiven, my friend."

The teachers of the Law and the Pharisees began to say to themselves, "Who is this man who speaks such blasphemy! God is the only one who can forgive sins!"

Jesus knew their thoughts and said to them, "Why do you think such things? Is it easier to say, 'Your sins are forgiven you,' or to say, 'Get up and walk'? I will prove to you, then, that the Son of Man has authority on earth to forgive sins." So he said to the paralysed man, "I tell you, get up, pick up your bed, and go home!"

At once the man got up in front of them all, took the bed he had been lying on, and went home, praising God. They were all completely amazed! Full of fear, they praised God, saying, "What marvellous things we have seen today."

Luke 5:17–26

✠

Jesus sees to the heart of our trouble. For the man lowered through the roof, the real problem isn't his paralysis but his guilt. He is riddled with regret and remorse over things he has done in the past. So, of course, Jesus deals with these first – and the Pharisees are scandalized. Who is Jesus to forgive sins? Does he think he is God?

✠

Lord Jesus, you are indeed the Son of God. Thank you that you see our real needs – our needs for forgiveness and peace of mind – and always attend to our deepest hurts first.

✠ ✠ ✠ ✠ ✠

June 26

After this, Jesus went to Jerusalem for a religious festival. Near the Sheep Gate in Jerusalem there is a pool with five porches. A large crowd of sick people were lying in the porches – the blind, the lame, and the paralysed. A man was there who had been ill for thirty-eight years. Jesus saw him lying there, and he knew that the man had been ill for such a long time; so he asked him, "Do you want to get well?"

The sick man answered, "Sir, I have no one here to put me in the pool when the water is stirred up; while I am trying to get in, somebody else gets there first."

Jesus said to him, "Get up, pick up your mat, and walk." Immediately the man got well; he picked up his mat and started walking.

The day this happened was a Sabbath, so the Jewish authorities told the man who had been healed, "This is a Sabbath, and it is against our Law for you to carry your mat."

He answered, "The man who made me well told me to pick up my mat and walk."

They asked him, "Who is the man who told you to do this?"

But the man who had been healed did not know who Jesus was, for there was a crowd in that place, and Jesus had slipped away.

John 5:1–13

✠

Again, Jesus sees to the heart of a man's problem. Does he really *want* to get well? Or does it quite suit him to be carried around by others and have them bring him food? Maybe he's given up trying to be first in the pool, and has settled for a life of leisure lying beside it instead?

Jesus asks the same searching questions today. Do we really *want* to be changed? Do we really want our lives to be in tune with God? If so, we must get up and do as he says.

✠

Lord, when we ask you for a change in ourselves or in our situation, help us to hear and obey your answering command.

✠ ✠ ✠ ✠ ✠

June 27

When Jesus had finished saying all these things to the people, he went to Capernaum. A Roman officer there had a servant who was very dear to him; the man was sick and about to die. When the officer heard about Jesus, he sent some Jewish elders to ask him to come and heal his servant. They came to Jesus and begged him earnestly, "This man really deserves your help. He loves our people and he himself built a synagogue for us."

So Jesus went with them. He was not far from the house when the officer sent friends to tell him, "Sir, don't trouble yourself. I do not deserve to have you come into my house, neither do I consider myself worthy to come to you in person. Just give the order, and my servant will get well. I, too, am a man placed under the authority of superior officers, and I have soldiers under me. I order this one, 'Go!' and he goes; I order that one, 'Come!' and he comes; and I order my slave, 'Do this!' and he does it."

Jesus was surprised when he heard this; he turned round and said to the crowd following him, "I tell you, I have never found faith like this, not even in Israel!"

The messengers went back to the officer's house and found his servant well.

Luke 7:1–10

✠

The Roman officer hadn't been brought up to believe in the God of the Jews. He had started to believe when his work placed him in Capernaum. His work had also taught him about the power of being in command of people, and how to give and receive orders.

The officer comes to Jesus because he believes Jesus has God's power over sickness and disease, and can tell them to be off! And Jesus is delighted to find such faith, especially in someone who isn't even a Jew.

✠

Lord Jesus, help us to surprise you with our faith today.

✠ ✠ ✠ ✠ ✠

June 28

Soon afterwards Jesus went to a town called Nain, accompanied by his disciples and a large crowd. Just as he arrived at the gate of the town, a funeral procession was coming out. The dead man was the only son of a woman who was a widow, and a large crowd from the town was with her. When the Lord saw her, his heart was filled with pity for her, and he said to her, "Don't cry." Then he walked over and touched the coffin, and the men carrying it stopped. Jesus said, "Young man! Get up, I tell you!" The dead man sat up and began to talk, and Jesus gave him back to his mother.

They all were filled with fear and praised God. "A great prophet has appeared among us!" they said; "God has come to save his people!"

Luke 7:11–16

✠

Imagine watching the funeral procession coming out of Nain.

Everyone feels so sad for the young man's mother. She has already lost her husband, and now her son has died. She is so alone that she must be wishing she could die herself.

And then Jesus walks towards her, and what a difference he makes! He shows that he not only has power over sickness and disease, but he can actually raise people from death.

✠

Lord Jesus, please be close to all who are sad today. May we look to you for comfort in our sadness, and thank you for your victory over death.

✠ ✠ ✠ ✠ ✠

June 29

A Pharisee invited Jesus to have dinner with him, and Jesus went to his house and sat down to eat. In that town was a woman who lived a sinful life. She heard that Jesus was eating in the Pharisee's house, so she brought an alabaster jar full of perfume and stood behind Jesus, by his feet, crying and wetting his feet with her tears. Then she dried his feet with her hair, kissed them, and poured the perfume on them. When the Pharisee saw this, he said to himself, "If this man really were a prophet, he would know who this woman is who is touching him; he would know what kind of sinful life she lives!"

But Jesus turned to the woman and said to Simon, "Do you see this woman? I came into your home, and you gave me no water for my feet, but she has washed my feet with her tears and dried them with her hair. You did not welcome me with a kiss, but she has not stopped kissing my feet since I came. You provided no olive-oil for my head, but she has covered my feet with perfume. I tell you, then, the great love she has shown proves that her many sins have been forgiven. But whoever has been forgiven little shows only a little love."

Then Jesus said to the woman, "Your sins are forgiven."

Luke 7:36–39,44–48

✠

It seems strange to us that such a notorious woman could wander into Simon the Pharisee's house and interrupt the meal. It was certainly embarrassing for everyone, and many of the guests must have been glad she was crying over Jesus and not over them!

But Jesus isn't embarrassed at all, because he knows what the woman is doing. He knows what's in her heart. She is showing how grateful she is to God for his forgiveness of her sins, and she is showing her thanks in the most wholehearted way she can.

✠

Lord Jesus, please flood our lives with love for you. And when we realize how much you have done for us, may we show our thanks in generous ways.

✠ ✠ ✠ ✠ ✠

June 30

Then Jesus left and went away to the territory near the city of Tyre. He went into a house and did not want anyone to know he was there, but he could not stay hidden. A woman, whose daughter had an evil spirit in her, heard about Jesus and came to him at once and fell at his feet. The woman was a Gentile, born in the region of Phoenicia in Syria. She begged Jesus to drive the demon out of her daughter. But Jesus answered, "Let us first feed the children. It isn't right to take the children's food and throw it to the dogs."

"Sir," she answered, "even the dogs under the table eat the children's leftovers!"

So Jesus said to her, "Because of that answer, go back home, where you will find that the demon has gone out of your daughter!"

She went home and found her child lying on the bed; the demon had indeed gone out of her.

Mark 7:24–30

Jesus feels that his mission in life is to tell the Jews that God's Kingdom has come, and that he must show the power of this Kingdom by healing diseases and casting out evil spirits.

But sometimes people who aren't Jews have such astonishing faith, that Jesus simply has to help them. The Roman officer was one such person, and this woman is another. It's strange to think of Jesus having to be persuaded to help, isn't it? But his resistance brings out a most wonderful faith in the woman – as well as a very lively wit!

✠

Lord, help us not to take "No" for an answer when we ask you for the very best.

✠ ✠ ✠ ✠ ✠

Jesus [illegible] his [illegible] to tell the [illegible] that God's kingdom has come, and that He must now [illegible] the [illegible] in this kingdom by healing [illegible] [illegible] your evil spirits.

But sometimes people who don't know Jesus [illegible] that Jesus surely has to help them. The Roman officer was one such person, and this [illegible] [illegible] be persuaded to help, [illegible] brings out a more wonderful faith in the woman [illegible] [illegible] even [illegible].

*

Let us [illegible] for an answer, then we ask you for the very best.

* * * *

A Psalm for
July

O God, you are my God,
  and I long for you.
My whole being desires you;
  like a dry, worn-out, and waterless land,
  my soul is thirsty for you.
Let me see you in the sanctuary;
  let me see how mighty and glorious you are.
Your constant love is better than life itself,
  and so I will praise you.
I will give you thanks as long as I live;
  I will raise my hands to you in prayer.
My soul will feast and be satisfied,
  and I will sing glad songs of praise to you.

As I lie in bed, I remember you;
  all night long I think of you,
  because you have always been my help.
In the shadow of your wings I sing for joy.
I cling to you,
  and your hand keeps me safe.

Psalm 63:1–8

July 1

As Jesus was walking along, he saw a man who had been born blind. His disciples asked him, "Teacher, whose sin caused him to be born blind? Was it his own or his parents' sin?"

Jesus answered "His blindness has nothing to do with his sins or his parents' sins. He is blind so that God's power might be seen at work in him. As long as it is day, we must keep on doing the work of him who sent me; night is coming when no one can work. While I am in the world, I am the light for the world."

After he said this, Jesus spat on the ground and made some mud with the spittle; he rubbed the mud on the man's eyes and said, "Go and wash your face in the Pool of Siloam."

So the man went, washed his face, and came back seeing.

John 9:1–7

✠

When things go wrong, we always look around for someone to blame.

The disciples think this man is blind because he deserves it – or perhaps it is a punishment for something his parents have done.

But Jesus says it is nothing of the sort. The man is blind so that the power of God can be seen at work in healing him. He is in darkness so that everyone will have the chance to realize that Jesus is the light.

✠

Lord, you are the light of the world. Please shine into every dark place, so that we can all find the way to God.

✠ ✠ ✠ ✠ ✠

July 2

As Jesus and his disciples went on their way, he came to a village where a woman named Martha welcomed him in her home. She had a sister named Mary, who sat down at the feet of the Lord and listened to his teaching. Martha was upset over all the work she had to do, so she came and said, "Lord, don't you care that my sister has left me to do all the work by myself? Tell her to come and help me!"

The Lord answered her, "Martha, Martha! You are worried and troubled over so many things, but just one is needed. Mary has chosen the right thing, and it will not be taken away from her."

Luke 10:38–42

✠

Martha is an excellent housekeeper and a wonderful hostess. It gives her great pleasure that Jesus stays at her home.

But on this occasion she starts to feel sorry for herself. She's having to work so hard, getting all hot and bothered about the meal, while her sister Mary just sits doing nothing – talking to Jesus.

But when Martha explodes in self-pity and jealousy, Jesus says something very special to her. He explains that Mary has been quite right to sit quietly listening. The housekeeping and cooking will always need to be done, but there are times when we must simply leave them to make space for Jesus instead.

✠

Lord, help us to give you our undivided attention even in the midst of our busy days.

✠ ✠ ✠ ✠ ✠

July 3

Some people brought their babies to Jesus for him to place his hands on them. The disciples saw them and scolded them for doing so, but Jesus called the children to him and said, "Let the children come to me and do not stop them, because the Kingdom of God belongs to such as these. Remember this! Whoever does not receive the Kingdom of God like a child will never enter it."

Luke 18:15–17

✠

The disciples think that children aren't important – that they should be kept at the back while Jesus talks to the adults.

But Jesus thinks differently. He says that there is something very special about children. Their simple trust and their willingness to learn make them just the kind of people he wants in his Kingdom. Indeed, the Kingdom's door is only open to people like this – children of all ages.

✠

Lord, thank you that you don't just look for strong, wise or clever people to come into your Kingdom. Thank you that you welcome anyone who comes to you in simple trust. Help us to be like that.

✠ ✠ ✠ ✠ ✠

July 4

A Jewish leader asked Jesus, "Good Teacher, what must I do to receive eternal life?"

"Why do you call me good?" Jesus asked him. "No one is good except God alone. You know the commandments: 'Do not commit adultery; do not commit murder; do not steal; do not accuse anyone falsely; respect your father and your mother.'"

The man replied, "Ever since I was young, I have obeyed all these commandments."

When Jesus heard this, he said to him, "There is still one more thing you need to do. Sell all you have and give the money to the poor, and you will have riches in heaven; then come and follow me." But when the man heard this, he became very sad, because he was very rich.

Luke 18:18–23

For most of us there is something we cling to which stops us trusting God completely.

Sometimes it's a bad habit or a sinful secret which we refuse to give up.

This young man has no problems at all in keeping the commandments, but he is absolutely devoted to his possessions. His treasures and home comforts are so dear to his heart, that he simply can't let them go – not even for the sake of following Jesus.

✠

Dear Lord, may we not be so fond of our possessions that they own us and dominate our lives. Help us to travel light, and to be able to put you first at all times.

✠ ✠ ✠ ✠ ✠

July 5

Jesus saw that the young man was sad and said, "How hard it is for rich people to enter the Kingdom of God! It is much harder for a rich person to enter the Kingdom of God than for a camel to go through the eye of a needle."

The people who heard him asked, "Who, then, can be saved?"

Jesus answered, "What is impossible for man is possible for God."

Then Peter said, "Look! We have left our homes to follow you."

"Yes," Jesus said to them, "and I assure you that anyone who leaves home or wife or brothers or parents or children for the sake of the Kingdom of God will receive much more in this present age and eternal life in the age to come."

Luke 18:24–30

✠

When we make Jesus our Lord, we have to put him first. He is more important to us than even our closest family.

But Jesus promises that whatever we give up for him, he will give us back many times over in this life – to say nothing of welcoming us to enjoy eternal life with him in heaven.

✠

Lord, thank you for our homes and families. Help us to love them best by loving you first.

✠ ✠ ✠ ✠ ✠

July 6

Once when large crowds of people were going along with Jesus, he turned and said to them, "Whoever comes to me cannot be my disciple unless he loves me more than he loves his father and his mother, his wife and his children, his brothers and his sisters, and himself as well. Whoever does not carry his own cross and come after me cannot be my disciple.

"If one of you is planning to build a tower, he sits down first and works out what it will cost, to see if he has enough money to finish the job. If he doesn't, he will not be able to finish the tower after laying the foundation; and all who see what happened will laugh at him. 'This man began to build but can't finish the job!' they will say.

"If a king goes out with ten thousand men to fight another king who comes against him with twenty thousand men, he will sit down first and decide if he is strong enough to face that other king. If he isn't, he will send messengers to meet the other king, to ask for terms of peace while he is still a long way off. In the same way," concluded Jesus, "none of you can be my disciple unless he gives up everything he has."

Luke 14:25–33

✠

Jesus wants people to think very carefully before becoming his disciples. It's just as serious as starting a building or going to war, and requires total commitment.

Unless Jesus is the most important person in our lives, we can't call him Lord. Unless we are completely given over to him, he can't rely on us – and so we aren't truly his disciples.

✠

Lord, help us thoughtfully, seriously, to put you first – weighing up the hard times that will come, as well as the joys.

✠ ✠ ✠ ✠ ✠

July 7

As Jesus was coming near Jericho, there was a blind man sitting by the road, begging. When he heard the crowd passing by, he asked, "What is this?"

"Jesus of Nazareth is passing by," they told him.

He cried out, "Jesus! Son of David! Take pity on me!"

The people in front scolded him and told him to be quiet. But he shouted even more loudly, "Son of David! Take pity on me!"

So Jesus stopped and ordered the blind man to be brought to him. When he came near, Jesus asked him, "What do you want me to do for you?"

"Sir," he answered, "I want to see again."

Jesus said to him, "Then see! Your faith has made you well."

At once he was able to see, and he followed Jesus, giving thanks to God. When the crowd saw it, they all praised God.

Luke 18:35–43

✠

Jesus won't be coming to Jericho again. Maybe the blind man senses that it's his last chance to be healed.

He attracts attention by shouting that Jesus is the "Son of David" – a dangerous political slogan. And not surprisingly, people try to get him to be quiet!

When Jesus calls for him, he asks him to put into words what it is that he really wants. Are the prayers we pray as short and to the point as the blind man's answer?

✠

Lord, you stopped in your tracks for a blind beggar. Thank you that you came to save us, no matter how ugly and helpless we are. Thank you that you hear and answer the deepest prayers of our hearts.

✠ ✠ ✠ ✠ ✠

July 8

Jesus went on into Jericho and was passing through. There was a chief tax collector there named Zacchaeus, who was rich. He was trying to see who Jesus was, but he was a little man and could not see Jesus because of the crowd. So he ran ahead of the crowd and climbed a sycomore tree to see Jesus, who was going to pass that way. When Jesus came to that place, he looked up and said to Zacchaeus, "Hurry down, Zacchaeus, because I must stay in your house today."

Zacchaeus hurried down and welcomed him with great joy. All the people who saw it started grumbling, "This man has gone as a guest to the home of a sinner!"

Zacchaeus stood up and said to the Lord, "Listen, sir! I will give half my belongings to the poor, and if I have cheated anyone, I will pay him back four times as much."

Jesus said to him, "Salvation has come to this house today, for this man, also, is a descendant of Abraham. The Son of Man came to seek and to save the lost."

Luke 19:1–10

✠

Zacchaeus is one of the richest men in Jericho – and certainly the most hated.

But Jesus loves him. He doesn't love his greed or his wealth – but he loves *him*.

And when Zacchaeus turns to God and starts to put things right, it's just as much of a miracle as a blind man seeing or a cripple starting to dance.

✠

Lord, we praise you for loving us despite everything – loving us back to God, and loving us into caring for others as well.

✠ ✠ ✠ ✠ ✠

July 9

Today we go back hundreds of years, to hear more about Jacob – and his favourite son, Joseph.

✠

Jacob loved Joseph more than all his other sons, because he had been born to him when he was old. He made a long robe with full sleeves for him. When his brothers saw that their father loved Joseph more than he loved them, they hated their brother so much that they would not speak to him in a friendly manner.

One night Joseph had a dream, and when he told his brothers about it, they hated him even more. He said, "Listen to the dream I had. We were all in the field tying up sheaves of wheat, when my sheaf got up and stood up straight. Yours formed a circle round mine and bowed down to it."

"Do you think you are going to be a king and rule over us?" his brothers asked. So they hated him even more because of his dreams and because of what he said about them.

Genesis 37:3–8

✠

Do you remember Jacob? Do you remember how he was his mother's favourite, and what a lot of trouble that caused?

Well, now Jacob makes the same mistake in bringing up his own children. He treats his youngest son, Joseph, like a prince. Only a prince would have a robe with sleeves (everyone else had to get their hands and arms dirty earning a living). And, of course, Joseph is proud. It comes out in his dreams, and his brothers are jealous. Favouritism in a family means that everyone gets hurt in the end.

✠

Lord, you have made us to be a family – a place where we all belong. May we love and value each other very highly indeed, not only today but in all the years to come.

✠ ✠ ✠ ✠ ✠

July 10

One day when Joseph's brothers had gone to Shechem to take care of their father's flock, Jacob said to Joseph,

"I want you to go to Shechem, where your brothers are taking care of the flock."

Joseph answered, "I am ready."

His father said, "Go and see if your brothers are safe and if the flock is all right; then come back and tell me." So Joseph went after his brothers and found them at Dothan.

They saw him in the distance, and before he reached them, they plotted against him and decided to kill him. They said to one another, "Here comes that dreamer. Come on now, let's kill him and throw his body into one of the dry wells. We can say that a wild animal killed him. Then we will see what becomes of his dreams."

Reuben heard them and tried to save Joseph. "Let's not kill him," he said. "Just throw him into this well in the wilderness, but don't hurt him." He said this, planning to save him from them and send him back to his father.

Genesis 37:12–14,17b–22

✠

The brothers can see Joseph coming a mile away – his sleeves billowing in the sunshine. They have plenty of time to hatch a plot to kill him.

But Reuben disagrees, and we begin to see that perhaps God is at work to rescue Joseph after all.

✠

Lord, we see again that our lives are quite safe until your particular purpose for each of us is fulfilled. We praise and thank you for your constant love.

✠ ✠ ✠ ✠ ✠

July 11

When Joseph came up to his brothers, they ripped off his long robe with full sleeves. Then they took him and threw him into the well, which was dry.

While they were eating, they suddenly saw a group of Ishmaelites travelling from Gilead to Egypt. Their camels were loaded with spices and resins. Judah said to his brothers, "What will we gain by killing our brother and covering up the murder? Let's sell him to these Ishmaelites. Then we won't have to hurt him; after all, he is our brother, our own flesh and blood." His brothers agreed, and when some Midianite traders came by, the brothers pulled Joseph out of the well and sold him for twenty pieces of silver to the Ishmaelites, who took him to Egypt.

Genesis 37:23–28

✠

On the face of it, Joseph has no chance of survival. He is in a desert, down a hole, and outnumbered ten to one by his angry brothers.

But such odds are nothing to God. First the brothers glimpse a group of Ishmaelites, and Judah has the idea of selling Joseph instead of murdering him. And then, by the time some Midianites come by, they are all agreed. They sell their brother for twenty pieces of silver. (Do you remember that Jesus was sold for silver when the priests paid Judas for betraying him? The whole story of Joseph is a Bible "trailer" for the life and death of Jesus. Like Joseph, Jesus was rejected, but in the end God made him Lord of all.)

✠

Mighty God, thank you that you rescue your people from hopeless situations, giving faith instead of fear and life instead of death.

✠ ✠ ✠ ✠ ✠

July 12

Now the Ishmaelites had taken Joseph to Egypt and sold him to Potiphar, one of the king's officers, who was the captain of the palace guard. The LORD was with Joseph and made him successful. He lived in the house of his Egyptian master, who saw that the LORD was with Joseph and had made him successful in everything he did. Potiphar was pleased with him and made him his personal servant; so he put him in charge of his house and everything he owned. From then on, because of Joseph the LORD blessed the household of the Egyptian and everything that he had in his house and in his fields. Potiphar handed over everything he had to the care of Joseph and did not concern himself with anything except the food he ate.

Genesis 39:1–6

✠

Once in Egypt, Joseph starts to do very well. He is clever, patient, hard-working – and an excellent manager.

But it's not because of any of these gifts that he succeeds. It's because the Lord is blessing him, as Potiphar can plainly see.

But trouble isn't far away. One day, Potiphar's wife accuses Joseph of trying to attack her while her husband was out. Potiphar has no choice but to believe his wife's word, and so he has Joseph thrown into prison.

✠

Lord, please bless us and make us a blessing in our lives today.

✠ ✠ ✠ ✠ ✠

July 13

After two years had passed, the king of Egypt dreamt that he was standing by the River Nile, when seven cows, fat and sleek, came up out of the river and began to feed on the grass. Then seven other cows came up; they were thin and bony. They came and stood by the other cows on the river-bank, and the thin cows ate up the fat cows. Then the king woke up. He fell asleep again and had another dream. Seven ears of corn, full and ripe, were growing on one stalk. Then seven other ears of corn sprouted, thin and scorched by the desert wind, and the thin ears of corn swallowed the full ones. The king woke up and realized that he had been dreaming. In the morning he was worried, so he sent for all the magicians and wise men of Egypt. He told them his dreams, but no one could explain them to him.

Genesis 41:1–8

Now we meet the king of Egypt, who is suffering from terrible dreams.

The fat cattle and bumper crops which make his country prosperous are being consumed by skinny cows and scrappy corn. The king knows that dreams can be important, and he tries to find out the meaning straight away. But no one can help – not even his wisest advisers.

✠

Mighty God, you are Lord of all the earth. The world of nature and the power of kings are all under your control. We praise you that your strength is matched by your wisdom, and your wisdom by your love.

✠ ✠ ✠ ✠ ✠

July 14

Then the wine steward said to the king, "I must confess today that I have done wrong. You were angry with the chief baker and me, and you put us in prison in the house of the captain of the guard. One night each of us had a dream, and the dreams had different meanings. A young Hebrew was there with us, a slave of the captain of the guard. We told him our dreams, and he interpreted them for us. Things turned out just as he said: you restored me to my position, but you executed the baker."

The king sent for Joseph, and he was immediately brought from the prison. After he had shaved and changed his clothes, he came into the king's presence.

The king said to him, "I have had a dream, and no one can explain it. I have been told that you can interpret dreams."

Joseph answered, "I cannot, Your Majesty, but God will give a favourable interpretation."

Genesis 41:9–16

✠

Suddenly the wine steward remembers that when he was in prison he met a young man who could tell the meaning of dreams. So, in one swift connection, Joseph is brought from the dungeons where he is an imprisoned slave, into the presence of the king himself. All of a sudden, he is a trusted adviser! And see how, in this amazing turn of events, he is quick to give all the credit for his gift to God.

✠

Lord God, your plans are marvellous and your timing is perfect. Help us to commit our own lives to you afresh – our situation, our gifts, and ourselves.

✠ ✠ ✠ ✠ ✠

July 15

Joseph said to the king, "The two dreams mean the same thing; God has told you what he is going to do. The seven fat cows are seven years, and the seven full ears of corn are also seven years; they have the same meaning. The seven thin cows which came up later and the seven thin ears of corn scorched by the desert wind are seven years of famine. It is just as I told you – God has shown you what he is going to do. There will be seven years of great plenty in all the land of Egypt. After that, there will be seven years of famine, and all the good years will be forgotten, because the famine will ruin the country. The time of plenty will be entirely forgotten, because the famine which follows will be so terrible. The repetition of your dream means that the matter is fixed by God and that he will make it happen in the near future."

Genesis 41:25–32

✠

The meaning of the dreams is simple – and just as the king had feared. His country stands on the brink of ruin.

But Joseph doesn't see ruin. He sees God at work. And he doesn't hesitate to talk to the king about this wonderful God. It is God who is speaking through the dreams. It is God who has decided what will happen. It is God who knows what can be done in the face of this crisis.

✠

Lord God, every trouble that threatens is also our chance to turn to you, and your opportunity to show your powerful deliverance. Thank you!

✠ ✠ ✠ ✠ ✠

July 16

Joseph said to the king: "Now you should choose some man with wisdom and insight and put him in charge of the country. You must also appoint other officials and take a fifth of the crops during the seven years of plenty. Order them to collect all the food during the good years that are coming, and give them authority to store up corn in the cities and guard it. The food will be a reserve supply for the country during the seven years of famine which are going to come on Egypt. In this way the people will not starve."

The king and his officials approved this plan, and he said to them, "We will never find a better man than Joseph, a man who has God's spirit in him." The king said to Joseph, "God has shown you all this, so it is obvious that you have greater wisdom and insight than anyone else. I will put you in charge of my country, and all my people will obey your orders. Your authority will be second only to mine. I now appoint you governor over all Egypt."

Genesis 41:33–41

✠

There is something special about Joseph. It shines out of him. Potiphar had noticed that God was blessing Joseph and that his home was a better place for having him around. Now the king entrusts Joseph with the government of all Egypt.

The pompous little boy who provoked his brothers by telling his dreams has now been transformed, through many hardships, into a remarkable man of God.

Living God, what a difference you can make if only we let you. Please make our lives a miracle of change for the better.

✠ ✠ ✠ ✠ ✠

July 17

The seven years of plenty that the land of Egypt had enjoyed came to an end, and the seven years of famine began, just as Joseph had said. There was famine in every other country, but there was food throughout Egypt. When the Egyptians began to be hungry, they cried out to the king for food. So he ordered them to go to Joseph and do what he told them. The famine grew worse and spread over the whole country, so Joseph opened all the storehouses and sold corn to the Egyptians. People came to Egypt from all over the world to buy corn from Joseph, because the famine was severe everywhere.

When Jacob learnt that there was corn in Egypt, he said to his sons, "Why don't you do something? I hear that there is corn in Egypt; go there and buy some to keep us from starving to death." So Joseph's ten half-brothers went to buy corn in Egypt, but Jacob did not send Joseph's full-brother Benjamin with them, because he was afraid that something might happen to him.

Genesis 41:53–42:4

✠

The God who can bring Joseph out of the dungeons and make him Prime Minister is now bringing Joseph's brothers all the way from Canaan. It's going to take a while, because Jacob now has another favourite son – Benjamin – whom he isn't letting out of his sight.

✠

Lord, everything is under your control. You used Joseph to bless the Egyptians and keep them from starvation. You used the famine to draw Joseph's family back together. Help us to see your hand in our own circumstances, and to work along with you today.

✠ ✠ ✠ ✠ ✠

July 18

When Joseph sees his brothers coming to buy food, he decides to test them. He himself is so different from when they last saw him as a young man being dragged off into slavery. Now he is full-grown, changed by suffering, and dressed in the regalia of an Egyptian noble.

✠

Although Joseph recognized his brothers, they did not recognize him. He remembered the dreams he had dreamt about them and said, "You are spies; you have come to find out where our country is weak."

"No, sir," they answered. "We have come as your slaves, to buy food. We are all brothers. We are not spies, sir, we are honest men."

Joseph said to them, "No! You have come to find out where our country is weak."

They said, "We were twelve brothers in all, sir, sons of the same man in the land of Canaan. One brother is dead, and the youngest is now with our father."

"It is just as I said," Joseph answered. "You are spies. This is how you will be tested: I swear by the name of the king that you will never leave unless your youngest brother comes here."

Genesis 42:8–15

✠

Joseph accuses his brothers of spying – which they aren't. But they do have a guilty secret, which isn't far below the surface, even after all these years. See how quickly they mention their "dead brother"!

✠

Lord, you know everything, you know the things we are ashamed of – even things that happened years ago. Sometimes you open old wounds of guilt and regret – but only so that you can forgive the past and heal our memories. Thank you.

✠ ✠ ✠ ✠ ✠

July 19

Joseph lets his brothers buy food and return home – and unbeknown to them, he has their money put back in their sacks. But, if they come again, they must bring

Benjamin – and that plunges old Jacob into a dilemma. Either they must take the risk of Benjamin travelling to Egypt, or they must starve.

✠

The famine in Canaan got worse, and when the family of Jacob had eaten all the corn which had been brought from Egypt, Jacob said to his sons, "Go back and buy a little food for us."

Judah said to him, "The man sternly warned us that we would not be admitted to his presence unless we had our brother with us. If you are willing to send our brother with us, we will go and buy food for you. If you are not willing, we will not go, because the man told us we would not be admitted to his presence unless our brother was with us."

Their father said to them, "If that is how it has to be, then take the best products of the land in your packs as a present for the governor: a little resin, a little honey, spices, pistachio nuts, and almonds. Take with you also twice as much money, because you must take back the money that was returned in the top of your sacks. Maybe it was a mistake. Take your brother and return at once. May Almighty God cause the man to have pity on you, so that he will give Benjamin and your other brother back to you. As for me, if I must lose my children, I must lose them."

So the brothers took the gifts and twice as much money, and set out for Egypt with Benjamin.

Genesis 43:1–5,11–15

✠

It's easy for us to see that there was nothing to worry about. But Jacob offers one of his great wrestling prayers, that God will change the governor's mind. And having prayed with all his heart, he lets his sons go on their journey and leaves the rest to God.

✠

Lord, even when we have known and trusted you for many years, there are still some agonizing decisions to face. Help us to lay all our cares at your feet – and leave them there.

✠ ✠ ✠ ✠ ✠

July 20

The servant took the brothers into the house. He gave them water so that they could wash their feet, and he fed their donkeys. They got their gifts ready to present to Joseph when he arrived at noon, because they had been told that they were to eat with him. When Joseph got home, they took the gifts into the house to him and bowed down to the ground before him. He asked about their health and then said, "You told me about your old father – how is he? Is he still alive and well?"

They answered, "Your humble servant, our father, is still alive and well." And they knelt and bowed down before him.

Genesis 43:24–28

✠

When the brothers arrive in Egypt, they find themselves treated as special guests. Not for them the long queue at the storehouses, but a bath and a meal at the Prime Minister's residence! Their minds are buzzing with questions. Why have they been singled out? How does this governor remember to ask after their father? Why does he care so much?

As for Joseph, he is delighted to see young Benjamin at last, and when his brothers bow to him – well, it's nothing less than a dream come true.

✠

Lord Jesus, you are the Lord of Glory, yet you call us your brothers and sisters. We don't know why you should care for us at all, but we thank you that you do.

✠ ✠ ✠ ✠ ✠

July 21

Joseph was no longer able to control his feelings in front of his servants, so he ordered them all to leave the room. No one else was with him when Joseph told his brothers who he was. He cried with such loud sobs that the Egyptians heard it, and the news was taken to the king's palace. Joseph said to his brothers, "I am Joseph. Is my father still alive?" But when his brothers heard this, they were so terrified that they could not answer. Then Joseph said to them, "Please come closer." They did, and he said, "I am your brother Joseph, whom you sold into Egypt. Now do not be upset or blame yourselves because you sold me here. It was really God who sent me ahead of you to save people's lives. This is only the second year of famine in the land; there will be five more years in which there will be neither ploughing nor reaping. God sent me ahead of you to rescue you in this amazing way and to make sure that you and your descendants survive. So it was not really you who sent me here, but God. He has made me the king's highest official. I am in charge of his whole country; I am the ruler of all Egypt."

Genesis 45:1–8

✠

So at last the secret is out. The governor of Egypt is their long-lost brother. How can they possibly escape the punishment they deserve for selling him as a slave?

But nothing is further from Joseph's mind. He sees all his suffering in the light of God's plan to save them. It was God who sent him to Egypt and promoted him to the highest place of honour. And all so that the sons of Jacob – the children of Israel – might be kept safe and well through the years of famine.

✠

Lord God, you promised to protect Jacob and his descendants – and you did. Thank you that you are a God who keeps your promises, even weaving our wilful errors and stupid mistakes into your perfect plan.

✠ ✠ ✠ ✠ ✠

July 22

When they arrived, Joseph got in his chariot and went to Goshen to meet his father. When they met, Joseph threw his arms round his father's neck and cried for a long time. Jacob said to Joseph, "I am ready to die, now that I have seen you and know that you are still alive."

Then Joseph said to his brothers and the rest of his father's family, "I must go and tell the king that my brothers and all my father's family, who were living in Canaan, have come to me. I will tell him that you are shepherds and take care of livestock and that you have brought your flocks and herds and everything else that belongs to you. When the king calls for you and asks what your occupation is, be sure to tell him that you have taken care of livestock all your lives, just as your ancestors did. In this way he will let you live in the region of Goshen."

Then Joseph settled his father and his brothers in Egypt, giving them property in the best of the land near the city of Rameses, as the king had commanded. Joseph provided food for his father, his brothers, and all the rest of his father's family, including the very youngest.

Genesis 46:28b–34; 47:11–12

✠

Old Jacob and the rest of his family come to Egypt, and Jacob and Joseph are reunited after so many years. Jacob is content, and feels that his life is now complete. As for his sons, Joseph's brothers, it is a new beginning. The king will want to be sure that they aren't just rogues passing through, stealing other men's cattle and grazing other men's pasture. When he understands that they are experienced shepherds, he gives them the very best of the land to settle in. And so the amazing story of Joseph comes to a happy end.

✠

Lord, thank you for your great faithfulness to your people over years and distances, and from one generation to another. You never break your promise to care.

✠ ✠ ✠ ✠ ✠

July 23

Then, a new king, who knew nothing about Joseph, came to power in Egypt. He said to his people, "These Israelites are so numerous and strong that they are a threat to us. In case of war they might join our enemies in order to fight against us, and might escape from the country. We must find some way to keep them from becoming even more numerous."

So the Egyptians put slave-drivers over them to crush their spirits with hard labour. The Israelites built the cities of Pithom and Rameses to serve as supply centres for the king. But the more the Egyptians oppressed the Israelites, the more they increased in number and the further they spread through the land. The Egyptians came to fear the Israelites and made their lives miserable by forcing them into cruel slavery. They made them work on their building projects and in their fields, and they had no mercy on them.

Finally the king issued a command to all his people: "Take every new-born Hebrew boy and throw him into the Nile, but let all the girls live."

Exodus 1:8–14,22

✠

Time has passed, and the memory of Joseph has faded.

Instead of feeling gratitude for the way Joseph had masterminded the fight against famine, the Egyptians now feel angry at the way the Israelites are growing in number – and afraid of what they might do.

So the Egyptians begin to oppress the Hebrews, reducing them to slavery and, in the end, drowning their baby boys.

How cruel we human beings can get once fear and bitterness take hold of us. The only antidote is *love.* "Love your neighbour as yourself," says Jesus – for perfect love casts out fear.

✠

Lord, in our nation, and between the nations, may we see love conquering fear, harmony overcoming tension, and peace reigning instead of war.

✠ ✠ ✠ ✠ ✠

July 24

During this time a man from the tribe of Levi married a woman of his own tribe, and she bore him a son. When she saw what a fine baby he was, she hid him for three months. But when she could not hide him any longer, she took a basket made of reeds and covered it with tar to make it watertight. She put the baby in it and then placed it in the tall grass at the edge of the river. The baby's sister stood some distance away to see what would happen to him.

The king's daughter came down to the river to bathe, while her servants walked along the bank. Suddenly she noticed the basket in the tall grass and sent a slave-girl to get it. The princess opened it and saw a baby boy. He was crying, and she felt sorry for him. "This is one of the Hebrew babies," she said.

Then his sister asked her, "Shall I go and call a Hebrew woman to act as a wet-nurse?"

"Please do," she answered. So the girl went and brought the baby's own mother. The princess told the woman, "Take this baby and nurse him for me, and I will pay you." So she took the baby and nursed him. Later, when the child was old enough, she took him to the king's daughter, who adopted him as her own son. She said to herself, "I pulled him out of the water, and so I name him Moses."

Exodus 2:1–10

✠

When her baby grew so big that his cries could be heard far and wide, the mother laid him gently in a tar-covered basket – knowing very well that the basket might become his coffin.

But the cries which might have meant that all was lost in fact result in him being found – and found by none other than the king's daughter! Soon Moses receives his name and is adopted as the princess's son – and his mother is given the best job in the world, being paid for looking after her own baby!

✠

Lord, when all seems lost we can still look to you and find that all is won.

✠ ✠ ✠ ✠ ✠

July 25

When Moses had grown up, he went out to visit his people, the Hebrews, and he saw how they were forced to do hard labour. He even saw an Egyptian kill a Hebrew, one of Moses' own people. Moses looked all round, and when he saw that no one was watching, he killed the Egyptian and hid his body in the sand.

The next day he went back and saw two Hebrew men fighting. He said to the one who was in the wrong, "Why are you beating up a fellow-Hebrew?"

The man answered, "Who made you our ruler and judge? Are you going to kill me just as you killed that Egyptian?" Then Moses was afraid and said to himself, "People have found out what I have done." When the king heard about what had happened, he tried to have Moses killed, but Moses fled and went to live in the land of Midian.

Exodus 2:11–16

✠

Moses has been brought up as a prince of Egypt: living in the royal palace, eating at the royal table, and enjoying the very best in education and leisure.

But he has always known from his real mother that he is a Hebrew – and now he feels it in his bones.

One day he goes to see for himself the kind of life the Hebrews live, and impetuously takes revenge on an Egyptian slave-driver whom he sees killing one of his people.

The next day he can hardly wait to get back and visit them again. It may be that he, a prince of Egypt, can help them in some way . . .

But it doesn't work out at all. Moses, who is both Hebrew and Egyptian, finds himself rejected by both peoples. He has to run for his life.

✠

Lord, sometimes you give us a glimpse of the work you want us to do. Help us to do that work in your good way and in your good time.

✠ ✠ ✠ ✠ ✠

July 26

One day while Moses was taking care of the sheep and goats of his father-in-law Jethro, the priest of Midian, he led the flock across the desert and came to Sinai, the holy mountain. There the angel of the LORD appeared to him as a flame coming from the middle of a bush. Moses saw that the bush was on fire but that it was not burning up. "This is strange," he thought. "Why isn't the bush burning up? I will go closer and see."

When the LORD saw that Moses was coming closer, he called to him from the middle of the bush and said, "Moses! Moses!"

He answered, "Yes, here I am."

God said, "Do not come any closer. Take off your sandals, because you are standing on holy ground. I am the God of your ancestors, the God of Abraham, Isaac, and Jacob." So Moses covered his face, because he was afraid to look at God.

Then the LORD said, "I have seen how cruelly my people are being treated in Egypt; I have heard them cry out to be rescued from their slave-drivers. I know all about their sufferings, and so I have come down to rescue them from the Egyptians and to bring them out of Egypt to a spacious land, one which is rich and fertile. I have indeed heard the cry of my people, and I see how the Egyptians are oppressing them. Now I am sending you to the king of Egypt so that you can lead my people out of his country."

Exodus 3:1–10

✠

For forty years Moses has lived and worked in the wilderness.

He has learned about love as he married and started a family. He has learned about God as he talked to his father-in-law. He has learned patience and responsibility in caring for his flocks day after day.

In it all, God has been preparing him for the most demanding job anybody ever had – to lead the Israelite slaves out of Egypt, across the Sinai desert, and on to a new life in the Promised Land. But it is not Moses who will do all this. It is God.

✠

Lord, please use us – our gifts and our experiences – in your work. But help us always to remember that it is your work, and give you the glory.

✠ ✠ ✠ ✠ ✠

July 27

But Moses said to God, "I am nobody. How can I go to the king and bring the Israelites out of Egypt?"

God answered, "I will be with you, and when you bring the people out of Egypt, you will worship me on this mountain. That will be the proof that I have sent you."

But Moses replied, "When I go to the Israelites and say to them, 'The God of your ancestors sent me to you,' they will ask me, 'What is his name?' So what can I tell them?"

God said, "I am who I am. This is what you must say to them: 'The one who is called I AM has sent me to you.' Tell the Israelites that I, the LORD, the God of their ancestors, the God of Abraham, Isaac, and Jacob, have sent you to them. This is my name for ever; this is what all future generations are to call me."

Exodus 3:11–15

✠

How different Moses is from the proud, strong prince who once went to inspect the Hebrews. Now he knows he is nothing – a nobody. But it is when we know we are nothing, that God can be everything to us.

God introduces himself to Moses, and reveals his secret name: "I AM". God is the one who is. He is who he is. He will be who he will be. He is the same God who walked with Abraham, Isaac and Jacob. He will be the God of Israel to all future generations.

✠

Immortal, invisible God, thank you for making yourself known to us, and for catching us up in your wonderful plan for mankind.

July 28

Moses is nervous about going back to Egypt and asking the king to let the Hebrews go. God allows him to take his brother Aaron as a companion.

✠

Then Moses and Aaron went to the king of Egypt and said, "The LORD, the God of Israel, says, 'Let my people go, so that they can hold a festival in the desert to honour me.'"

"Who is the LORD?" the king demanded. "Why should I listen to him and let Israel go? I do not know the LORD; and I will not let Israel go."

Moses and Aaron replied, "The God of the Hebrews has revealed himself to us. Allow us to travel for three days into the desert to offer sacrifices to the LORD our God. If we don't do so, he will kill us with disease or by war."

The king said to Moses and Aaron, "What do you mean by making the people neglect their work? Get those slaves back to work! You people have become more numerous than the Egyptians. A Egyptian slave-drivers and the Israelite foremen: "Stop giving the people straw for making bricks. Ma one brick less. They haven't enough work to do, and that is why they keep asking me to let them go and offer sacrifices to their God! Make these men work harder and keep them busy, so that they won't have time to listen to a pack of lies."

Exodus 5:1–9

✠

Of course, the king sees that if the Hebrews leave, he will lose all his cheap labour. The Egyptians don't like the Hebrews, but they have come to depend on them to do their heavy building work and to plough the fields. So the king heaps more work on the slaves – and life gets harder.

✠

Lord God, we live for you in a world that hates you. Help us to carry on patiently and joyfully when times get hard.

✠ ✠ ✠ ✠ ✠

July 29

Then the LORD said to Moses, "The king is very stubborn and refuses to let the people go. So go and meet him in the morning when he goes down to the Nile. Take with you the stick that was turned into a snake, and wait for him on the bank of the river. Then say to the king, 'The LORD, the God of the Hebrews, sent me to tell you to let his people go, so that they can worship him in the desert. But until now you have not listened. Now, Your Majesty, the LORD says that you will find out who he is by what he is going to do. Look, I am going to strike the surface of the river with this stick, and the water will be turned into blood. The fish will die, and the river will stink so much that the Egyptians will not be able to drink from it.'"

The LORD said to Moses, "Tell Aaron to take his stick and hold it out over all the rivers, canals, and pools in Egypt. The water will become blood, and all over the land there will be blood, even in the wooden tubs and stone jars."

Then Moses and Aaron did as the LORD commanded. In the presence of the king and his officers, Aaron raised his stick and struck the surface of the river, and all the water in it was turned into blood.

Exodus 7:14–20

✠

Now God starts to reveal his power, and life is about to get very hard for the Egyptians.

Egypt is a hot, dry country, whose lifeline is the river Nile. For all the water to be turned to blood is a national disaster. But the king is so stubborn, that there will be worse things happening yet.

✠

Lord, when we refuse your love we plunge ourselves into many difficulties – but it's our own choice! Help us not to be stubborn towards you, but to accept that your way leads to life.

✠ ✠ ✠ ✠ ✠

July 30

As time goes by, the people of Egypt endure many plagues – frogs, lice, flies, boils, hail, locusts, darkness . . . Moses forecast each one and said it was God's doing, but the king still wouldn't let the Hebrews out of his sight, not even for a few days.

Then the LORD said to Moses, "I will send only one more punishment on the king of Egypt and his people. After that he will let you leave. In fact, he will drive all of you out of here. Now speak to the people of Israel and tell all of them to ask their neighbours for gold and silver jewellery." The LORD made the Egyptians respect the Israelites. Indeed, the officials and all the people considered Moses to be a very great man.

Moses then said to the king, "The LORD says, 'At about midnight I will go through Egypt, and every first-born son in Egypt will die, from the king's son, who is heir to the throne, to the son of the slave-woman, who grinds corn. The first-born of all the cattle will die also. There will be loud crying all over Egypt, such as there has never been before or ever will be again. But not even a dog will bark at the Israelites or their animals. Then you will know that I, the LORD, make a distinction between the Egyptians and the Israelites.'" Moses concluded by saying, "All your officials will come to me and bow down before me, and they will beg me to take all my people and go away. After that, I will leave." Then in great anger Moses left the king.

Exodus 11:1–8

✠

The last and most dreadful plague is that the first-born son of every Egyptian family – and the first-born of the cattle – will die. How could God do such a thing, even to his enemies? It almost seems that he was left with no choice, for the king of Egypt had rejected every attempt at persuasion. But how true it is that when leaders are opposed to God's will, their people suffer.

Lord God, please bless those who lead the nations of the world. Give them ears to hear your word and hearts to obey your commands.

✠ ✠ ✠ ✠ ✠

July 31

The Lord spoke to Moses and Aaron in Egypt: "This month is to be the first month of the year for you. Give these instructions to the whole community of Israel: On the tenth day of this month each man must choose either a lamb or a young goat for his household. If his family is too small to eat a whole animal, he and his next-door neighbour may share an animal, in proportion to the number of people and the amount that each person can eat. You may choose either a sheep or a goat, but it must be a one-year-old male without any defects. Then, on the evening of the fourteenth day of the month, the whole community of Israel will kill the animals. The people are to take some of the blood and put it on the door-posts and above the doors of the houses in which the animals are to be eaten. That night the meat is to be roasted, and eaten with bitter herbs and with bread made without yeast. Do not eat any of it raw or boiled, but eat it roasted whole, including the head, the legs, and the internal organs. You must not leave any of it until morning; if any is left over, it must be burnt. You are to eat it quickly, for you are to be dressed for travel, with your sandals on your feet and your stick in your hand. It is the Passover Festival to honour me, the Lord."

Exodus 12:1–11

This is the story of the very first Passover meal – the most important night in the history of Israel, and one of their most important annual festivals to this very day.

The blood on the door-posts is to be a sign that a life has already been paid so that the first-born son shall be spared. The bitter herbs are a symbol of the bitterness of slavery in Egypt, and the bread is made without yeast, because it is made in a hurry, and there is no time to let it rise. It is the Hebrews' last meal in slavery. They eat with their bags packed, ready to leave.

✠

Lord, as we thank you for rescuing your people from slavery, we thank you for that greater day when Jesus, the perfect Lamb, gave up his life for us all.

✠ ✠ ✠ ✠ ✠

A Psalm for
August

God, be merciful to us and bless us;
  look on us with kindness,
so that the whole world may know your will;
  so that all nations may know your salvation.

May the peoples praise you, O God;
  may all the peoples praise you!

May the nations be glad and sing for joy,
  because you judge the peoples with justice
  and guide every nation on earth.

May the peoples praise you, O God;
  may all the peoples praise you!

The land has produced its harvest;
  God, our God, has blessed us.
God has blessed us;
  may all people everywhere honour him.

Psalm 67:1–7

August 1

At midnight the LORD killed all the first-born sons in Egypt, from the king's son, who was heir to the throne, to the son of the prisoner in the dungeon; all the first-born of the animals were also killed. That night, the king, his officials, and all the other Egyptians were awakened. There was loud crying throughout Egypt, because there was not one home in which there was not a dead son.

That same night the king sent for Moses and Aaron and said, "Get out, you and your Israelites! Leave my country; go and worship the LORD, as you asked. Take your sheep, goats, and cattle, and leave. Also pray for a blessing on me."

The Egyptians urged the people to hurry and leave the country; they said, "We will all be dead if you don't leave."

So the people filled their baking-pans with unleavened dough, wrapped them in clothing, and carried them on their shoulders. The Israelites had done as Moses had said, and had asked the Egyptians for gold and silver jewellery and for clothing. The LORD made the Egyptians respect the people and give them what they asked for. In this way the Israelites carried away the wealth of the Egyptians.

Exodus 12:29–36

Whoever would have thought that such a turnabout was possible? Who could have forecast that the day would come when the king of Egypt would command the Israelites to leave, and that they would depart laden with the jewellery and clothes of the Egyptians?

Such things are impossible – even for a great man like Moses. But with God, all things are possible. It is his doing. And to this day, the Jews don't mention Moses at all when they tell the story of Passover, for they want all the glory to belong to God.

✠

Lord, thank you that you are on the side of the weak and the poor. Thank you that you choose those without hope to be your own people. Thank you for defeating our enemies and heaping blessings upon us.

✠ ✠ ✠ ✠ ✠

August 2

When the king of Egypt was told that the people had escaped, he and his officials changed their minds and said, "What have we done? We have let the Israelites escape, and we have lost them as our slaves!" The king got his war chariot and his army ready. He set out with all his chariots, including the six hundred finest, commanded by their officers. The LORD made the king stubborn, and he pursued the Israelites, who were leaving triumphantly. The Egyptian army, with all the horses, chariots, and drivers, pursued them and caught up with them where they were camped by the Red Sea.

When the Israelites saw the king and his army marching against them, they were terrified and cried out to the LORD for help. They said to Moses, "Weren't there any graves in Egypt? Did you have to bring us out here in the desert to die? Look what you have done by bringing us out of Egypt! Didn't we tell you before we left that this would happen? We told you to leave us alone and let us go on being slaves of the Egyptians. It would be better to be slaves there than to die here in the desert."

Moses answered, "Don't be afraid! Stand your ground, and you will see what the LORD will do to save you today; you will never see these Egyptians again. The LORD will fight for you, and there is no need for you to do anything."

Exodus 14:5–14

✠

Suddenly the king of Egypt realizes that his work-force has escaped. In a brutal (and typical) change of mind, he gives chase with his army.

But it's not only the king who changes his mind. The Israelites are already pleading with Moses to let them remain in slavery!

In all the turmoil, Moses is the one whose mind is clear and cool. He tells them to keep calm and see what God will do.

✠

Lord, in the changes and chances of life, give us a sure faith like Moses, so that we look for your victory in every crisis.

August 3

The LORD said to Moses, "Why are you crying out for help? Tell the people to move forward. Lift up your stick and hold it out over the sea. The water will divide, and the Israelites will be able to walk through the sea on dry ground. I will make the Egyptians so stubborn that they will go in after them, and I will gain honour by my victory over the king, his army, his chariots, and his drivers. When I defeat them, the Egyptians will know that I am the LORD."

The angel of God, who had been in front of the army of Israel, moved and went to the rear. The pillar of cloud also moved until it was between the Egyptians, and the Israelites. The cloud made it dark for the Egyptians, but gave light to the people of Israel, and so the armies could not come near each other all night.

Moses held out his hand over the sea, and the LORD drove the sea back with a strong east wind. It blew all night and turned the sea into dry land. The water was divided, and the Israelites went through the sea on dry ground, with walls of water on both sides. The Egyptians pursued them and went after them into the sea with all their horses, chariots, and drivers. Just before dawn the LORD looked down from the pillar of fire and cloud at the Egyptian army and threw them into a panic. He made the wheels of their chariots get stuck, so that they moved with great difficulty. The Egyptians said, "The LORD is fighting for the Israelites against us. Let's get out of here!"

On that day the LORD saved the people of Israel from the Egyptians, and the Israelites saw them lying dead on the seashore. When the Israelites saw the great power with which the LORD had defeated the

Egyptians, they stood in awe of the LORD; and they had faith in the LORD and in his servant Moses.

Exodus 14:15–25,30–31

✠

The Exodus is the greatest event in the history of Israel. It is nothing less than the birthday of the nation. And it is so clearly an act of God, that the Jews never cease to wonder at what he did that day.

✠

Lord, by your mighty power you give us freedom and victory – freedom from the slavery of sin and victory even over death. We praise you!

✠ ✠ ✠ ✠ ✠

August 4

The LORD said to Moses, "Now I am going to make food rain down from the sky for all of you. The people must go out every day and gather enough for that day. In this way I can test them to find out if they will follow my instructions. On the sixth day they are to bring in twice as much as usual and prepare it."

In the evening a large flock of quails flew in, enough to cover the camp, and in the morning there was dew all round the camp. When the dew evaporated, there was something thin and flaky on the surface of the desert. It was as delicate as frost. When the Israelites saw it, they didn't know what it was and asked each other, "What is it?"

Moses said to them, "This is the food that the LORD has given you to eat. The LORD has commanded that each of you is to gather as much of it as he needs, two litres for each member of his household."

The Israelites did this, some gathering more, others less. When they measured it, those who had gathered more did not have too much, and those who had gathered less did not have too little. Each had gathered just what he needed.

The people of Israel called the food manna. It was like a small white seed, and tasted like biscuits made with honey.

Exodus 16:4–5,13–18,31

✠

Just as Moses had learned so much during his years in the wilderness, now the Israelites are going to learn important lessons as well.

First of all, they will discover that God can supply all their needs. That doesn't mean that they have all they *want* (they are soon dreaming of the lush vegetables of Egypt and hankering to go back for a good meal), but they certainly have all they *need*. Manna is "enough". Day by day the Lord provides enough for everyone.

When Jesus taught a prayer, it included some words which seemed to have manna in mind: "Give us this day our daily bread", or in other words, "Give us each day enough for the day".

✠

Lord, thank you for providing all our needs.

✠ ✠ ✠ ✠✠

August 5

The whole Israelite community left the desert of Sin, moving from one place to another at the command of the LORD. They made camp at Rephidim, but there was no water there to drink. They complained to Moses and said, "Give us water to drink."

Moses answered, "Why are you complaining? Why are you putting the LORD to the test?"

But the people were very thirsty and continued to complain to Moses. They said, "Why did you bring us out of Egypt? To kill us and our children and our livestock with thirst?"

Moses prayed earnestly to the LORD and said, "What can I do with these people? They are almost ready to stone me."

The LORD said to Moses, "Take some of the leaders of Israel with you, and go on ahead of the people. Take along the stick with which you struck the Nile. I will stand before you on a rock at Mount Sinai. Strike the rock, and water will come out of it for the people to drink." Moses did so in the presence of the leaders of Israel.

The place was named Massah and Meribah, because the Israelites complained and put the LORD to the test when they asked, "Is the LORD with us or not?"

Exodus 17:1–7

✠

After food, the problem is water. Again, the people have to learn that they have a God who provides. He sees ahead, and meets the need. Surely the water had been there in the rocks for thousands of years!

Moses is finding that being a leader can hurt. The people gossip about him, criticize him, and blame him when things go wrong. His is a lonely task.

Lord, help us to value and respect our leaders. Bless them today in the work they do and in the decisions they have to make.

✠ ✠ ✠ ✠ ✠

August 6

The people of Israel left Rephidim, and on the first day of the third month after they had left Egypt they came to the desert of Sinai. There they set up camp at the foot of Mount Sinai, and Moses went up the mountain to meet with God.

The LORD called to him from the mountain and told him to say to the Israelites, Jacob's descendants: "You saw what I, the LORD, did to the Egyptians and how I carried you as an eagle carries her young on her wings, and brought you here to me. Now, if you will obey me and keep my covenant, you will be my own people. The whole earth is mine, but you will be my chosen people, a people dedicated to me alone, and you will serve me as priests." So Moses went down and called the leaders of the people together and told them everything that the LORD had commanded him. Then all the people answered together, "We will do everything that the LORD has said," and Moses reported this to the LORD.

Exodus 19:1–8

✠

God has rescued the Israelites from slavery and shown his power in bringing them safely through the Red Sea.

He has provided them with food and water. Now he unfolds his plan . . .

If the people will keep faith with him, and obey his laws, then they will be his Chosen Race – his own nation. This means that God will entrust his reputation to the Israelites. The rest of the world will be able to see what he is like by looking at them.

✠

Lord, as we are your people today, help us to live in a way that does you credit, and not in ways that make you angry or ashamed.

✠ ✠ ✠ ✠ ✠

August 7

There are many rules for right living in the Bible, but they are all summed up in the Ten Commandments. Here are the first two.

✠

God spoke, and these were his words: "I am the LORD your God who brought you out of Egypt, where you were slaves.

"Worship no god but me.

"Do not make for yourselves images of anything in heaven or on earth or in the water under the earth. Do not bow down to any idol or worship it, because I am the LORD your God and I tolerate no rivals. I bring punishment on those who hate me and on their descendants down to the third and fourth generation. But I show my love to thousands of generations of those who love me and obey my laws."

Exodus 20:1–6

✠

The Israelites know that other nations worship other gods. The Egyptians, for example, have legends of gods and goddesses going back thousands of years. The Canaanites have idols to make sure that the rains come and that the crops grow.

But the Living God tells Israel that he is the only God for them. They know him through what he has done, and must never try to make models of him. An idol or statue is small and powerless. It can never begin to portray the majesty of the invisible God.

✠

Lord, we can never reduce you to fit our tiny minds. Instead, we worship you in spirit and in truth.

✠ ✠ ✠ ✠ ✠

August 8

The Commandments continue with two more about how to behave towards God, and then six about how to behave towards other people.

✠

The Lord continued:

"Do not use my name for evil purposes, for I, the LORD your God, will punish anyone who misuses my name.

"Observe the Sabbath and keep it holy. You have six days in which to do your work, but the seventh day is a day of rest dedicated to me. On that day no one is to work – neither you, your children, your slaves, your animals, nor the foreigners who live in your country. In six days I, the LORD, made the earth, the sky, the sea, and everything in them, but on the seventh day I rested. That is why I, the LORD, blessed the Sabbath and made it holy.

"Respect your father and your mother, so that you may live a long time in the land that I am giving you.

"Do not commit murder.

"Do not commit adultery.

"Do not steal.

"Do not accuse anyone falsely.

"Do not desire another man's house; do not desire his wife, his slaves, his cattle, his donkeys, or anything else that he owns."

Exodus 20:7–17

✠

God's name is holy, and isn't to be used as a swear-word, or as a guarantee on empty promises.

One day each week is to be kept as a holy day (a holiday!), so that all can take a rest and enjoy free time to worship God.

The commandments about each other tell us to respect our elders (although we may not always agree with them or even like them!); and we must respect the lives, marriages and possessions of others. We must tell the truth, and guard against every kind of jealousy.

✠

Lord, your law was given so that we might enjoy your freedom. Help us to love your commands and keep them in glad obedience, because you know what's best for us.

✠ ✠ ✠ ✠ ✠

August 9

When the people saw that Moses had not come down from the mountain but was staying there a long time, they gathered round Aaron and said to him, "We do not know what has happened to this man Moses, who led us out of Egypt; so make us a god to lead us."

Aaron said to them, "Take off the gold earrings which your wives, your sons, and your daughters are wearing, and bring them to me." So all the people took off their gold earrings and brought them to Aaron. He took the earrings, melted them, poured the gold into a mould, and made a gold bull.

The people said, "Israel, this is our god, who led us out of Egypt!"

Exodus 32:1–4

✠

While Moses is on Mount Sinai receiving God's law, there is trouble in the Israelite camp. The people put pressure on Aaron to produce a god they can *see* – something like the idols other nations worship.

Aaron is nothing like the strong leader that Moses is, and he quickly gives in. The result is disaster.

✠

Lord, we are often tempted to make other gods – gods of money, or possessions, or fame. Sometimes we even give our worship to other people. Help us to turn back to you, for you are the only one worth worshipping, and the only one who can help.

✠ ✠ ✠ ✠ ✠

August 10

The LORD said to Moses, "Go back down at once, because your people, whom you led out of Egypt, have sinned and rejected me. They have already left the way that I commanded them to follow; they have made a bull out of melted gold and have worshipped it and offered sacrifices to it. They are saying that this is their god, who led them out of Egypt. I know how stubborn these people are. Now, don't try to stop me. I am angry with them, and I am going to destroy them. Then I will make you and your descendants into a great nation."

But Moses pleaded with the LORD his God and said, "LORD, why should you be so angry with your people, whom you rescued from Egypt with great might and power? Why should the Egyptians be able to say that you led your people out of Egypt, planning to kill them in the mountains and destroy them completely? Stop being angry; change your mind and do not bring this disaster on your people. Remember your servants Abraham, Isaac, and Jacob. Remember the solemn promise you made to them to give them as many descendants as there are stars in the sky and to give their descendants all that land you promised would be their possession for ever." So the LORD changed his mind and did not bring on his people the disaster he had threatened.

Exodus 32:7–14

✠

While chaos reigns in the Israelite camp, Moses pleads with God that the people might be spared. What an extraordinary prayer! He reminds God that his reputation is at stake, and that his promises to Abraham, Isaac and Jacob will be broken!

✠

Lord, thank you for being so patient with us, although we don't deserve it. And thank you for all those who pray for us that we might be kept in your way.

✠ ✠ ✠ ✠ ✠

August 11

When Moses came close enough to the camp to see the bull and to see the people dancing, he was furious. There at the foot of the mountain, he threw down the tablets he was carrying and broke them. He took the bull which they had made, melted it, ground it into fine powder, and mixed it with water. Then he made the people of Israel drink it. He said to Aaron, "What did these people do to you, that you have made them commit such a terrible sin?"

Aaron answered, "Don't be angry with me; you know how determined these people are to do evil. They said to me, 'We don't know what has happened to this man Moses, who brought us out of Egypt; so make us a god to lead us.' I asked them to bring me their gold ornaments, and those who had any took them off and gave them to me. I threw the ornaments into the fire and out came this bull!"

Exodus 32:19–24

✠

The law of God is broken straight away, before the stone tablets are even safely in the camp.

Moses shows what he thinks of the golden bull by destroying it utterly. He doesn't even give the people back their gold, except to make them drink it.

Aaron, with a shrug, tries to explain that it wasn't his fault – it just happened. So much for being left in charge!

✠

Lord, forgive us that sometimes we do wrong in order to be popular with certain people. Help us to want to please you more than anyone else in the world.

✠ ✠ ✠ ✠ ✠

August 12

God wants his people to enjoy a life filled with his blessings. Here is a batch of lovely promises.

✠

The LORD said, "Do not make idols or set up statues, stone pillars, or carved stones to worship. I am the LORD your God. Keep the religious festivals and honour the place where I am worshipped. I am the LORD.

"If you live according to my laws and obey my commands, I will send you rain at the right time, so that the land will produce crops and the trees will bear fruit. Your crops will be so plentiful that you will still be harvesting corn when it is time to pick grapes, and you will still be picking grapes when it is time to sow corn. You will have all that you want to eat, and you will live in safety in your land.

"I will give you peace in your land, and you will sleep without being afraid of anyone. I will get rid of the dangerous animals in the land, and there will be no more war there. You will be victorious over your enemies; five of you will be able to defeat a hundred, and a hundred will be able to defeat ten thousand. I will bless you and give you many children; I will keep my part of the covenant that I made with you. Your harvests will be so plentiful that they will last for a year, and even then you will have to throw away what is left of the old harvest to make room for the new. I will live among you in my sacred tent, and I will never turn away from you. I will be with you; I will be your God, and you will be my people. I, the LORD your God, brought you out of Egypt, so that you would no longer be slaves. I broke the power that held you down and let you walk with your head held high."

Leviticus 26:1–13

It is God's will that his people should have health and safety, peace and plenty. But there is a condition. We must live "according to his laws" – in other words, we must live *his* way in *his* world. And we must put him first.

✠

Lord, everything comes from you. Help us to live in such a way that we enjoy a glimpse of heaven here on earth.

✠ ✠ ✠ ✠ ✠

August 13

One day, when Moses realized that his life was coming to an end, he said these solemn words to the people.

✠

"These are all the laws that the LORD your God commanded me to teach you. Obey them in the land that you are about to enter and occupy. As long as you live, you and your descendants are to honour the LORD your God and obey all his laws that I am giving you, so that you may live in that land a long time. Listen to them, people of Israel, and obey them! Then all will go well with you, and you will become a mighty nation and live in that rich and fertile land, just as the LORD, the God of our ancestors, has promised.

"Israel, remember this! The LORD – and the LORD alone – is our God. Love the LORD your God with all your heart, with all your soul, and with all your strength. Never forget these commands that I am giving you today. Teach them to your children. Repeat them when you are at home and when you are away, when you are resting and when you are working. Tie them on your arms and wear them on your foreheads as a reminder. Write them on the door-posts of your houses and on your gates."

Deuteronomy 6:1–9

✠

God's most precious gift to the Israelites is not the land, but the law. The law is the key to a happy life. If they keep it, treasure it, learn it, and pass it on, then it will be a blessing to them and their children for ever.

✠

Lord, it is such a relief to have your commandments – to know how it is that you want us to behave, and how it is that we can discover real freedom and peace of mind. Thank you most of all for Jesus, who fulfilled the law and showed us your heart of love.

✠ ✠ ✠ ✠ ✠

August 14

Moses went up from the plains of Moab to Mount Nebo, to the top of Mount Pisgah east of Jericho, and there the LORD showed him the whole land.

Then the LORD said to Moses, "This is the land that I promised Abraham, Isaac, and Jacob I would give to their descendants. I have let you see it, but I will not let you go there."

So Moses, the LORD's servant, died there in the land of Moab, as the LORD had said he would. The LORD buried him in a valley in Moab, opposite the town of Bethpeor, but to this day no one knows the exact place of his burial. Moses was a hundred and twenty years old when he died; he was as strong as ever, and his eyesight was still good. The people of Israel mourned for him for thirty days in the plains of Moab.

Joshua son of Nun was filled with wisdom, because Moses had appointed him to be his successor. The people of Israel obeyed Joshua and kept the commands that the LORD had given them through Moses.

There has never been a prophet in Israel like Moses; the LORD spoke with him face to face. No other prophet has ever done miracles and wonders like those that the LORD sent Moses to perform against the king of Egypt, his officials, and the entire country. No other prophet has been able to do the great and terrifying things that Moses did in the sight of all Israel.

Deuteronomy 34:1,4–12

✠

It's sad to read of Moses dying without entering the Promised Land. But he entered into the presence of God, which is far better. We know that he lives on with God, for he and Elijah met with Jesus on a mountain many years later (see the reading for March 6).

What a great man Moses was – surely one of the greatest leaders the world has ever seen. But it was God who made him great, as we know from the mistakes of his early days.

Lord, thank you for the example of those who have totally given their lives to you. May their experience encourage us to do the same.

✠ ✠ ✠ ✠ ✠

August 15

After the death of the LORD's servant Moses, the LORD spoke to Moses' helper, Joshua son of Nun. He said, "My servant Moses is dead. Get ready now, you and all the people of Israel, and cross the River Jordan into the land that I am giving them. As I told Moses, I have given you and all my people the entire land that you will be marching over. Joshua, no one will be able to defeat you as long as you live. I will be with you as I was with Moses. I will always be with you; I will never abandon you. Be determined and confident, for you will be the leader of these people as they occupy this land which I promised their ancestors. Just be determined, be confident; and make sure that you obey the whole Law that my servant Moses gave you. Do not neglect any part of it and you will succeed wherever you go. Be sure that the book of the Law is always read in your worship. Study it day and night, and make sure that you obey everything written in it. Then you will be prosperous and successful. Remember that I have commanded you to be determined and confident! Don't be afraid or discouraged, for I, the LORD your God, am with you wherever you go."

Joshua 1:1–3,5–9

✠

Joshua must be very nervous! Moses had led the people ever since anyone could remember. He had known God so closely and trusted him so completely.

But now God speaks to Joshua. He assures Joshua that he will never leave him, and that all will be well. In particular, he must hold fast to the whole law – studying it and applying it all the time. After all, it's no good having God's law in a book if we never read it, and no benefit to read it unless we do what it says!

✠

Lord, as you have given us your law, help us to take it in and to live it out, every day.

✠ ✠ ✠ ✠ ✠

August 16

The gates of Jericho were kept shut and guarded to keep the Israelites out. No one could enter or leave the city. The LORD said to Joshua, "I am putting into your hands Jericho, with its king and all its brave soldiers. You and your soldiers are to march round the city once a day for six days. Seven priests, each carrying a trumpet, are to go in front of the Covenant Box. On the seventh day you and your soldiers are to march round the city seven times while the priests blow the trumpets. Then they are to sound one long note. As soon as you hear it, all the men are to give a loud shout, and the city walls will collapse. Then the whole army will go straight into the city."

Joshua 6:1–5

There is only one way for Joshua and his people to capture the mighty stronghold of Jericho – and that is for God to give them victory. Marching round the city blowing trumpets will make no difference at all! But by the power of God, the walls collapse!

The people who have dug up the ruins of Jericho have found that there were two walls round the city, and the inner one was twelve feet thick! They have also discovered that the walls did indeed collapse – the outer wall falling outwards and the inner wall falling inwards, as though demolished by an earthquake.

✠

Lord, some of the things we do for you may seem strange. But they are ways of showing that we want to obey you, and they help us to stop worrying about our own reputation and success.

✠ ✠ ✠ ✠ ✠

August 17

On the seventh day they got up at daybreak and marched seven times round the city in the same way – this was the only day that they marched round it seven times. The seventh time round, when the priests were about to sound the trumpets, Joshua ordered his men to shout, and he said, "The LORD has given you the city! The city and everything in it must be totally destroyed as an offering to the LORD. Only the prostitute Rahab and her household will be spared, because she hid our spies. But you are not to take anything that is to be destroyed; if you do, you will bring trouble and destruction on the Israelite camp. Everything made of silver, gold, bronze, or iron is set apart for the LORD. It is to be put in the LORD's treasury."

So the priests blew the tumpets. As soon as the men heard it, they gave a loud shout, and the walls collapsed. Then all the army went straight up the hill into the city and captured it.

Joshua 6:15–20

✠

Why was everything and everyone in Jericho destroyed? The answer is that the Israelites were not to mix with pagan peoples *at all*. They weren't to intermarry with such people or adopt their way of life. God wanted to settle his Chosen Race in the Promised Land as a strong, pure and holy people.

✠

Lord, thank you for giving your people victory against all the odds. We ask today that we might share your victory over every kind of evil.

✠ ✠ ✠ ✠ ✠

August 18

After many years of campaigning and settlement, Joshua summons the Israelites together at the two mountains of Ebal and Gerizim. Here he challenges them about the idols they still have and the superstitions they hold. And he presents them with a clear choice – to worship man-made idols or to be faithful to the Living God.

✠

"Now then," Joshua continued, "honour the LORD and serve him sincerely and faithfully. Get rid of the gods which your ancestors used to worship in Mesopotamia and in Egypt, and serve only the LORD. If you are not willing to serve him, decide today whom you will serve, the gods your ancestors worshipped in Mesopotamia or the gods of the Amorites, in whose land you are now living. As for my family and me, we will serve the LORD."

The people replied, "We would never leave the LORD to serve other gods! The LORD our God brought our fathers and us out of slavery in Egypt, and we saw the miracles that he performed. He kept us safe wherever we went among all the nations through which we passed. As we advanced into this land, the LORD drove out all the Amorites who lived here. So we also will serve the LORD; he is our God."

Joshua 24:14–18

✠

Lord, help us to choose you afresh at each turning point of life, both as individuals and as a family.

✠ ✠ ✠ ✠ ✠

August 19

Now we look at some of the stories Jesus told. They are called "parables" – short, colourful stories with a twist in them. And the twist always says something about the challenge of God's Kingdom. The first is the Parable of the Good Samaritan.

✠

A teacher of the Law came up and tried to trap Jesus. "Teacher," he asked, "what must I do to receive eternal life?"

Jesus answered him, "What do the scriptures say? How do you interpret them?"

The man answered, "'Love the Lord your God with all your heart, with all your soul, with all your strength, and with all your mind'; and 'Love your neighbour as you love yourself.'"

"You are right," Jesus replied; "do this and you will live."

But the teacher of the Law wanted to justify himself, so he asked Jesus, "Who is my neighbour?"

Jesus answered, "There was once a man who was going down from Jerusalem to Jericho when robbers attacked him, stripped him, and beat him up, leaving him half dead. It so happened that a priest was going down that road; but when he saw the man, he walked on by, on the other side. In the same way a Levite also came along, went over and looked at the man, and then walked on by, on the other side."

Luke 10:25–32

✠

Jesus has been asked a question that everyone is asking. If we're supposed to "love our neighbour as we love ourselves" where do we stop? Is our neighbour the person next door, or everyone in the same community, or what?

Jesus answers with a story about a Jew who is attacked and robbed on the road to Jericho. The first two travellers who come by are both religious people – a priest and a Levite. But for some reason they don't stop to help. Either they are in a hurry, or they don't want to touch someone who is bleeding or may even be dead. And so they leave him lying in the road . . .

✠

Lord, we will see someone who needs help today. May we not be too busy or fearful to stop and see what we can do.

✠ ✠ ✠ ✠ ✠

August 20

Jesus continued: "But a Samaritan who was travelling that way came upon the man, and when he saw him, his heart was filled with pity. He went over to him, poured oil and wine on his wounds and bandaged them; then he put the man on his own animal and took him to an inn, where he took care of him. The next day he took out two silver coins and gave them to the innkeeper. 'Take care of him,' he told the innkeeper, 'and when I come back this way, I will pay you whatever else you spend on him.'"

And Jesus concluded, "In your opinion, which one of

these three acted like a neighbour towards the man attacked by the robbers?"

The teacher of the Law answered, "The one who was kind to him."

Jesus replied, "You go, then, and do the same."

Luke 10:33–37

✠

The Samaritans and the Jews have hated each other for years. They don't have anything to do with each other at all. But when this particular Samaritan finds the wounded Jew, he helps him in every way he can. He not only saves his life, but takes him somewhere comfortable, and pays a lot of money for him to stay there.

Jesus says that this is what it means to love our neighbour as ourselves. Our neighbour is *anyone* we have a chance to help, no matter what kind of person it is.

✠

Lord, help us to see each person in need as someone we can care for. And may we be thoughtful, patient and generous in the kind of help we give.

✠ ✠ ✠ ✠ ✠

August 21

Jesus told this parable: "There was once a rich man who had land which bore good crops. He began to think to himself, 'I haven't anywhere to keep all my crops. What can I do? This is what I will do,' he told himself; 'I will tear down my barns and build bigger ones, where I will store my corn and all my other goods. Then I will say to myself, Lucky man! You have all the good things you need for many years. Take life easy, eat, drink, and enjoy yourself!' But God said to him, 'You fool! This very night you will have to give up your life; then who will get all these things you have kept for yourself?'"

And Jesus concluded, "This is how it is with those who pile up riches for themselves but are not rich in God's sight."

Luke 12:16–21

✠

Jesus often warned people not to worship money or possessions. This story is about a wise man – a farmer who has worked hard and successfully all his life. Now he can afford to retire. He even plans his retirement wisely, and looks forward to every moment of it.

But God says that the man is not at all wise – far from it. He's a fool. And the reason he's a fool is that in all his busy life he has never given a thought to God. He is about to die, leaving all his riches behind him. And all he has to take to God is a self-centred, bankrupt soul.

✠

Lord, help us to turn to you while we have time. Set us free from love of money, and make us rich in the things that really matter – putting others first, enjoying peace of mind, and knowing what it is that you want us to do for you.

August 22

Jesus said, "There was once a man who was giving a great feast to which he invited many people. When it was time for the feast, he sent his servant to tell his guests, 'Come, everything is ready!' But they all began, one after another, to make excuses. The first one told the servant, 'I have bought a field and must go and look at it; please accept my apologies.' Another one said, 'I have bought five pairs of oxen and am on my way to try them out; please accept my apologies.' Another one said, 'I have just got married, and for that reason I cannot come.'

"The servant went back and told all this to his master. The master was furious and said to his servant, 'Hurry out to the streets and alleys of the town, and bring back the poor, the crippled, the blind, and the lame.' Soon the servant said, 'Your order has been carried out, sir, but there is room for more.' So the master said to the servant, 'Go out to the country roads and lanes and make people come in, so that my house will be full. I tell you all that none of those men who were invited will taste my dinner!'"

Luke 14:16–24

✠

Jesus says that God is like a man who has prepared a banquet for his friends. Heaven is an open house to all who turn from their own life and come to God.

But some of those who seem close to God are in fact full of excuses – and not very good excuses. Jesus says that their invitation will be given to others – the poor, the outcast, the sick and the suffering. For God is determined that his heaven shall be full!

Lord, help us not to be so busy day after day that we miss your invitation.

✠ ✠ ✠ ✠ ✠

August 23

One day when many tax collectors and other outcasts came to listen to Jesus, the Pharisees and the teachers of the Law started grumbling, "This man welcomes outcasts and even eats with them!" So Jesus told them this parable:

"Suppose one of you has a hundred sheep and loses one of them – what does he do? He leaves the other ninety-nine sheep in the pasture and goes looking for the one that got lost until he finds it. When he finds it, he is so happy that he puts it on his shoulders and carries it back home. Then he calls his friends and neighbours together and says to them, 'I am so happy I found my lost sheep. Let us celebrate!' In the same way, I tell you, there will be more joy in heaven over one sinner who repents than over ninety-nine respectable people who do not need to repent."

Luke 15:1–7

✠

The Pharisees and teachers of the Law are very respectable people. They keep the law in every tiny detail – and look down on everyone who can't or won't do the same.

But Jesus doesn't look down on such people. He goes out of his way to be with them – just as a shepherd goes out of his way to find, rescue and bring home any lost sheep.

This is why Jesus is such a wonderful Saviour. He comes all the way to reach us, however far from God we are. And when he brings us back to God, heaven overflows with joy.

✠

Lord, thank you for mixing with people like us, so that we can come home to heaven.

✠ ✠ ✠ ✠ ✠

August 24

Jesus said: "Suppose a woman who has ten silver coins loses one of them – what does she do? She lights a lamp, sweeps her house, and looks carefully everywhere until she finds it. When she finds it, she calls her friends and neighbours together, and says to them, 'I am so happy I found the coin I lost. Let us celebrate!' In the same way, I tell you, the angels of God rejoice over one sinner who repents."

Luke 15:8–10

✠

This is another "searching" story, like the one we read yesterday about the lost sheep. Although, unlike the sheep, the coin couldn't help getting lost!

Perhaps this was one of the precious coins given to the woman by her father when she got married, and which she always wore on her forehead. Jesus describes the joy she has when she finds it again. He says that's how it is in heaven when even one sinful person turns to God.

✠

Lord, thank you for being such a wonderful Saviour, and not giving up until you find us.

✠ ✠ ✠ ✠ ✠

August 25

Jesus went on to say, "There was once a man who had two sons. The younger one said to him, 'Father, give me my share of the property now.' So the man divided his property between his two sons. After a few days the younger son sold his part of the property and left home with the money. He went to a country far away, where he wasted his money in reckless living. He spent everything he had. Then a severe famine spread over that country, and he was left without a thing. So he went to work for one of the citizens of that country, who sent him out to his farm to take care of the pigs. He wished he could fill himself with the bean pods the pigs ate, but no one gave him anything to eat. At last he came to his senses and said, 'All my father's hired workers have more than they can eat, and here I am about to starve! I will get up and go to my father and say, Father, I have sinned against God and against you. I am no longer fit to be called your son; treat me as one of your hired workers.' So he got up and started back to his father."

Luke 15:11–20

Again, something is lost. This time it isn't a sheep or a coin, but a son!

The young man has asked his father to split the property between himself and his brother. Then straight away he squanders his share, and ends up in poverty – feeding pigs. He begins to wonder if there's any way he can get back home, and maybe work for his father.

This story is a picture of ourselves. We are like the self-centred young man, spoiling God's world and running away from his love. But it's never too late to turn round and go back.

✠

Lord, please forgive us for snatching your blessings but rejecting your love. Please accept us back and help us to start afresh.

✠ ✠ ✠ ✠ ✠

August 26

Jesus went on: "He was still a long way from home when his father saw him; his heart was filled with pity, and he ran, threw his arms round his son, and kissed him. 'Father,' the son said, 'I have sinned against God and against you. I am no longer fit to be called your son.' But the father called his servants. 'Hurry!' he said. 'Bring the best robe and put it on him. Put a ring on his finger and shoes on his feet. Then go and get the prize calf and kill it, and let us celebrate with a feast! For this son of mine was dead, but now he is alive; he was lost, but now he has been found.' And so the feasting began."

Luke 15:20–24

The father is on the look-out for his son, and comes running to meet him. The young man only manages to blurt out half his little speech before his father interrupts him. There's no question of turning him away, or even of making his son become one of his workers. He is to have the best robe in the house, the ring of sonship, and the shoes of a free man. And, of course, a party to welcome him home.

What a wonderful picture this is of God – that he comes running to meet us. He is so ready to forgive us when we turn to him and say we are sorry for the wrong things we have done.

✠

Lord, thank you that you don't make us earn our place in heaven, for we could never do it. Thank you that it is your loving gift to all who simply turn to you.

✠ ✠ ✠ ✠ ✠

August 27

Then Jesus told the rest of the story: "In the meantime the elder son was out in the field. On his way back, when he came close to the house, he heard the music and dancing. So he called one of the servants and asked him, 'What's going on?' 'Your brother has come back home,' the servant answered, 'and your father has killed the prize calf, because he got him back safe and sound.'

"The elder brother was so angry that he would not go into the house; so his father came out and begged him to come in. But he answered his father, 'Look, all these years I have worked for you like a slave, and I have never disobeyed your orders. What have you given me? Not even a goat for me to have a feast with my friends! But this son of yours wasted all your property, and when he comes back home, you kill the prize calf for him!' 'My son,' the father answered, 'you are always here with me, and everything I have is yours. But we had to celebrate and be happy, because your brother was dead, but now he is alive; he was lost, but now he has been found.'"

Luke 15:25–32

✠

It's strange but true that some of the people who are already safe home with God can resent others turning to him and receiving a welcome.

The Pharisees were like this in Jesus' day – wanting to slam God's door in the face of outsiders such as tax collectors and Samaritans.

When we find ourselves doing this today, it means we haven't yet realized just how much God loves *everyone*. He doesn't limit his love to those who go to church, or to any other group. He longs that every man, woman and child in the world should turn to him and know his love. So let's make sure we don't stand in anyone's way!

✠

Lord, may we share your searching eyes and loving heart, and reach out to other people with your welcoming arms.

✠ ✠ ✠ ✠ ✠

August 28

Jesus said: "There was once a rich man who dressed in the most expensive clothes and lived in great luxury every day. There was also a poor man named Lazarus, covered with sores, who used to be brought to the rich man's door, hoping to eat the bits of food that fell from the rich man's table. Even the dogs would come and lick his sores.

"The poor man died and was carried by the angels to sit beside Abraham at the feast in heaven. The rich man died and was buried, and in Hades, where he was in great pain, he looked up and saw Abraham, far away, with Lazarus at his side. So he called out, 'Father Abraham! Take pity on me, and send Lazarus to dip his finger in some water and cool my tongue, because I am in great pain in this fire!'

"But Abraham said, 'Remember, my son, that in your lifetime you were given all the good things, while Lazarus got all the bad things. But now he is enjoying himself here, while you are in pain. Besides all that, there is a deep pit lying between us, so that those who want to cross over from here to you cannot do so, nor can anyone cross over to us from where you are.'"

Luke 16:19–26

✠

Life isn't very fair, is it? There are people who enjoy immense wealth because they were born into a rich family, or have a simple idea which makes them a lot of money. There are others who, through no fault of their own, never have a chance of good food, nice clothes and a happy time.

But God knows! And he cares very deeply about the way we use our wealth, and whether or not we share his gifts with those in need. And in heaven he is well able to put things right – to make it up to those who are lonely and destitute in this life.

✠

Lord, you have given us many things to enjoy, and we enjoy them best when we share them with others. Help us to be sharing people.

✠ ✠ ✠ ✠ ✠

August 29

Jesus continued the story: "The rich man said, 'Then I beg you, father Abraham, send Lazarus to my father's house, where I have five brothers. Let him go and warn them so that they, at least, will not come to this place of pain.'

"Abraham said, 'Your brothers have Moses and the prophets to warn them; your brothers should listen to what they say.' The rich man answered, 'That is not enough, father Abraham! But if someone were to rise from death and go to them, then they would turn from their sins.' But Abraham said, 'If they will not listen to Moses and the prophets, they will not be convinced even if someone were to rise from death.'"

Luke 16:27–31

✠

In his suffering, the rich man realizes how wrong he has been. He fears for his brothers who are still living in the same greedy, selfish and careless way. Is there some way he can send them a message to warn them?

Abraham tells him that the message has already gone out and is to be found in the scriptures. But some people are so set on their course, that nothing will make them change their mind.

✠

Lord, help us to change our ways while we have time, and to share the Good News of your love with others.

✠ ✠ ✠ ✠ ✠

August 30

Jesus also told this parable to people who were sure of their own goodness and despised everybody else. "Once there were two men who went up to the Temple to pray: one was a Pharisee, the other a tax collector.

"The Pharisee stood apart by himself and prayed, 'I thank you, God, that I am not greedy, dishonest, or an adulterer, like everybody else. I thank you that I am not like that tax collector over there. I fast two days a week, and I give you a tenth of all my income.'

"But the tax collector stood at a distance and would not even raise his face to heaven, but beat on his breast and said, 'God, have pity on me, a sinner!' I tell you," said Jesus, "the tax collector, and not the Pharisee, was in the right with God when he went home. For everyone who makes himself great will be humbled, and everyone who humbles himself will be made great."

Luke 18:9–14

✠

When the Pharisee goes to the Temple, he doesn't pray at all! He just makes a long speech telling God what a wonderful man he is. He wants to be seen, heard and admired for his very religious life.

The tax collector, on the other hand, wants to hide away. He is so sorry and ashamed that he hangs his head, and his prayer is only a whisper. But because it is a real prayer, from his heart, God accepts him – and Jesus holds him up as an example to us.

✠

Lord, help us to come to you as we really are, and not as we pretend to be.

✠ ✠ ✠ ✠ ✠

August 31

Today we read a psalm. It describes the difference between those who live their lives according to God's law, and those who do evil.

✠

Happy are those
who reject the advice of evil men,
who do not follow the example of sinners
or join those who have no use for God.
Instead, they find joy in obeying the
Law of the LORD,
and they study it day and night.
They are like trees that grow beside a stream,
that bear fruit at the right time,
and whose leaves do not dry up.
They succeed in everything they do.

But evil men are not like this at all;
they are like straw that the wind
blows away.
Sinners will be condemned by God
and kept apart from God's own people.
The righteous are guided and protected
by the LORD,
but the evil are on the way to their
doom.

Psalm 1

✠

There is joy in obeying God's law – for God's word gives life and health and peace. We need God's life like a tree needs water. He makes us strong, fruitful and fresh. But those who reject God are without any firm roots. They have nothing to hold them steady or nourish them, and in the end they are destroyed.

✠

Lord, help us always to live and grow in the deep soil of your word, the fresh water of your blessings, and the good air of your Spirit.

A Psalm for

September

Come, let us praise the LORD!
Let us sing for joy to God, who protects us!
Let us come before him with thanksgiving
and sing joyful songs of praise.
For the LORD is a mighty God,
a mighty king over all the gods.
He rules over the whole earth,
from the deepest caves to the highest hills.
He rules over the sea, which he made;
the land also, which he himself formed.

Come, let us bow down and worship him;
let us kneel before the LORD, our Maker!
He is our God;
we are the people he cares for,
the flock for which he provides.

Psalm 95:1–7

September 1

Jesus describes himself in some very special ways. Here, for example, he says, "I AM the bread of life".

As we know from the story of Moses (the reading we had on July 27), "I AM" is God's own name, and here Jesus hints that this is his name too.

✠

When the people found Jesus on the other side of the lake, they said to him, "Teacher, when did you get here?"

Jesus answered, "I am telling you the truth: you are looking for me because you ate the bread and had all you wanted, not because you understood my miracles.

"I am the bread of life," Jesus told them. "He who comes to me will never be hungry; he who believes in me will never be thirsty. Now, I told you that you have seen me but will not believe. Everyone whom my Father gives me will come to me. I will never turn away anyone who comes to me, because I have come down from heaven to do not my own will but the will of him who sent me. And it is the will of him who sent me that I should not lose any of all those he has given me, but that I should raise them all to life on the last day. For what my Father wants is that all who see the Son and believe in him should have eternal life. And I will raise them to life on the last day."

John 6:25–26,35–40

✠

In John's gospel, the ways Jesus describes himself go together with the miracles he performs. They are "signs" of who he is. In this reading, Jesus has just fed a great crowd from a few loaves and fishes. Now he explains that he is "the bread of life". Just as the Israelites were given manna by God in the old days, so now Jesus has come to satisfy the hunger of all those who long for God.

✠

Lord, feed us with your eternal life now and always.

✠ ✠ ✠ ✠ ✠

September 2

Jesus said: "I am the good shepherd, who is willing to die for the sheep. When the hired man, who is not a shepherd and does not own the sheep, sees a wolf coming, he leaves the sheep and runs away; so the wolf snatches the sheep and scatters them. The hired man runs away because he is only a hired man and does not care about the sheep. I am the good shepherd. As the Father knows me and I know the Father, in the same way I know my sheep and they know me. And I am willing to die for them. There are other sheep which belong to me that are not in this sheepfold. I must bring them, too; they will listen to my voice, and they will become one flock with one shepherd."

John 10:11–16

✠

What's the difference between a good shepherd and a bad shepherd? Jesus says the good shepherd is willing to die for his sheep. He counts their lives more important than his own. The bad shepherd runs away at the first sign of danger, and leaves the sheep without help or defence.

Jesus is our Good Shepherd, and we are his sheep. He looks after us all the time, and knows each of us by name. And he counts our life as more important than his own, as he showed when he gave up his life on the cross to rescue us from sin and death.

✠

Lord, thank you for your loving care. Thank you for laying down your life for us.

✠ ✠ ✠ ✠ ✠

September 3

For the next few days we will be listening to some of the things Jesus taught in his Sermon on the Mount.

Jesus said: "Do not think that I have come to do away with the Law of Moses and the teachings of the prophets. I have not come to do away with them, but to make their teachings come true. Remember that as long as heaven and earth last, not the least point nor the smallest detail of the Law will be done away with – not until the end of all things. So then, whoever disobeys even the least important of the commandments and teaches others to do the same, will be least in the Kingdom of heaven. On the other hand, whoever obeys the Law and teaches others to do the same, will be great in the Kingdom of heaven. I tell you, then, that you will be able to enter the Kingdom of heaven only if you are more faithful than the teachers of the Law and the Pharisees in doing what God requires."

Matthew 5:17–20

✠

Sometimes people think that Jesus came to cancel the old laws of Moses. They feel that there is no need for those rules any more, because Jesus has come to make us free.

But Jesus says here that what God taught in the past still holds good. Jesus came to build on the foundation laid by Moses and the prophets, and to complete what they had started.

✠

Lord, help us to love your law and keep it faithfully – not to earn your love, but to show our love for you.

✠ ✠ ✠ ✠ ✠

September 4

Jesus said: "You have heard that people were told in the past, 'Do not commit murder; anyone who does will be brought to trial.' But now I tell you: whoever is angry with his brother will be brought to trial, whoever calls his brother 'You good-for-nothing!' will be brought before the Council, and whoever calls his brother a worthless fool will be in danger of going to the fire of hell. So if you are about to offer your gift to God at the altar and there you remember that your brother has something against you, leave your gift there in front of the altar, go at once and make peace with your brother, and then come back and offer your gift to God."

Matthew 5:21–24

✠

Jesus talks about the old commandment "Do not commit murder". He explains that at the heart of murder is anger. And so he tells us that we must not even be angry, but instead be quick to forgive those who have wronged us, and to make up quarrels. After all, how can we expect to be at peace with God if we are at odds with each other?

✠

Lord, you know that we get angry – perhaps many times a day. Please help us to be quick to forgive, and to be patient in situations which we find frustrating. And may we be your secret agents for peace.

✠ ✠ ✠ ✠ ✠

September 5

Jesus said: "You have heard that it was said, 'Do not commit adultery.' But now I tell you: anyone who looks at a woman and wants to possess her is guilty of committing adultery with her in his heart. So if your right eye causes you to sin, take it out and throw it away! It is much better for you to lose a part of your body than to have your whole body thrown into hell. If your right hand causes you to sin, cut it off and throw it away! It is much better for you to lose one of your limbs than for your whole body to go to hell."

Matthew 5:27–30

✠

Jesus talks about the old commandment "Do not commit adultery" – that means "Don't take someone else's husband or wife". He explains that adultery starts in our minds and imaginations. So if we are to avoid adultery, we must sometimes behave as though we can't see or touch that particular person. That's what Jesus means by plucking out an eye or cutting off a hand – that we must "disable" ourselves when we are tempted.

✠

Lord, help us to keep your law in our minds, so that all our behaviour will arise from good thoughts.

✠ ✠ ✠ ✠ ✠

September 6

Jesus said: "You have also heard that people were told in the past, 'Do not break your promise, but do what you have vowed to the Lord to do.' But now I tell you: do not use any vow when you make a promise. Do not swear by heaven, because it is God's throne; nor by earth, because it is the resting place for his feet; not by Jerusalem, because it is the city of the great King. Do not even swear by your head, because you cannot make a single hair white or black. Just say 'Yes' or 'No' – anything else you say comes from the Evil One."

Matthew 5:33–37

✠

Jesus talks about keeping our word. He says there's no need to add God's name to what we say when we make promises. Indeed, there's no need to add anything at all if our word is true. A simple "Yes" or "No" is quite sufficient. People will soon learn whether or not our word is to be trusted.

✠

Lord, help us to be people who know the truth, tell the truth, and live the truth.

✠ ✠ ✠ ✠ ✠

September 7

Jesus said: "You have heard that it was said, 'An eye for an eye, and a tooth for a tooth.' But now I tell you: do not take revenge on someone who wrongs you. If anyone slaps you on the right cheek, let him slap your left cheek too. And if someone takes you to court to sue you for your shirt, let him have your coat as well. And if one of the occupation troops forces you to carry his pack one kilometre, carry it two kilometres. When someone asks you for something, give it to him; when someone wants to borrow something, lend it to him."

Matthew 5:38–42

✠

Jesus talks about the old regulation "An eye for an eye, and a tooth for a tooth". It was a law designed to make sure that punishments were exact and fair (*only* an eye for an eye, and *only* a tooth for a tooth), and so to stop revenge from getting out of hand.

But now Jesus says that his people shouldn't take revenge at all. We must take the knocks that others give and not return them or pass them on. Jesus did this himself when he died on the cross – accepting all the cruelty and spite that was heaped upon him, without retaliating in any way. Now he calls us to do the same.

✠

Lord, help us to take anger and injustice out of circulation when it comes our way – laying it instead at the foot of your cross.

✠ ✠ ✠ ✠ ✠

September 8

Jesus continued: "You have heard that it was said, 'Love your friends, hate your enemies.' But now I tell you: love your enemies and pray for those who persecute you, so that you may become the sons of your Father in heaven. For he makes his sun to shine on bad and good people alike, and gives rain to those who do good and to those who do evil. Why should God reward you if you love only the people who love you? Even the tax collectors do that! And if you speak only to your friends, have you done anything out of the ordinary? Even the pagans do that! You must be perfect – just as your Father in heaven is perfect!"

Matthew 5:43–48

✠

What a standard Jesus has for us! We must be perfect!

Here he talks about the old attitudes of love and hate. Most people love their friends and hate their enemies. But Jesus says, "Love your enemies – yes, *love them*! And pray for those who persecute you!"

If we do this, we shall be like God our Father, who is kind to everyone – showering his blessings on those who hate him as well as on those who love him.

✠

Lord, you know that we have enemies. People who are mean to us, bitter about us, or exploit us in some way. Help us to surround them with our love and prayer, because this is how you feel about them, and you want us to be like you.

✠ ✠ ✠ ✠ ✠

September 9

Jesus said: "Do not store up riches for yourselves here on earth, where moths and rust destroy, and robbers break in and steal. Instead, store up riches for yourselves in heaven, where moths and rust cannot destroy, and robbers cannot break in and steal. For your heart will always be where your riches are."

Matthew 6:19–21

✠

Jesus talks about wealth – our money and our belongings. He points out that none of our goods will last for ever, and nothing is safe from accident or theft.

So he tells us not to worry about possessions, but to store our riches in heaven. The riches he means are the treasures of trusting God for everything, the priceless wealth of forgiveness, and the beautiful jewels of love, care and service to others.

✠

Lord, set our hearts on things that make us truly rich.

✠ ✠ ✠ ✠ ✠

September 10

Jesus said: "No one can be a slave of two masters; he will hate one and love the other; he will be loyal to one and despise the other. You cannot serve both God and money.

"This is why I tell you not to be worried about the food and drink you need in order to stay alive, or about clothes for your body. After all, isn't life worth more than food? And isn't the body worth more than clothes? Look at the birds flying around: they do not sow seeds, gather a harvest and put it in barns; yet your Father in heaven takes care of them! Aren't you worth much more than birds? Can any of you live a bit longer by worrying about it?"

Matthew 6:24–27

✠

Jesus says that if we try to love God and money at the same time, we will be torn in two directions at once. So we must make up our minds!

He urges us to stop fretting about what we're going to eat and drink, and what we're going to wear. The God who gave us life and set us in this wonderful world wants us to trust him for our everyday needs. If we spend all our time being eaten up with worry, it shows we don't think too much of God's promise to provide for us!

✠

Almighty God, father and provider, we look to you for the things we need each day.

✠ ✠ ✠ ✠ ✠

September 11

Jesus went on: "And why worry about clothes? Look how the wild flowers grow: they do not work or make clothes for themselves. But I tell you that not even King Solomon with all his wealth had clothes as beautiful as one of these flowers. It is God who clothes the wild grass – grass that is here today and gone tomorrow, burnt up in the oven. Won't he be all the more sure to clothe you? How little faith you have!

"So do not start worrying: 'Where will my food come from? or my drink? or my clothes?' (These are the things the pagans are always concerned about.) Your Father in heaven knows that you need all these things. Instead, be concerned above everything else with the Kingdom of God and with what he requires of you, and he will provide you with all these other things. So do not worry about tomorrow; it will have enough worries of its own. There is no need to add to the troubles each day brings."

Matthew 6:28–34

✠

Jesus is still talking about our worries. Why do so many people say "I haven't got a thing to wear" when really they have plenty of clothes? Is it because we worry too much about what other people think of us? We don't want to be the odd ones out – the only one at the party without a new dress, or the only one at school without the latest gear . . .

But Jesus says that if we put the life of the Kingdom of God first – sharing God's goodness with others and doing the things he wants – then we'll find we have quite enough for each day as it comes.

Heavenly Father, help us to live this day the Kingdom way.

✠ ✠ ✠ ✠ ✠

September 12

Jesus said: "Do not judge others, so that God will not judge you, for God will judge you in the same way as you judge others, and he will apply to you the same rules you apply to others. Why, then, do you look at the speck in your brother's eye, and pay no attention to the log in your own eye? How dare you say to your brother, 'Please, let me take that speck out of your eye,' when you have a log in your own eye? You hypocrite! First take the log out of your own eye, and then you will be able to see clearly to take the speck out of your brother's eye."

Matthew 7:1–5

✠

We are sometimes far too quick to criticize other people – saying where they are going wrong, either to their face or (more often) behind their back.

Jesus says we shouldn't do this. Only God is wise enough to make judgements, and only he knows all the facts. So we should leave criticism to him!

And then Jesus turns the spotlight on us. After all, "it takes one to know one". The chances are we're picking on something in another person that's all too evident in ourselves. So let's deal with ourselves first.

Lord, may we be quick to care, but slow to judge. And help us to put our own lives in order before we presume to tell other people how they should behave.

✠ ✠ ✠ ✠ ✠

September 13

Jesus concluded: "So anyone who hears these words of mine and obeys them is like a wise man who built his house on rock. The rain poured down, the rivers overflowed, and the wind blew hard against that house. But it did not fall, because it was built on rock.

"But anyone who hears these words of mine and does not obey them is like a foolish man who built his house on sand. The rain poured down, the rivers overflowed, the wind blew hard against that house, and it fell. And what a terrible fall that was!"

Matthew 7:24–27

✠

At the end of the Sermon on the Mount, Jesus tells his hearers that his teaching is a sure foundation for life – at least, it is if they do what he says.

If we hear the words of Jesus and take no notice, then we're as foolish as a man trying to build a house on sand. It will look all right for a while, but when the storms of life come – doubt, temptation, hardship and suffering – we'll fall apart.

✠

Lord, you are the rock, our sure foundation. Help us to hear what you have to say, and do it.

✠ ✠ ✠ ✠ ✠

September 14

The Jews had many hundreds of laws by which they tried to live. Some were to be found in the scriptures, and others had been added over the years. In the end, they were in a muddle as to what was really important and what wasn't.

✠

A teacher of the Law was there who heard the discussion. He saw that Jesus had given the Sadducees a good answer, so he came to him with a question: "Which commandment is the most important of all?"

Jesus replied, "The most important one is this: 'Listen, Israel! The Lord our God is the only Lord. Love the Lord your God with all your heart, with all your soul, with all your mind, and with all your strength.' The second most important commandment is this: 'Love your neighbour as you love yourself.' There is no other commandment more important than these two."

Mark 12:28–31

✠

When a teacher of the Law asks Jesus about the most important law, he receives a clear answer. Jesus takes two verses from scripture – one about loving God with every part of us, and one about loving others and accepting them as we would like to be accepted. When these two commandments lead the way, every other rule and regulation follows in its rightful place.

✠

Lord, you are a wonderful teacher. Help us to put God first in everything and to love and care for others for his sake.

✠ ✠ ✠ ✠ ✠

September 15

Today we go back over a thousand years to dip into the lovely story of Ruth.

✠

Long ago, in the days before Israel had a king, there was a famine in the land. So a man named Elimelech, who belonged to the clan of Ephrath and who lived in Bethlehem in Judah, went with his wife Naomi and their two sons Mahlon and Chilion to live for a while in the country of Moab. While they were living there, Elimelech died, and Naomi was left alone with her two sons, who married Moabite girls, Orpah and Ruth. About ten years later, Mahlon and Chilion also died, and Naomi was left all alone, without husband or sons.

Some time later Naomi heard that the LORD had blessed his people by giving them a good harvest; so she got ready to leave Moab with her daughters-in-law. They started out together to go back to Judah, but on the way she said to them, "Go back home and stay with your mothers. May the LORD be as good to you as you have been to me and to those who have died. And may the LORD make it possible for each of you to marry again and have a home."

So Naomi kissed them good-bye. But they started crying and said to her, "No! We will go with you to your people."

Ruth 1:1–10

✠

This is one of the great love stories of the Bible, but it begins with a triple tragedy. Not only does Naomi lose her husband, but both her sons die as well. She is left without anyone to support her – for there were no widows' pensions in those days, and her daughters-in-law are widows too. The best thing seems to be for them each to go back to their own part of the world – Naomi to Bethlehem, and Orpah and Ruth to their families in Moab. But the thought of leaving each other almost breaks their hearts.

✠

Lord, you know all our sorrows. Thank you that you are with us to share our sadness, and even weave our tragedies into your beautiful eternal plan.

✠ ✠ ✠ ✠ ✠

September 16

"You must go back, my daughters," Naomi answered. "Why do you want to come with me? Do you think I could have sons again for you to marry? Go back home, for I am too old to get married again. Even if I thought there was still hope, and so got married tonight and had sons, would you wait until they had grown up? Would this keep you from marrying someone else? No, my daughters, you know that's impossible. The LORD has turned against me, and I feel very sorry for you."

Again they started crying. Then Orpah kissed her mother-in-law good-bye and went back home, but Ruth held on to her. So Naomi said to her, "Ruth, your sister-in-law has gone back to her people and to her god. Go back home with her."

But Ruth answered, "Don't ask me to leave you! Let me go with you. Wherever you go, I will go; wherever you live, I will live. Your people will be my people, and your God will be my God. Wherever you die, I will die, and that is where I will be buried. May the LORD's worst punishment come upon me if I let anything but death separate me from you!"

When Naomi saw that Ruth was determined to go with her, she said nothing more.

They went on until they came to Bethlehem.

Ruth 1:11–19

✠

In the end, Orpah decides to go back home, where she hopes to find a new husband and make a new life. But Ruth insists on staying with Naomi, sharing her life and worshipping her God. And Naomi gives in. They go on together, two helpless widows, without support or protection, but trusting in the living God.

As it turned out, Ruth met Boaz in Bethlehem – a wonderful man who asked her to marry him. And looking back, we can see that they were the grandparents of the great King David, and ancestors of Jesus himself!

✠

Lord, thank you for Ruth's example. Help us to do what's right, even when it looks as though we might miss out. At least we won't miss out on pleasing you.

✠ ✠ ✠ ✠ ✠

September 17

There was a man named Elkanah, from the tribe of Ephraim, who lived in the town of Ramah in the hill-country of Ephraim. Elkanah had two wives, Hannah and Peninnah. Peninnah had children, but Hannah had none. Every year Elkanah went from Ramah to worship and offer sacrifices to the LORD Almighty at Shiloh, where Hophni and Phinehas, the two sons of Eli, were priests of the LORD. Each time Elkanah offered his sacrifice, he would give one share of the meat to Peninnah and one share to each of her children. And even though he loved Hannah very much he would give her only one share, because the LORD had kept her from having children. Peninnah, her rival, would torment and humiliate her, because the LORD had kept her childless. This went on year after year; whenever they went to the house of the LORD, Peninnah would upset Hannah so much that she would cry and refuse to eat anything.

1 Samuel 1:1–7

✠

Here is another person who is part of God's plan. Her name is Hannah. She is near to despair.

It isn't that she has no husband, because she has. And he loves her very much. But he has two wives, and it is the other wife, Peninnah, whom God is blessing with children. People thought in those days that if you couldn't have children, you must have done something wrong and that God was punishing you. But God wasn't punishing Hannah at all. He was putting a longing in her heart which he was going to meet in a wonderful way – as we shall see.

Lord, when we're stuck in a bad situation, or life is full of friction and hurt, help us to look for the new thing you want to do.

✠ ✠ ✠ ✠ ✠

September 18

One day, after they had finished their meal in the house of the LORD at Shiloh, Hannah got up. She was deeply distressed, and she cried bitterly as she prayed to the LORD. Meanwhile, Eli the priest was sitting in his place by the door. Hannah made a solemn promise: "Almighty LORD, look at me, your servant! See my trouble and remember me! Don't forget me! If you give me a son, I promise that I will dedicate him to you for his whole life and that he will never have his hair cut."

Hannah continued to pray to the LORD for a long time, and Eli watched her lips. She was praying silently; her lips were moving, but she made no sound. So Eli thought that she was drunk, and said to her, "Stop making a drunken show of yourself! Stop your drinking and sober up!"

"No, I'm not drunk, sir," she answered. "I haven't been drinking! I am desperate, and I have been praying, pouring out my troubles to the LORD. Don't think I am a worthless woman. I have been praying like this because I'm so miserable."

"Go in peace," Eli said, "and may the God of Israel give you what you have asked him for."

"May you always think kindly of me," she replied. Then she went away, ate some food, and was no longer sad.

1 Samuel 1:9–18

Hannah knew what to do in her distress. She went to God's house and poured out her heart in prayer. She felt – and looked – a mess. But in her great need she made a promise to God – a promise she would faithfully keep. And God gave her Eli to talk to her, to listen to her troubles, and assure her of God's care.

✠

Lord, please help us to come to you with our deepest needs. And thank you for people who are good listeners, or who give good advice.

✠ ✠ ✠ ✠ ✠

September 19

So it was that Hannah became pregnant and gave birth to a son. She named him Samuel, and explained, "I asked the LORD for him."

The time came again for Elkanah and his family to go to Shiloh and offer to the LORD the yearly sacrifice and the special sacrifice he had promised. But this time Hannah did not go. She told her husband, "As soon as the child is weaned, I will take him to the house of the LORD, where he will stay all his life."

Elkanah answered, "All right, do whatever you think best; stay at home until you have weaned him. And may the LORD make your promise come true." So Hannah stayed at home and nursed her child.

After she had weaned him, she took him to Shiloh, taking along a three-year-old bull, ten kilogrammes of flour, and a leather bag full of wine. She took Samuel, young as he was, to the house of the LORD at Shiloh. After they had killed the bull, they took the child to Eli. Hannah said to him, "Excuse me, sir. Do you remember me? I am the woman you saw standing here, praying to the LORD. I asked him for this child, and he gave me what I asked for. So I am dedicating him to the LORD. As long as he lives, he will belong to the LORD."

1 Samuel 1:20–28

✠

It must have been the hardest thing imaginable for Hannah to take her precious son to Shiloh and leave him there. The only thing we can give to the Lord which is more than our own life is the life of our children. And doesn't this tell us something about God's love for us? He loved the world so much that he gave *his only Son* that all who believe in him shall not perish but have everlasting life.

✠

Lord, thank you for loving us so much. Help us to keep our word – especially the promises we make to you.

✠ ✠ ✠ ✠ ✠

September 20

In those days, when the boy Samuel was serving the LORD under the direction of Eli, there were very few messages from the LORD, and visions from him were quite rare. One night Eli, who was now almost blind, was sleeping in his own room; Samuel was sleeping in the sanctuary, where the sacred Covenant Box was. Before dawn, while the lamp was still burning, the LORD called Samuel. He answered, "Yes, sir!" and ran to Eli and said, "You called me, and here I am." But Eli answered, "I didn't call you; go back to bed." So Samuel went back to bed.

The LORD called Samuel again. The boy did not know that it was the LORD, because the LORD had never spoken to him before. So he got up, went to Eli, and said, "You called me, and here I am." But Eli answered, "My son, I didn't call you; go back to bed."

The LORD called Samuel a third time; he got up, went to Eli, and said, "You called me, and here I am."

Then Eli realized that it was the LORD who was calling the boy, so he said to him, "Go back to bed; and if he calls you again, say, 'Speak, LORD, your servant is listening.'" So Samuel went back to bed.

The LORD came and stood there, and called as he had before, "Samuel! Samuel!"

Samuel answered, "Speak; your servant is listening."

1 Samuel 3:1–10

✠

God speaks to Samuel in a voice that can be heard. Not just a quiet voice inside his head, but a voice which sounds like someone nearby calling to him. This was very rare in those days, and it is very rare today.

God has chosen Samuel to talk to, and to give messages for him to pass on to other people.

✠

Lord, help us to learn to recognize your voice, whichever way you speak to us. Help us to be open to your words and willing to do what you say.

✠ ✠ ✠ ✠ ✠

September 21

The LORD said to Samuel, "Some day I am going to do something to the people of Israel that is so terrible that everyone who hears about it will be stunned. On that day I will carry out all my threats against Eli's family, from beginning to end. I have already told him that I am going to punish his family for ever because his sons have spoken evil things against me. Eli knew they were doing this, but he did not stop them. So I solemnly declare to the family of Eli that no sacrifice or offering will ever be able to remove the consequences of this terrible sin."

Samuel stayed in bed until morning; then he got up and opened the doors of the house of the LORD. He was afraid to tell Eli about the vision. Eli called him, "Samuel, my boy!"

"Yes, sir," answered Samuel.

"What did the LORD tell you?" Eli asked. "Don't keep anything from me. God will punish you severely if you don't tell me everything he said." So Samuel told him everything; he did not keep anything back. Eli said, "He is the LORD; he will do whatever seems best to him."

As Samuel grew up, the LORD was with him and made everything that Samuel said come true. So all the people of Israel, from one end of the country to the other, knew that Samuel was indeed a prophet of the LORD. The LORD continued to reveal himself at Shiloh, where he had appeared to Samuel and had spoken to him. And when Samuel spoke, all Israel listened.

1 Samuel 3:11–21

✠

The first message that the Lord has for Samuel is that he is angry with Eli's sons. They are corrupt priests who have been using their position to rob people. Their lives are a blasphemy God can never forgive.

Eli, too, has played his part by being a weak father who has failed to correct his sons. When Samuel tells Eli the message, the old man knows that it is all too true.

✠

Lord, thank you for caring about the way we live. Please forgive the wrong things we have said, thought and done. And help us in our family to honour you from generation to generation.

✠ ✠ ✠ ✠ ✠

September 22

When Samuel grew old, he made his sons judges in Israel. The elder son was named Joel and the younger one Abijah; they were judges in Beersheba. But they did not follow their father's example; they were interested only in making money, so they accepted bribes and did not decide cases honestly.

Then all the leaders of Israel met together, went to Samuel in Ramah, and said to him, "Look, you are getting old and your sons don't follow your example. So then, appoint a king to rule over us, so that we will have a king, as other countries have." Samuel was displeased with their request for a king; so he prayed to the LORD, and the LORD said, "Listen to everything the people say to you. You are not the one they have rejected; I am the one they have rejected as their king. Ever since I brought them out of Egypt, they have turned away from me and worshipped other gods; and now they are doing to you what they have always done to me. So then, listen to them, but give them strict warnings and explain how their kings will treat them."

1 Samuel 8:1–9

✠

Just as Eli's sons had followed him as priests, Samuel's sons follow him as judges. But their hearts are not truly set on the Lord's way, and they make their decisions according to who pays them most.

The result is that the people begin to ask for a real king – not an invisible king like God, but a king they can see and hear and follow. Samuel is hurt by their request, but it is only a shadow of the rejection God feels.

✠

Lord, when other people reject us or let us down, it gives us a glimpse of how you must often feel about us. Please forgive us, and help us to live as you want us to.

September 23

Samuel told the people who were asking him for a king everything that the LORD had said to him. "This is how your king will treat you," Samuel explained. "He will make soldiers of your sons; some of them will serve in his war chariots, others in his cavalry, and others will run before his chariots. He will make some of them officers in charge of a thousand men, and others in charge of fifty men. Your sons will have to plough his fields, harvest his crops, and make his weapons and the equipment for his chariots. Your daughters will have to make perfumes for him and work as his cooks and his bakers. He will take your best fields, vineyards, and olive-groves, and give them to his officials. He will take a tenth of your corn and of your grapes for his court officers and other officials. He will take your servants and your best cattle and donkeys, and make them work for him. He will take a tenth of your flocks. And you yourselves will become his slaves. When that time comes, you will complain bitterly because of your king, whom you yourselves chose, but the LORD will not listen to your complaints."

The people paid no attention to Samuel, but said "No! We want a king, so that we will be like other nations, with our own king to rule us and to lead us out to war and to fight our battles." Samuel listened to everything they said and then went and told the LORD. The LORD answered, "Do what they want and give them a king."

1 Samuel 8:10–22

✠

Samuel doesn't want Israel to have a king, because God himself is their king for ever. But they insist on having a ruler, because they want to be like the other nations.

Sometimes we decide we want something, and we just won't take "No" for an answer!

But Samuel warns the people very clearly that a king will make demands on them and that they will soon be complaining about him. But they simply refuse to listen.

✠

Dear God our Father, you are the perfect king, your service is perfect freedom. We give our lives into your hands today.

✠ ✠ ✠ ✠ ✠

September 24

There was a wealthy and influential man named Kish, from the tribe of Benjamin; he was the son of Abiel and grandson of Zeror, and belonged to the family of Becorath, a part of the clan of Aphiah. He had a son named Saul, a handsome man in the prime of life. Saul was a head taller than anyone else in Israel and more handsome as well.

Some donkeys belonging to Kish had wandered off, so he said to Saul, "Take one of the servants with you and go and look for the donkeys." They went through the hill-country of Ephraim and the region of Shalishah, but did not find them; so they went on through the region of Shaalim, but the donkeys were not there. Then they went through the territory of

Benjamin, but still did not find them. When they came into the region of Zuph, Saul said to his servant, "Let's go back home, or my father might stop thinking about the donkeys and start worrying about us."

The servant answered, "Wait! In this town there is a holy man who is highly respected because everything he says comes true. Let's go to him, and maybe he can tell us where we can find the donkeys."

Saul replied, "A good idea! Let's go." So they went to the town where the holy man lived.

1 Samuel 9:1–6,9

✠

And so we meet Saul. Saul is to become the first king of Israel, and the hunt for the donkeys is just God's way of introducing him to Samuel.

It's strange how God can use all kinds of situations to guide us. Mistakes, interruptions, accidents – God uses anything that will shake us out of our routine, lead us to meet new people, or help us to see things differently.

✠

Lord, no experience or adventure you give us is ever wasted. Help us to look for your loving purpose even in the things that go "wrong".

✠ ✠ ✠ ✠ ✠

September 25

When Samuel caught sight of Saul, the LORD said to him, "This is the man I told you about. He will rule my people." Then Saul went over to Samuel, who was near the gate, and asked, "Tell me, where does the seer live?"

Samuel answered, "I am the seer. Go on ahead of me to the place of worship. Both of you are to eat with me today. Tomorrow morning I will answer all your questions and send you on your way. As for the donkeys that were lost three days ago, don't worry about them; they have already been found. But who is it that the people of Israel want so much? It is you – you and your father's family."

So Saul ate with Samuel that day. When they went down from the place of worship to the town, they made up a bed for Saul on the roof, and he slept there.

At dawn Samuel called to Saul on the roof, "Get up, and I will send you on your way." Saul got up, and he and Samuel went out to the street together. When they arrived at the edge of the town, Samuel said to Saul, "Tell the servant to go on ahead of us." The servant left, and Samuel continued, "Stay here a minute, and I will tell you what God has said."

Then Samuel took a jar of olive-oil and poured it on Saul's head, kissed him, and said, "The LORD anoints you as ruler of his people Israel. You will rule his people and protect them from all their enemies. And this is the proof to you that the LORD has chosen you to be the ruler of his people."

1 Samuel 9:17–20,25–27; 10:1

✠

So Saul is anointed as king, with Samuel pouring oil over his head as a sign of God's abundant blessing.

It was a strange day for both of them. They had never met before, and Saul had no idea when he went in search of his father's donkeys that the journey would end like this. And how must Samuel have felt? No doubt he was excited at meeting God's chosen leader, but surely he was also sad that the people had insisted on having a human king at all. Anyway, on this special day both Saul and Samuel were completely open to God and ready for whatever he had in store.

✠

Dear Lord, give us a special openness to your plans. Thank you for the leaders you have given us, and the work you have for us to do.

✠ ✠ ✠ ✠ ✠

September 26

Saul is tall and good-looking, and he makes a striking king. But his heart is never really in tune with God. He disobeys some of God's most important commands, and suffers periods of black depression. Meanwhile, Samuel is very torn. He had warned the people against wanting a king, and yet now he longs that Saul will rule successfully.

✠

The LORD said to Samuel, "How long will you go on grieving over Saul? I have rejected him as king of Israel. But now get some olive-oil and go to Bethlehem, to a man named Jesse, because I have chosen one of his sons to be king."

"How can I do that?" Samuel asked. "If Saul hears about it, he will kill me!"

The LORD answered, "Take a calf with you and say that you are there to offer a sacrifice to the LORD. Invite Jesse to the sacrifice, and I will tell you what to do. You will anoint as king the man I tell you to."

Samuel did what the LORD told him to do and went to Bethlehem, where the city leaders came trembling to meet him and asked, "Is this a peaceful visit, seer?"

"Yes," he answered. "I have come to offer a sacrifice to the LORD. Purify yourselves and come with me." He also told Jesse and his sons to purify themselves, and he invited them to the sacrifice.

1 Samuel 16:1–5

✠

When the local people see Samuel riding into town, they wonder what's going to happen! But Samuel assures them he has come in peace. And he invites them all to a service.

When we want to know God's way forward, we cannot do better than to come with open hearts and worship him.

✠

Lord God, today is the first day of the rest of our lives. Please make us clean from all our sins and take us the next step along your way.

September 27

When they arrived, Samuel saw Jesse's son Eliab and said to himself, "This man standing here in the LORD's presence is surely the one he has chosen." But the LORD said to him, "Pay no attention to how tall and handsome he is. I have rejected him, because I do not judge as man judges. Man looks at the outward appearance, but I look at the heart."

Then Jesse called his son Abinadab and brought him to Samuel. But Samuel said, "No, the LORD hasn't chosen him either." Jesse then brought Shammah. "No, the LORD hasn't chosen him either," Samuel said. In this way, Jesse brought seven of his sons to Samuel. And Samuel said to him, "No, the LORD hasn't chosen any of these." Then he asked him, "Have you any more sons?"

Jesse answered, "There is still the youngest, but he is out taking care of the sheep."

"Tell him to come here," Samuel said. "We won't offer the sacrifice until he comes." So Jesse sent for him. He was a handsome, healthy young man, and his eyes sparkled. The LORD said to Samuel, "This is the one – anoint him!" Samuel took the olive-oil and anointed David in front of his brothers. Immediately the spirit of the LORD took control of David and was with him from that day on. Then Samuel returned to Ramah.

1 Samuel 16:6–13

✠

Even Samuel, the greatest holy man of his day, still has important lessons to learn. He has to realize that God chooses people by what he sees in their hearts, and not by the way they look – however strong or beautiful they may be. (Remember Saul had been tall and good-looking, but his heart was far from God. Samuel isn't to make the same mistake again!)

And so, listening for the Lord's guiding voice, Samuel discovers David. David who will grow up to be Israel's greatest king.

✠

Lord, we come to you with all our faults and weaknesses, and ask that you will take our lives and use us for your glory.

✠ ✠ ✠ ✠ ✠

September 28

The LORD's spirit left Saul, and an evil spirit sent by the LORD tormented him. His servants said to him, "We know that an evil spirit sent by God is tormenting you. So give us the order, sir, and we will look for a man who knows how to play the harp. Then when the evil spirit comes on you, the man can play his harp, and you will be all right again."

Saul ordered them, "Find me a man who plays well and bring him to me."

One of his attendants said, "Jesse, of the town of Bethlehem, has a son who is a good musician. He is also a brave and handsome man, a good soldier, and an able speaker. The LORD is with him."

So Saul sent messengers to Jesse to say, "Send me your son David, the one who takes care of the sheep." Jesse sent David to Saul with a young goat, a donkey loaded with bread, and a leather bag full of wine. David came to Saul and entered his service. Saul liked him very much and chose him as the man to carry his weapons. Then Saul sent a message to Jesse: "I like David. Let him stay here in my service." From then on, whenever the evil spirit sent by God came on Saul, David would get his harp and play it. The evil spirit would leave, and Saul would feel better and be all right again.

1 Samuel 16:14–23

✠

God always knows where we are. Although David is the youngest of eight brothers and expects to spend his life guarding sheep on the hills of Bethlehem, God has a way of changing everything.

God uses David's gift of music-making to bring him into the royal palace. The music which has passed the time while the sheep graze is now to be used to soothe Saul's torment. And the same music will one day blossom in the writing of psalms – many of which are in the Bible to this very day.

✠

Lord, thank you for the gifts you give us. Help us to develop our talents so that we can live interesting lives, give pleasure to others, and be useful to you at any time.

✠ ✠ ✠ ✠ ✠

September 29

The Philistines gathered for battle in Socoh, a town in Judah; Saul and the Israelites assembled and camped in the Valley of Elah, where they got ready to fight the Philistines. The Philistines lined up on one hill and the Israelites on another, with a valley between them.

A man named Goliath, from the city of Gath, came out from the Philistine camp to challenge the Israelites. He was nearly three metres tall and wore bronze armour that weighed about fifty-seven kilogrammes and a bronze helmet. His legs were also protected by bronze armour, and he carried a bronze javelin slung over his shoulder. His spear was as thick as the bar on a weaver's loom, and its iron head weighed about seven kilogrammes. A soldier walked in front of him carrying his shield. Goliath stood and shouted at the Israelites, "What are you doing there, lined up for battle? I am a Philistine, you slaves of Saul! Choose one of your men to fight me. If he wins and kills me, we will be your slaves; but if I win and kill him, you will be our slaves. Here and now I challenge the Israelite army. I dare you to pick someone to fight me!" When Saul and his men heard this, they were terrified.

1 Samuel 17:1–11

✠

Goliath is the biggest man the Israelites have ever seen – and they had thought that Saul was tall! What's more, Goliath is armed with the very latest weaponry, so there's no way anyone can possibly hurt him.

Sometimes we have problems of our own which are a bit like Goliath. Problems so big that we tremble with terror. But the Israelites are about to discover that however great their problem, their God is greater still.

✠

Lord, help us to look at our problems through your eyes, and see how small they are to you, and how well you are able to help.

✠ ✠ ✠ ✠ ✠

September 30

Goliath challenged the Israelites every morning and evening for forty days.

One day Jesse said to David, "Take ten kilogrammes of this roasted grain and these ten loaves of bread, and hurry with them to your brothers in the camp. And take these ten cheeses to the commanding officer. Find out how your brothers are getting on and bring back something to show that you saw them and that they are well."

David got up early the next morning, left someone else in charge of the sheep, took the food, and went as Jesse had told him to. He arrived at the camp just as the Israelites were going out to their battle line, shouting the war-cry. David left the food with the officer in charge of the supplies, ran to the battle line, went to his brothers and asked how they were getting on. As he was talking to them, Goliath came forward and challenged the Israelites as he had done before. And David heard him. When the Israelites saw Goliath, they ran away in terror.

"Look at him!" they said to each other. "Listen to his challenge! King Saul has promised to give a big reward to the man who kills him; the king will also give him his daughter to marry and will not require his father's family to pay taxes."

David asked the men who were near him, "What will the man get who kills this Philistine and frees Israel from this disgrace? After all, who is this heathen Philistine to defy the army of the living God?" They told him what would be done for the man who killed Goliath.

1 Samuel 17:16–18,20,22–27

✠

King Saul is desperate for someone to take on Goliath. (Really he should be going out to fight the giant himself, as he is tall and has a fine suit of bronze armour.) As for David, he can hardly believe that a reward is being offered for killing Goliath – after all, he may be an incredible hulk, but he is nothing compared with the army of the Living God.

✠

Lord, forgive us when we live as though you don't exist. When we try to tackle problems in our own strength, or wait for them to go away. May today's challenges make us turn to you, and may we have no doubts at all that your strength will win.

✠ ✠ ✠ ✠ ✠

A Psalm for

October

Praise the LORD, my soul!
  All my being, praise his holy name!
Praise the LORD, my soul,
  and do not forget how kind he is.
He forgives all my sins
  and heals all my diseases.
He keeps me from the grave
  and blesses me with love and mercy.
He fills my life with good things,
  so that I stay young and strong like
    an eagle.

The LORD judges in favour of the
    oppressed
  and gives them their rights.
He revealed his plans to Moses
  and let the people of Israel see his
    mighty deeds.
The LORD is merciful and loving,
  slow to become angry and full of
    constant love.
He does not keep on rebuking;
  he is not angry for ever.
He does not punish us as we deserve
  or repay us for our sins and wrongs.
As high as the sky is above the earth,
  so great is his love for those who
    honour him.

As far as the east is from the west,
so far does he remove our sins from us.
As kind as a father is to his children,
so kind is the LORD to those who
honour him.

Psalm 103:1–13

October 1

Eliab, David's eldest brother, heard David talking to the men. He was angry with David and said, "What are you doing here? Who is taking care of those sheep of yours out there in the wilderness? You cheeky brat, you! You just came to watch the fighting!"

"Now what have I done?" David asked. "Can't I even ask a question?" He turned to another man and asked him the same question, and every time he asked, he got the same answer.

Some men heard what David had said, and they told Saul, who sent for him. David said to Saul, "Your Majesty, no one should be afraid of this Philistine! I will go and fight him."

"No," answered Saul. "How could you fight him? You're just a boy, and he has been a soldier all his life!"

"Your Majesty," David said, "I take care of my father's sheep. Whenever a lion or a bear carries off a lamb, I go after it, attack it, and rescue the lamb. And if the lion or bear turns on me, I grab it by the throat and beat it to death. I have killed lions and bears, and I will do the same to this heathen Philistine, who has defied the army of the living God. The LORD has saved me from lions and bears; he will save me from this Philistine."

"All right," Saul answered. "Go, and the LORD be with you." He gave his own armour to David for him to wear: a bronze helmet, which he put on David's head, and a coat of armour. David strapped Saul's sword over the armour and tried to walk, but he couldn't, because he wasn't used to wearing them. "I can't fight with all this," he said to Saul. "I'm not used to it." So he took it all off. He took his shepherd's stick and then picked up five smooth stones from the stream and put them in his bag. With his catapult ready, he went out to meet Goliath.

1 Samuel 17:28–40

✠

Some people would have thought that David was mad, going out to fight an armoured giant with only a catapult. But David's real armour was his faith in the Living God, and in his memories of what God had done for him in the past.

Are we able to look at all that God has done for us up to now, and so step out in confident faith today?

✠

Lord, thank you that your love always surrounds us and your strength protects us, whatever our circumstances.

✠ ✠ ✠ ✠ ✠

October 2

Goliath started walking towards David, with his shield-bearer walking in front of him. He kept coming closer, and when he got a good look at David, he was filled with scorn for him because he was just a nice, good-looking boy. He said to David, "What's that stick for? Do you think I'm a dog?" And he called down curses from his god on David. "Come on," he challenged David, "and I will give your body to the birds and animals to eat."

David answered, "You are coming against me with sword, spear, and javelin, but I come against you in the name of the LORD Almighty, the God of the Israelite armies, which you have defied. This very day the LORD will put you in my power; I will defeat you and cut off your head. And I will give the bodies of the Philistine soldiers to the birds and animals to eat. Then the whole world will know that Israel has a God, and everyone here will see that the LORD does not need swords or spears to save his people. He is victorious in battle, and he will put all of you in our power."

Goliath started walking towards David again, and David ran quickly towards the Philistine battle line to fight him. He put his hand into his bag and took out a stone, which he slung at Goliath. It hit him on the forehead and broke his skull, and Goliath fell face downwards on the ground. And so, without a sword, David defeated and killed Goliath with a catapult and a stone! He ran to him, stood over him, took Goliath's sword out of its sheath, and cut off his head and killed him.

When the Philistines saw that their hero was dead, they ran away.

1 Samuel 17:41–51

What an extraordinary battle! Although we know the story so well, it still amazes us to see how God gives victory to David. He *uses* David – David's courage, David's wit and David's skill – to reveal his glorious power and rescue his people against all the odds.

✠

Mighty God, no matter what the odds, we are always on the victory side when we trust our lives to you.

✠ ✠ ✠ ✠ ✠

October 3

Of course, David became a national hero overnight after his conquest of Goliath. But Saul, instead of being delighted and sharing his joy, was consumed with jealousy. In the end, David had to go into hiding – and he was soon joined by others.

✠

Saul took three thousand of the best soldiers in Israel and went looking for David and his men east of Wild Goat Rocks. He came to a cave close to some sheep pens by the road and went in to relieve himself. It happened to be the very cave in which David and his men were hiding far back in the cave. They said to him, "This is your chance! The LORD has told you that he would put your enemy in your power and you could do to him whatever you wanted to." David crept over and cut off a piece of Saul's robe without Saul's knowing it. But then David's conscience began to trouble him, and he said to his men, "May the LORD keep me from doing any harm to my master, whom the LORD chose as king! I must not harm him in the least, because he is the king chosen by the LORD!" So David convinced his men that they should not attack Saul.

1 Samuel 24:2–7

✠

David has Saul in his power, but he refuses to take any advantage. Saul is God's king. If God doesn't want Saul as king any more, then he can remove him at any time. It's not for David or anyone else to take the law into their own hands.

✠

Lord, thank you for the leaders you have given us – in our church, in our community, and in our country. As you have chosen them, may we give them our support and encouragement to do the things that are right.

✠ ✠ ✠ ✠ ✠

October 4

Saul got up, left the cave, and started on his way. Then David went out after him and called to him, "Your Majesty!" Saul turned round, and David bowed down to the ground in respect and said, "Why do you listen to people who say that I am trying to harm you? You can see for yourself that just now in the cave the LORD put you in my power. Some of my men told me to kill you, but I felt sorry for you and said that I would not harm you in the least, because you are the one whom the LORD chose to be king. Look, my father, look at the piece of your robe I am holding! I could have killed you, but instead I only cut this off. This should convince you that I have no thought of rebelling against you or of harming you. You are hunting me down to kill me, even though I have not done you any wrong. May the LORD judge which one of us is wrong!"

When David had finished speaking, Saul said, "Is that really you, David my son?" And he started crying. Then he said to David, "You are right, and I am wrong. You have been so good to me, while I have done such wrong to you! Now I am sure that you will be king of Israel and that the kingdom will continue under your rule."

1 Samuel 24:7–12,16–17,20

✠

David knows that "two wrongs don't make a right". Saul may be a bad king, but it would still be quite wrong to kill him. He must be replaced only in God's way and in God's time.

✠

Lord, it seems that some rulers you appoint, but some you merely allow. Help us to respect and pray for them all; and when we have a chance to choose new leaders, help us to look and listen for your choice.

✠ ✠ ✠ ✠ ✠

October 5

Then all the tribes of Israel came to David at Hebron and said to him, "We are your own flesh and blood. In the past, even when Saul was still our king, you led the people of Israel in battle, and the LORD promised you that you would lead his people and be their ruler." So all the leaders of Israel came to King David at Hebron. He made a sacred alliance with them, they anointed him, and he became king of Israel. David was thirty years old when he became king, and he ruled for forty years. He ruled in Hebron over Judah for seven and a half years and in Jerusalem over all Israel and Judah for thirty-three years.

The time came when King David and his men set out to attack Jerusalem. The Jebusites, who lived there, thought that David would not be able to conquer the city, and so they said to him, "You will never get in here; even the blind and the crippled could keep you out." But David did capture their fortress of Zion, and it became known as "David's City".

2 Samuel 5:1–7

✠

And so at last David's hour has come. He is king by God's anointing and by the people's choice. This too is how Jesus will be king of our world – when all nations accept that he is God's Saviour and Lord.

✠

Heavenly Father, we thank you for making Jesus our king. We give him pride of place in our hearts and in our homes today.

October 6

When David was about to die, he called his son Solomon and gave him his last instructions: "My time to die has come. Be confident and determined, and do what the LORD your God orders you to do. Obey all his laws and commands, as written in the Law of Moses, so that wherever you go you may prosper in everything you do. If you obey him, the LORD will keep the promise he made when he told me that my descendants would rule Israel as long as they were careful to obey his commands faithfully with all their heart and soul."

1 Kings 2:1–4

✠

David has lived a long life and learned many hard lessons. In it all he has *known* God – not just known *about* God, but enjoyed God's protection and walked in his light.

Now David tells Solomon the secret of success. If he keeps God's law and obeys God's commands, then all will go well for him and his people.

✠

Lord, it is so exciting that you have shown us the path of life. You have told us how to live safely and well in this complex and bewildering world. And you have given us Jesus, the true and living way. Thank you!

✠ ✠ ✠ ✠ ✠

October 7

David wrote many psalms, but by far the best known is this beautiful song about God's care for each of us.

✠

The LORD is my shepherd;
 I have everything I need.
He lets me rest in fields of green grass
 and leads me to quiet pools of fresh water.
He gives me new strength.
He guides me in the right paths,
 as he has promised.
Even if I go through the deepest darkness,
 I will not be afraid, LORD,
 for you are with me.
Your shepherd's rod and staff protect me.

You prepare a banquet for me,
 where all my enemies can see me;
you welcome me as an honoured guest
 and fill my cup to the brim.
I know that your goodness and love will
  be with me all my life;
 and your house will be my home as
  long as I live.

Psalm 23

✠

God is like a shepherd to us. He is with us all the time – guiding us, guarding us, and providing all our needs. And from all that we have seen of his love for us each day, we can surely look forward to spending the rest of our lives in his safe keeping.

Dear Lord our Shepherd, thank you that you know each one of us and care for us in every way. Help us to follow in your steps and listen for your voice today.

✠ ✠ ✠ ✠ ✠

October 8

The LORD appeared to Solomon in a dream and asked him, "What would you like me to give you?"

Solomon answered, "O LORD God, you have let me succeed my father as king, even though I am very young and don't know how to rule. Here I am among the people you have chosen to be your own, a people who are so many that they cannot be counted. So give me the wisdom I need to rule your people with justice and to know the difference between good and evil. Otherwise, how would I ever be able to rule this great people of yours?"

The LORD was pleased that Solomon had asked for this, and so he said to him, "Because you have asked for the wisdom to rule justly, instead of long life for yourself or riches or the death of your enemies, I will do what you have asked. I will give you more wisdom and understanding than anyone has ever had before or will ever have again. I will also give you what you have not asked for: all your life you will have wealth and honour, more than that of any other king. And if you obey me and keep my laws and commands, as your father David did, I will give you a long life."

1 Kings 3:5,7–14

✠

Solomon is given a blank cheque by God. He can ask for *anything*. And yet God cares very much about Solomon's reply.

The new king is an example to all of us in his prayer. He knows that he is tiny, weak, and ignorant. So he tells God how he feels, and asks for the gift of wisdom that he so greatly needs if he is to rule wisely and well. And God is delighted with such a prayer. In answer, he not only grants wisdom to Solomon, but long life, wealth and honour as well.

When we pray, do we ask God for the kind of blessings which will enable us to help others?

✠

Dear God our Father, please bless us and make us a blessing to others today.

✠ ✠ ✠ ✠ ✠

October 9

One day two women came and presented themselves before King Solomon. One of them said, "Your Majesty, this woman and I live in the same house, and I gave birth to a baby boy at home while she was there. Two days after my child was born she also gave birth to a baby boy. Only the two of us were there in the house – no one else was present. Then one night she accidentally rolled over on her baby and smothered it. She got up during the night, took my son from my side while I was asleep, and carried him to her bed; then she put the dead child in my bed. The next morning, when I woke up and was going to feed my baby, I saw that it was dead. I looked at it more closely and saw that it was not my child."

Then King Solomon said, "Each of you claims that the living child is hers and that the dead child belongs to the other one." He sent for a sword, and when it was brought, he said, "Cut the living child in two and give each woman half of it."

The real mother, her heart full of love for her son, said to the king, "Please, Your Majesty, don't kill the child! Give it to her!"

But the other woman said, "Don't give it to either of us; go ahead and cut it in two."

Then Solomon said, "Don't kill the child! Give it to the first woman – she is its real mother."

When the people of Israel heard of Solomon's decision, they were all filled with deep respect for him, because they knew then that God had given him the wisdom to settle disputes fairly.

1 Kings 3:16–21,23–28

✠

Solomon's decision isn't just clever – it is *wise.* Wisdom is a priceless gift which applies truth to difficult situations and sets people free. And do you notice that wisdom has a "feelright" about it, and that everyone rejoices in the outcome?

✠

Lord God, please give wisdom to all in authority, especially those leaders who are faced with incredibly difficult decisions today.

✠ ✠ ✠ ✠ ✠

October 10

God gave Solomon unusual wisdom and insight, and knowledge too great to be measured. Solomon was wiser than the wise men of the East or the wise men of Egypt. He was the wisest of all men, and his fame spread throughout all the neighbouring countries. He composed three thousand proverbs and more than a thousand songs. He spoke of trees and plants, from the Lebanon cedars to the hyssop that grows on walls; he talked about animals, birds, reptiles, and fish. Kings all over the world heard of his wisdom and sent people to listen to him.

1 Kings 4:29–34

✠

How wonderfully God answered Solomon's request for wisdom. And how greatly that wisdom benefited the rest of the world, both in Solomon's lifetime and in every generation since.

✠

Lord God, giver of all wisdom, thank you that your truth stands from place to place and from age to age. Help us to discover and live your truth right where we are in the situations that arise today.

✠ ✠ ✠ ✠ ✠

October 11

As Solomon studied, observed and reflected, he distilled his wisdom into pithy proverbs. We can read them in the Bible today, and enjoy their truth for ourselves.

✠

Don't forget what I teach you, my son. Always remember what I tell you to do. My teaching will give you a long and prosperous life. Never let go of loyalty and faithfulness. Tie them round your neck; write them on your heart. If you do this, both God and man will be pleased with you.

Trust in the LORD with all your heart. Never rely on what you think you know. Remember the LORD in everything you do, and he will show you the right way. Never let yourself think that you are wiser than you are; simply obey the LORD and refuse to do wrong. If you do, it will be like good medicine, healing your wounds and easing your pains. Honour the LORD by making him an offering from the best of all that your land produces. If you do, your barns will be filled with grain, and you will have too much wine to be able to store it all.

Proverbs 3:1–10

✠

Solomon says that the heart of all wisdom is to put God first, and to depend completely on him. To trust the Lord, to look for his guidance at every stage, and steadfastly to obey his law – these are the keys to life and health and peace.

✠

Lord God, forgive us when we spurn your wise and loving purposes, and stubbornly insist on our futile ideas. Help us to put you at the centre of our lives, to think your thoughts and to love your ways.

✠ ✠ ✠ ✠ ✠

October 12

Here are just a few of Solomon's proverbs. They are like random jigsaw pieces taken from a vast picture of God's wisdom.

✠

Reverence for the LORD gives confidence and security to a man and his family.

Do you want to avoid death? Reverence for the LORD is a fountain of life.

A king's greatness depends on how many people he rules; without them he is nothing.

If you stay calm, you are wise, but if you have a hot temper, you only show how stupid you are.

Peace of mind makes the body healthy, but jealousy is like a cancer.

If you oppress poor people, you insult the God who made them; but kindness shown to the poor is an act of worship.

Wicked people bring about their own downfall by their evil deeds, but good people are protected by their integrity.

Wisdom is in every thought of an intelligent man; fools know nothing about wisdom.

Righteousness makes a nation great; sin is a disgrace to any nation.

Proverbs 14:26–34

✠

Lord, your word is truth. Truth for us in our own lives, and truth to guide us in our dealings with each other. May your wisdom spread into every part of us, so that we live "together" lives of unselfish love, integrity and peace.

✠ ✠ ✠ ✠ ✠

October 13

A gentle answer quietens anger, but a harsh one stirs it up.

When wise people speak, they make knowledge attractive, but stupid people spout nonsense.

The LORD sees what happens everywhere; he is watching us, whether we do good or evil.

Kind words bring life, but cruel words crush your spirit.

It is foolish to ignore what your father taught you; it is wise to accept his correction.

Righteous men keep their wealth, but wicked men lose theirs when hard times come.

Knowledge is spread by people who are wise, not by fools.

The LORD is pleased when good men pray, but hates the sacrifices that wicked men bring him.

The LORD hates the ways of evil people, but loves those who do what is right.

Proverbs 15:1–9

Isn't it amazing how the things we say (and the way we say them) show up what is in our hearts? When we speak, we reveal not only our nationality and education, but our thoughts and emotions as well.

✠

Lord, give us love and understanding in our hearts and minds, so that the things we say may be wholesome, helpful and kind.

✠ ✠ ✠ ✠ ✠

October 14

Today we turn to Jesus' teaching about true religion. The first thing he has to say is that our giving is a secret between us and God. Any other motive is merely showing off.

✠

"Make certain you do not perform your religious duties in public so that people will see what you do. If you do these things publicly, you will not have any reward from your Father in heaven.

"So when you give something to a needy person, do not make a big show of it, as the hypocrites do in the houses of worship and on the streets. They do it so that people will praise them. I assure you, they have already been paid in full. But when you help a needy person, do it in such a way that even your closest friend will not know about it. Then it will be a private matter. And your Father, who sees what you do in private, will reward you."

Matthew 6:1–4

Most of us aren't content with doing good. We want other people to notice how good we are (hopefully without guessing our many shortcomings!).

But Jesus was different. He never worried about how he appeared to others. The only person he wanted to please was God.

✠

Lord, help us to do good – promptly, secretly, and without fanfare or fuss.

✠ ✠ ✠ ✠ ✠

October 15

Jesus says that our praying should be secret, too.

✠

"When you pray, do not be like the hypocrites! They love to stand up and pray in the houses of worship and on the street corners, so that everyone will see them. I assure you, they have already been paid in full. But when you pray, go to your room, close the door, and pray to your Father, who is unseen. And your Father, who sees what you do in private, will reward you."

Matthew 6:5–6

✠

Hypocrites are people who pretend to be something they aren't. And the biggest temptation for all of us is to pretend to be better than we are. So, says Jesus, when we pray we should try to keep it private – between ourselves and God. Prayer is talking to God – just as we are, in our own words, in secret.

✠

Dear God our Father, help us to spend hidden time with you – discarding all thought of impressing other people, and loving you for your own sake.

✠ ✠ ✠ ✠ ✠

October 16

Some teachers had model prayers which they taught their followers. Here we read of the time when Jesus' disciples asked him for such a prayer.

✠

One day Jesus was praying in a certain place. When he had finished, one of his disciples said to him, "Lord, teach us to pray, just as John taught his disciples."

Jesus said to them, "When you pray, say this:

'Father:
May your holy name be honoured;
may your Kingdom come.
Give us day by day the food we need.
Forgive us our sins,
for we forgive everyone who does
us wrong.
And do not bring us to hard testing.'"

Luke 11:1–4

Jesus' prayer puts God at the very centre of our lives and asks that the day will come when he will be acknowledged as Lord of all creation. We pray that everyone everywhere will come to worship him.

And after this, we ask for our own needs – enough food for each day, forgiveness of our sins, and protection from evil.

✠

Lord, thank you for this wonderful prayer. May we learn to ask for the things that please you.

✠ ✠ ✠ ✠ ✠

October 17

And Jesus said to his disciples, "Suppose one of you should go to a friend's house at midnight and say to him, 'Friend, let me borrow three loaves of bread. A friend of mine who is on a journey has just come to my house, and I haven't got any food for him!' And suppose your friend should answer from inside, 'Don't bother me! The door is already locked, and my children and I are in bed. I can't get up and give you anything.' Well, what then? I tell you that even if he will not get up and give you the bread because you are his friend, yet he will get up and give you everything you need because you are not ashamed to keep on asking."

Luke 11:5–8

✠

Jesus says time and again that God wants to hear from us! He's not like a human friend who gets irritable if we knock and get him out of bed in the middle of the night. God is our heavenly Father – he loves to hear our prayers, and he longs to give us good things.

✠

Lord, we miss so many blessings and endure so many miseries because we so often can't be bothered to bring our requests to you. Please forgive us, and help us to ask for great things – the great things you want to give us – from now on.

✠ ✠ ✠ ✠ ✠

October 18

Jesus said to his disciples: "Ask, and you will receive; seek, and you will find; knock, and the door will be opened to you. For everyone who asks will receive, and he who seeks will find, and the door will be opened to anyone who knocks. Would any of you who are fathers give your son a snake when he asks for fish? Or would you give him a scorpion when he asks for an egg? Bad as you are, you know how to give good things to your children. How much more, then, will the Father in heaven give the Holy Spirit to those who ask him!"

Luke 11:9–13

✠

The disciples believe that God is good, but they haven't realized how much God wants to be good to *them*. God isn't like a con-man who tricks and deceives. He is like a father who loves his children and longs to give them the very best. Most of all, God wants to give us his own Holy Spirit to fill our hearts and lives. But we have to ask!

✠

Dear God and Father, please give us the gift of your Holy Spirit, the Spirit of Jesus, to fill our hearts with love for you and to help us to serve you in the family of your Church.

✠ ✠ ✠ ✠ ✠

October 19

Jesus looked round and saw rich men dropping their gifts in the temple treasury, and he also saw a very poor widow dropping in two little copper coins. He said, "I tell you that this poor widow put in more than all the others. For the others offered their gifts from what they had to spare of their riches; but she, poor as she is, gave all she had to live on."

Luke 21:1–4

✠

When we give to God – whether it be money, time or talents – there is something else he sees as well. He sees what we hold back!

This poor woman gave very little – just two tiny coins. But she held nothing back. That meant that she was in fact one of the most generous people of all time.

Lord, what we give to you is no one else's business. But between ourselves, it is important. Help us to give generously to your work – the right amounts in the right ways and for the right reasons.

✠ ✠ ✠ ✠ ✠

October 20

When Jesus finished speaking, a Pharisee invited him to eat with him; so he went in and sat down to eat. The Pharisee was surprised when he noticed that Jesus had not washed before eating. So the Lord said to him, "Now then, you Pharisees clean the outside of your cup and plate, but inside you are full of violence and evil. Fools! Did not God, who made thc outside, also make the inside? But give what is in your cups and plates to the poor, and everything will be ritually clean for you.

"How terrible for you Pharisees! You give God a tenth of the seasoning herbs, such as mint and rue and all the other herbs, but you neglect justice and love for God. These you should practise, without neglecting the others."

Luke 11:37–42

✠

The Pharisees were a group of Jews who were very particular about keeping God's law. By this they meant not just the Law of Moses, but hundreds of extra rules they had made up since. For example, they spent a lot of time washing things, and they spent ages counting out their tithes – giving God ten per cent of everything, from coins and cattle to mint and mustard.

But Jesus tells them straight: it's their hearts that need to be clean, and other people who need their time and energy.

✠

Dear Father, make us more like Jesus in every way. Give us clean hearts and loving lives – and spare us from trying to get right with you by keeping silly little rules.

✠ ✠ ✠ ✠ ✠

October 21

"Do not be worried and upset," Jesus told them. "Believe in God and believe also in me. There are many rooms in my Father's house, and I am going to prepare a place for you. I would not tell you this if it were not so. And after I go and prepare a place for you, I will come back and take you to myself, so that you will be where I am. You know the way that leads to the place where I am going."

Thomas said to him, "Lord, we do not know where you are going; so how can we know the way to get there?"

Jesus answered him, "I am the way, the truth, and the life; no one goes to the Father except by me. Now that you have known me," he said to them, "you will know my Father also, and from now on you do know him and you have seen him."

John 14:1–7

Jesus tells his friends that they needn't be afraid of dying. Heaven is God's home, and we'll find a lovely welcome there – with room for everyone.

When Thomas, with a shrug, says, "Lord, how can we get to heaven?", Jesus says very simply, "I am the way".

We don't get to heaven by passing tests or exams, or even by trying to be good. We get to heaven by trusting Jesus, sharing his life and going his way.

✠

Lord Jesus, thank you for looking after us. Thank you for getting a place ready for us in heaven, and bringing us safely home to God.

✠ ✠ ✠ ✠ ✠

October 22

Now we go back a thousand years to the time of King Solomon. Solomon, you remember, was David's son. He was known throughout the world for his wise sayings and shrewd judgements. But most of all, he wanted to build a temple in Jerusalem for the Living God.

✠

King Hiram of Tyre had always been a friend of David's, and when he heard that Solomon had succeeded his father David as king he sent ambassadors to him. Solomon sent back this message to Hiram: "You know that because of the constant wars my father David had to fight against the enemy countries all round him, he could not build a temple for the worship of the LORD his God until the LORD had given him victory over all his enemies. But now the LORD my God has given me peace on all my borders. I have no enemies, and there is no danger of attack. The LORD promised my father David, 'Your son, whom I will make king after you, will build a temple for me.' And I have now decided to build that temple for the worship of the LORD my God. So send your men to Lebanon to cut down cedars for me. My men will work with them, and I will pay your men whatever you decide. As you well know, my men don't know how to cut down trees as well as yours do."

Hiram was extremely pleased when he received Solomon's message, and he said, "Praise the LORD today for giving David such a wise son to succeed him as king of that great nation!"

1 Kings 5:1–7

✠

Solomon wants to use the years of peace to build a beautiful temple – the very best that money can buy, that stonemasons can build, and that craftsmen can decorate. And right from the beginning, he draws other people into this great work.

✠

Lord God, when you give us years of peace, help us to use the time well – to worship you in freedom, and to draw others into the life and work of your Kingdom.

October 23

Hiram supplied Solomon with all the cedar and pine logs that he wanted, and Solomon provided Hiram with two thousand metric tons of wheat and four hundred thousand litres of pure olive-oil every year to feed his men.

The LORD kept his promise and gave Solomon wisdom. There was peace between Hiram and Solomon, and they made a treaty with each other.

King Solomon drafted thirty thousand men as forced labour from all over Israel, and put Adoniram in charge of them. He divided them into three groups of ten thousand men, and each group spent one month in Lebanon and two months back home.

Solomon also had eighty thousand men in the hill-country quarrying stone, with seventy thousand men to carry it, and he placed three thousand three hundred foremen in charge of them to supervise their work.

At King Solomon's command they quarried fine large stones for the foundation of the Temple. Solomon's and Hiram's workmen and men from the city of Byblos prepared the stones and the timber to build the Temple.

1 Kings 5:10–18

✠

What an amazing project! Not only did Solomon have the vision of a beautiful building, but he was able to do the organizing as well. Notice how careful he is to give the labourers time at home, so that they can continue to look after their farms and families.

✠

Lord God, please give our leaders vision for your work today. And give us all the strength, patience and love we need to play our part.

✠ ✠ ✠ ✠ ✠

October 24

The stones with which the Temple was built had been prepared at the quarry, so that there was no noise made by hammers, axes, or any other iron tools as the Temple was being built.

In the rear of the Temple an inner room was built, where the LORD's Covenant Box was to be placed. This inner room was nine metres long, nine metres wide, and nine metres high, all covered with pure gold. The altar was covered with cedar panels. The inside of the Temple was covered with gold, and gold chains were placed across the entrance of the inner room, which was also covered with gold. The whole interior of the Temple was covered with gold, as well as the altar in the Most Holy Place.

1 Kings 6:7,19–22

✠

The Temple was built of the very best materials – and even the way in which it was built was important. There was to be no crashing and banging, but instead a quiet and peaceful reverence.

At the heart of the building was the Most Holy Place, where God was especially present, and where only the High Priest would be able to go.

Lord God, nothing but the best is good enough for you. Please forgive us the many times that our worship has been off-hand, our work has been careless, or our methods have been unworthy of you. Help us to be the best and to do our best for you today.

✠ ✠ ✠ ✠ ✠

October 25

King Solomon and all the people of Israel assembled in front of the Covenant Box and sacrificed a large number of sheep and cattle – too many to count. Then the priests carried the Covenant Box into the Temple and put it in the Most Holy Place, beneath the winged creatures. Their outstretched wings covered the box and the poles it was carried by. There was nothing inside the Covenant Box except the two stone tablets which Moses had placed there at Mount Sinai, when the LORD made a covenant with the people of Israel as they were coming from Egypt.

As the priests were leaving the Temple, it was suddenly filled with a cloud shining with the dazzling light of the LORD's presence, and they could not go back in to perform their duties. Then Solomon prayed:

"You, LORD, have placed the sun in the
  sky,
 yet you have chosen to live in clouds
  and darkness.
Now I have built a majestic temple
  for you,
 a place for you to live in for ever."

1 Kings 8:5–7,9–13

At last the wonderful building is completed, and with great ceremony the Covenant Box is brought in. But the light that dazzled the congregation was not the effect of torches and burnished gold. It was the glory of the presence of God himself.

What a thrilling confirmation it was that all these years of labour had been part of God's perfect plan. After all, if the Lord had not come to his Temple, it would have been known for ever as Solomon's Folly!

✠

Lord, we are your temples today. Please dwell in our hearts and let your glory be seen in our lives.

✠ ✠ ✠ ✠ ✠

October 26

Then in the presence of the people Solomon went and stood in front of the altar, where he raised his arms and prayed, "LORD God of Israel, there is no god like you in heaven above or on earth below! You keep your covenant with your people and show them your love when they live in whole-hearted obedience to you. You have kept the promise you made to my father David; today every word has been fulfilled..

"But can you, O God, really live on earth? Not even all heaven is large enough to hold you, so how can this Temple that I have built be large enough? LORD my God, I am your servant. Listen to my prayer, and grant the requests I make to you today. Watch over this Temple day and night, this place where you have chosen to be worshipped. Hear me when I face this Temple and pray. Hear my prayers and the prayers of your people when they face this place and pray. In your home in heaven hear us and forgive us."

1 Kings 8:22–24,27–30

✠

Despite his great wealth and wisdom, Solomon has a humble heart. He knows that even this fabulous Temple is a mere speck in the universe, and that no building on earth can ever really begin to express the greatness and grandeur of God.

Nevertheless, Solomon asks that God will guard and bless the Temple, and that it will be a focal point of repentance, forgiveness and praise for all the people.

✠

Lord, thank you for all the buildings where you are worshipped and your word is taught. May our cathedrals, churches and chapels not become museums of what you have done in the past, but spiritual power houses for the present and launching pads for mission in the future.

✠ ✠ ✠ ✠ ✠

October 27

The queen of Sheba heard of Solomon's fame, and she travelled to Jerusalem to test him with difficult questions. She brought with her a large group of attendants, as well as camels loaded with spices, jewels, and a large amount of gold. When she and Solomon met, she asked him all the questions that she could think of. He answered them all; there was nothing too difficult for him to explain. The queen of Sheba heard Solomon's wisdom and saw the palace he had built. She saw the food that was served at his table, the living quarters for his officials, the organization of his palace staff and the uniforms they wore, the servants who waited on him at feasts, and the sacrifices he offered in the Temple. It left her breathless and amazed. She said to King Solomon, "What I heard in my own country about you and your wisdom is true! But I couldn't believe it until I had come and seen it all for myself. But I didn't hear even half of it; your wisdom and wealth are much greater than what I was told."

1 Kings 10:1–7

✠

When God blesses a person or a project, other people are curious to see for themselves. The Queen of Sheba came from Africa to probe Solomon's wisdom and to see whether all that was said about him was true. And of course she found that it was not only true, but that Solomon's wealth and wisdom were even greater than she had ever imagined.

✠

Lord Jesus, may the people we know be attracted to you by the things they hear and see. For you are the one who is greater than Solomon. You are all our wealth and all our wisdom.

✠ ✠ ✠ ✠ ✠

October 28

Solomon loved many foreign women. He married them even though the LORD had commanded the Israelites not to intermarry with these people, because they would cause the Israelites to give their loyalty to other gods. They made him turn away from God, and by the time he was old they had led him into the worship of foreign gods. He was not faithful to the LORD his God, as his father David had been. He worshipped Astarte the goddess of Sidon, and Milcom the disgusting god of Ammon. He sinned against the LORD and was not true to him as his father David had been. On the mountain east of Jerusalem he built a place to worship Chemosh, the disgusting god of Moab, and a place to worship Milcom, the disgusting god of Ammon. He also built places of worship where all his foreign wives could burn incense and offer sacrifices to their own gods.

Even though the LORD, the God of Israel, had appeared to Solomon twice and had commanded him not to worship foreign gods, Solomon did not obey the LORD, but turned away from him. So the LORD was angry with Solomon and said to him, "Because you have deliberately broken your covenant with me and disobeyed my commands, I promise that I will take the kingdom away from you and give it to one of your officials. However, for the sake of your father David I will not do this in your lifetime, but during the reign of your son."

1 Kings 11:1–12

✠

What a tragedy! Solomon, who was so wise in many ways, was a fool at the last.

In his efforts to make peace treaties with other nations, he married many foreign princesses – and they brought their pagan gods and goddesses with them into the royal palace in Jerusalem.

It hurts us to see Solomon's failure, but how very honest of the Bible writers to record it. We all have dreadful defeats, but we can learn so much even from the bad times, and God is always ready to forgive those who sincerely turn to him.

✠

Lord, help us to be on our guard, lest complacency or wrong desires destroy all the good you have done in our lives.

✠ ✠ ✠ ✠ ✠

October 29

When Solomon died, his son Rehoboam became king. Naturally, the people were anxious to know what kind of ruler he intended to be. Gentle and caring, or ruthless and bullying?

The people of the northern tribes sent for Jeroboam, and then they all went together to Rehoboam and said to him, "Your father Solomon treated us harshly and placed heavy burdens on us. If you make these burdens lighter and make life easier for us, we will be your loyal subjects."

"Come back in three days and I will give you my answer," he replied. So they left.

King Rehoboam consulted the older men who had served as his father Solomon's advisers. "What answer do you advise me to give these people?" he asked.

They replied, "If you want to serve this people well, give a favourable answer to their request, and they will always serve you loyally."

But he ignored the advice of the older men and went instead to the young men who had grown up with him and who were now his advisers. "What do you advise me to do?" he asked. "What shall I say to the people who are asking me to make their burdens lighter?"

They replied, "This is what you should tell them: 'My little finger is thicker than my father's waist!' Tell them, 'My father placed heavy burdens on you; I will make them even heavier. He beat you with a whip; I'll flog you with a horsewhip!'"

1 Kings 12:3–11

✠

Rehoboam is different from his father Solomon and his grandfather David. They had both looked for God's wisdom when they had to make hard decisions. But Rehoboam listens to his hot-headed friends. And that's a formula for disaster.

✠

Lord God, we ask you to bless and guide those who lead, especially when they are tempted to use their power selfishly. May they quickly discover your better way of selfless service and care for others.

✠ ✠ ✠ ✠ ✠

October 30

Three days later Jeroboam and all the people returned to King Rehoboam, as he had instructed them. The king ignored the advice of the older men and spoke harshly to the people, as the younger men had advised. He said, "My father placed heavy burdens on you; I will make them even heavier. He beat you with a whip; I'll flog you with a horsewhip!"

When the people saw that the king would not listen to them, they shouted, "Down with David and his family! What have they ever done for us? Men of Israel, let's go home! Let Rehoboam look out for himself!"

So the people of Israel rebelled, leaving Rehoboam as king only of the people who lived in the territory of Judah.

When the people of Israel heard that Jeroboam had returned from Egypt, they invited him to a meeting of the people and made him king of Israel. Only the tribe of Judah remained loyal to David's descendants.

1 Kings 12:12–14,16–17,20

✠

So Rehoboam makes a fatal decision. And because he threatens his people, some of them refuse to be ruled by him at all.

The kingdom of David and Solomon is split in two – Israel in the north, and Judah in the south. Things will never be the same again.

✠

Lord, when our leaders turn their backs on you, everybody suffers. Please have mercy on our perplexed and divided world. May all nations learn to look to you, and find the unity and peace for which we long.

✠ ✠ ✠ ✠ ✠

October 31

Ahab son of Omri became king of Israel, and he ruled in Samaria for twenty-two years. He sinned against the LORD more than any of his predecessors. It was not enough for him to sin like King Jeroboam; he went further and married Jezebel, the daughter of King Ethbaal of Sidon, and worshipped Baal. He built a temple to Baal in Samaria, made an altar for him, and put it in the temple. He also put up an image of the goddess Asherah. He did more to arouse the anger of the LORD, the God of Israel, than all the kings of Israel before him.

A prophet named Elijah, from Tishbe in Gilead, said to King Ahab, "In the name of the LORD, the living God of Israel, whom I serve, I tell you that there will be no dew or rain for the next two or three years until I say so."

Then the LORD said to Elijah, "Leave this place and go east and hide yourself near the brook of Cherith, east of the Jordan. The brook will supply you with water to drink, and I have commanded ravens to bring you food there."

Elijah obeyed the LORD's command, and went and stayed by the brook of Cherith. He drank water from the brook, and ravens brought him bread and meat every morning and every evening. After a while the brook dried up because of the lack of rain.

1 Kings 16:29–33; 17:1–7

✠

Ahab brings the kingdom of Israel to an all-time low. Not only does he ignore God's laws, but he marries the most wicked woman ever mentioned in the Bible – Jezebel! She is steeped in the violent and disgusting worship of Baal, and she wants the whole nation to follow her.

But into this dreadful situation steps one of God's greatest and most fearless servants – Elijah. Elijah is a prophet who will make sure that King Ahab can never get the Living God out of his mind. For a start, there's going to be a drought. No rain for three years – not a drop!

✠

Lord, thank you for those people who remind us of you – even those who make us feel a bit uncomfortable, because we know they are usually right.

✠ ✠ ✠ ✠ ✠

A Psalm for
November

I look to the mountains;
   where will my help come from?
My help will come from the LORD,
   who made heaven and earth.

He will not let you fall;
   your protector is always awake.

The protector of Israel
   never dozes or sleeps.
The LORD will guard you;
   he is by your side to protect you.
The sun will not hurt you during the day,
   nor the moon during the night.

The LORD will protect you from all danger;
   he will keep you safe.
He will protect you as you come and go
   now and for ever.

Psalm 121:1–8

November 1

Then the LORD said to Elijah, "Now go to the town of Zarephath, near Sidon, and stay there. I have commanded a widow who lives there to feed you." So Elijah went to Zarephath, and as he came to the gate of the town, he saw a widow gathering firewood. "Please bring me a drink of water," he said to her. And as she was going to get it, he called out, "And please bring me some bread, too."

She answered, "By the living LORD your God I swear that I haven't got any bread. All I have is a handful of flour in a bowl and a drop of olive-oil in a jar. I came here to gather some firewood to take back home and prepare what little I have for my son and me. That will be our last meal, and then we will starve to death."

"Don't worry," Elijah said to her. "Go ahead and prepare your meal. But first make a small loaf from what you have and bring it to me, and then prepare the rest for you and your son. For this is what the LORD, the God of Israel, says: 'The bowl will not run out of flour or the jar run out of oil before the day that I, the LORD, send rain.'"

The widow went and did as Elijah had told her, and all of them had enough food for many days. As the

LORD had promised through Elijah, the bowl did not run out of flour nor did the jar run out of oil.

1 Kings 17:8–16

✠

God promises to provide the everyday needs of those who trust him simply and completely. The widow dared to believe Elijah's message of hope, even to the extent of giving him the last of her food.

✠

Lord, help us to put you first, others next, and ourselves last. Then we will see that your way of love is the only style of life that really works.

✠ ✠ ✠ ✠ ✠

November 2

Some time later the widow's son fell ill; he got worse and worse, and finally he died. She said to Elijah, "Man of God, why did you do this to me? Did you come here to remind God of my sins and so cause my son's death?"

"Give the boy to me," Elijah said. He took the boy from her arms, carried him upstairs to the room where he was staying, and laid him on the bed. Then he prayed aloud, "O LORD my God, why have you done such a terrible thing to this widow? She has been kind enough to take care of me, and now you kill her son!" Then Elijah stretched himself out on the boy three times and prayed, "O LORD my God, restore this child to life!"

The LORD answered Elijah's prayer; the child started breathing again and revived.

Elijah took the boy back downstairs to his mother and said to her, "Look, your son is alive!"

She answered, "Now I know that you are a man of God and that the LORD really speaks through you!"

1 Kings 17:17–24

✠

When the widow's son becomes ill and dies, Elijah doesn't hesitate to give God a piece of his mind! Are we as honest with God when something terrible happens?

But God has allowed the boy to die so that his power may be seen more clearly. Sometimes this is the only good thing to be said about tragedy – that it forces us to rely on God more completely than we have ever done before.

✠

Lord God our Father, we pray that you will give health and safety to those we love. And if you ever do allow tragedy to befall us, please give us the faith to look to you. You are the one who can bring good out of evil and life out of death.

✠ ✠ ✠ ✠ ✠

November 3

Ahab set off to meet Elijah. When Ahab saw him, he said, "So there you are – the worst troublemaker in Israel!"

"I'm not the troublemaker," Elijah answered. "You are – you and your father. You are disobeying the LORD's commands and worshipping the idols of Baal. Now order all the people of Israel to meet me at Mount Carmel. Bring along the 450 prophets of Baal and the 400 prophets of the goddess Asherah who are supported by Queen Jezebel."

So Ahab summoned all the Israelites and the prophets of Baal to meet at Mount Carmel. Elijah went up to the people and said, "How much longer will it take you to make up your minds? If the LORD is God, worship him; but if Baal is God, worship him!" But the people didn't say a word. Then Elijah said, "I am the only prophet of the LORD still left, but there are 450 prophets of Baal. Bring two bulls; let the prophets of Baal take one, kill it, cut it in pieces, and put it on the wood – but don't light the fire. I will do the same with the other bull. Then let the prophets of Baal pray to their god, and I will pray to the LORD, and the one who answers by sending fire – he is God."

The people shouted their approval.

1 Kings 18:16–24

For many months the struggle has been going on between the followers of Baal and those who worship the Lord. Baal was supposed to be the god who gave the rainy season and the annual growth, but at the word of the Lord there has been a long drought.

Elijah sees that the people have been in two minds about which god is real. The time has come for a show-down!

✠

Lord, please forgive us for those times when we haven't fully trusted you. You have said you would provide our needs, but we have still been anxious. You have told us to forgive others, but we have still nursed grudges and complaints. Help us today to be as bold as Elijah in our stand for you.

✠ ✠ ✠ ✠ ✠

November 4

Then Elijah said to the prophets of Baal, "Since there are so many of you, you take a bull and prepare it first. Pray to your god, but don't set fire to the wood."

They took the bull that was brought to them, prepared it, and prayed to Baal until noon. They shouted, "Answer us, Baal!" and kept dancing round the altar they had built. But no answer came.

At noon Elijah started making fun of them: "Pray louder! He is a god! Maybe he is day-dreaming or relieving himself, or perhaps he's gone on a journey! Or maybe he's sleeping, and you've got to wake him up!" So the prophets prayed louder and cut themselves with knives and daggers, according to their ritual, until blood flowed. They kept on ranting and raving until the middle of the afternoon; but no answer came, not a sound was heard.

Then Elijah said to the people, "Come closer to me," and they all gathered round him. He set about repairing the altar of the LORD which had been torn down. He took twelve stones, one for each of the twelve tribes named after the sons of Jacob, the man to whom the LORD had given the name Israel. With these stones he rebuilt the altar for the worship of the LORD. He dug a trench round it, large enough to hold almost fourteen litres of water. Then he placed the wood on the altar, cut the bull in pieces, and laid it on the wood. He said, "Fill four jars with water and pour it on the offering and the wood." They did so, and he said, "Do it again" – and they did. "Do it once more," he said – and they did.

The water ran down round the altar and filled the trench.

1 Kings 18:25–35

✠

Elijah is hopelessly outnumbered by 450 prophets of Baal and 400 prophets of the goddess Asherah. The king and queen are against him, and the rest of the people are undecided.

Even so, Elijah lets his enemies have their turn first. And when it is time for him to call on the Living God for fire, he thoroughly douses the altar and the sacrifice with water. If God answers, it will not be by fluke, accident, or trickery!

✠

Lord, our Living God, may we not be afraid to speak and act for you, even when everyone else disagrees.

November 5

At the hour of the afternoon sacrifice the prophet Elijah approached the altar and prayed, "O LORD, the God of Abraham, Isaac, and Jacob, prove now that you are the God of Israel and that I am your servant and have done all this at your command. Answer me, LORD, answer me, so that this people will know that you, the LORD, are God, and that you are bringing them back to yourself."

The LORD sent fire down, and it burnt up the sacrifice, the wood, and the stones, scorched the earth and dried up the water in the trench. When the people saw this, they threw themselves on the ground and exclaimed, "The LORD is God; the LORD alone is God!"

Elijah ordered, "Seize the prophets of Baal; don't let any of them get away!" The people seized them all, and Elijah led them down to the River Kishon and killed them.

1 Kings 18:36–40

✠

Elijah prays and everyone else holds their breath. No one knows better than Elijah that his own life is on the line, for if God doesn't answer with fire, there will be no escape from his enemies.

And then the fire falls! It burns not just the wood and the sacrifice, but the very stones of the altar and the earth around. Everyone sees without a shadow of doubt that God is with his servant Elijah – and that one man with God is a majority!

✠

Lord, thank you that everything is possible for you, and that you promise to be closest to us at the times of our greatest need.

✠ ✠ ✠ ✠ ✠

November 6

Then Elijah said to King Ahab, "Now, go and eat. I hear the roar of rain approaching." While Ahab went to eat, Elijah climbed to the top of Mount Carmel, where he bowed down to the ground, with his head between his knees. He said to his servant, "Go and look towards the sea."

The servant went and returned, saying, "I didn't see anything." Seven times in all Elijah told him to go and look. The seventh time he returned and said, "I saw a little cloud no bigger than a man's hand, coming up from the sea."

Elijah ordered his servant, "Go to King Ahab and tell him to get into his chariot and go back home before the rain stops him."

In a little while the sky was covered with dark clouds, the wind began to blow, and heavy rain began to fall. Ahab got into his chariot and started back to Jezreel. The power of the LORD came on Elijah; he fastened his clothes tight round his waist and ran ahead of Ahab all the way to Jezreel.

1 Kings 18:41–46

✠

Just as certainly as he had promised fire, Elijah now forecasts rain. A hard rain is going to fall, and the king and his servants had best get themselves and their chariots home before the flood.

So the long drought ends. Not just the years of dearth and famine, but the spiritual dryness of people's hearts. All over Israel men and women are talking excitedly of the great things God is doing among them.

✠

Lord, give us the faith which looks for what you are doing and listens for what you are saying. May we be landmarks and beacons for you, so that others may be attracted to your love.

✠ ✠ ✠ ✠ ✠

November 7

King Ahab told his wife Jezebel everything that Elijah had done and how he had put all the prophets of Baal to death. She sent a message to Elijah: "May the gods strike me dead if by this time tomorrow I don't do the same thing to you that you did to the prophets." Elijah was afraid, and fled for his life; he took his servant and went to Beersheba in Judah.

Leaving the servant there, Elijah walked a whole day into the wilderness. He stopped and sat down in the shade of a tree and wished he would die. "It's too much, LORD," he prayed. "Take away my life; I might as well be dead!"

He lay down under the tree and fell asleep. Suddenly an angel touched him and said, "Wake up and eat." He looked round, and saw a loaf of bread and a jar of water near his head. He ate and drank, and lay down again. The LORD's angel returned and woke him up a second time, saying, "Get up and eat, or the journey will be too much for you." Elijah got up, ate and drank, and the food gave him enough strength to walk forty days to Sinai, the holy mountain. There he went into a cave to spend the night.

1 Kings 19:1–9

✠

After the epic battle at Mount Carmel and the long run back to the palace, Elijah is exhausted. And when he hears of Jezebel's terrible threat, he panics. Torn between fear and faith, he runs for his life – and yet he longs to die.

None of us can go on for ever without getting tired. We have "high" times of excitement and success, but we need "quiet" times of rest and reflection as well.

And it's when we come to the end of our own energies that God can come close and minister to us.

✠

Lord, please help us to live balanced lives. Keep us from overwork on the one hand and laziness on the other. May we take our lives at your chosen pace for us today.

✠ ✠ ✠ ✠ ✠

November 8

Suddenly the LORD spoke to him, "Elijah, what are you doing here?"

He answered, "LORD God Almighty, I have always served you – you alone. But the people of Israel have broken their covenant with you, torn down your altars, and killed all your prophets. I am the only one left – and they are trying to kill me!"

"Go out and stand before me on top of the mountain," the LORD said to him. Then the LORD passed by and sent a furious wind that split the hills and shattered the rocks – but the LORD was not in the wind. The wind stopped blowing, and then there was an earthquake – but the LORD was not in the earthquake.

After the earthquake, there was a fire – but the LORD was not in the fire. And after the fire, there was the soft whisper of a voice.

When Elijah heard it, he covered his face with his cloak and went out and stood at the entrance of the cave. A voice said to him, "Elijah, what are you doing here?"

He answered, "LORD God Almighty, I have always served you – you alone. But the people of Israel have broken their covenant with you, torn down your altars, and killed all your prophets. I am the only one left – and they are trying to kill me."

The LORD said, "Return to the wilderness near Damascus, then enter the city and anoint Hazael as king of Syria; anoint Jehu son of Nimshi as king of Israel, and anoint Elisha son of Shaphat from Abel Meholah to succeed you as prophet. Anyone who escapes being put to death by Hazael will be killed by Jehu, and anyone who escapes Jehu will be killed by Elisha. Yet I will leave seven thousand people alive in Israel – all those who are loyal to me and have not bowed to Baal or kissed his idol."

1 Kings 19:9–18

✠

Elijah feels so totally alone. Surely he is the only one in all Israel who is faithful to the Living God. And where *is* the Living God anyway? Why doesn't he speak in earthquake, wind and fire, like he did to Moses on this mountain long ago?

And then God *does* speak to Elijah, but in a new way. After all the noise of Elijah's anger and self-pity, there comes the quiet whisper of God. And in the quietness Elijah receives assurance of God's care and clear guidance for the future. God's instructions include the very things Elijah longs to see: a new king for the people, and a new companion for himself.

✠

Lord, if only we will stop clamouring at you with our own plans and wait quietly so that you can tell us yours! Please help us to be still and attentive, so that you can speak to us in new ways.

✠ ✠ ✠ ✠ ✠

November 9

Elijah left and found Elisha ploughing with a team of oxen; there were eleven teams ahead of him, and he was ploughing with the last one. Elijah took off his cloak and put it on Elisha. Elisha then left his oxen, ran after Elijah, and said, "Let me kiss my father and mother good-bye, and then I will go with you."

Elijah answered, "All right, go back. I'm not stopping you!"

Then Elisha went to his team of oxen, killed them, and cooked the meat, using the yoke as fuel for the fire. He gave the meat to the people, and they ate it. Then he went and followed Elijah as his helper.

1 Kings 19:19–21

✠

God is giving Elijah a most precious gift – a young man to keep him company and share his load; someone ready to carry on his work when he dies.

Elijah's way of "catching" Elisha is to throw his battered old cloak over him – and he seems a bit put out when the young man wants to go and say goodbye to his family. But, like Jesus many centuries later, Elijah's call is straight and uncompromising. This was no time for Elisha to hesitate. And just look how he shows that he's made up his mind!

✠

Lord, when you call us to follow you, help us to respond gladly, wholeheartedly, and promptly.

✠ ✠ ✠ ✠ ✠

November 10

The time came for the LORD to take Elijah up to heaven in a whirlwind. Elijah and Elisha set out from Gilgal, and on the way Elijah said to Elisha, "Now stay here; the LORD has ordered me to go to Bethel."

But Elisha answered, "I swear by my loyalty to the living LORD and to you that I will not leave you." So they went on to Bethel.

A group of prophets who lived there went to Elisha and asked him, "Do you know that the LORD is going to take your master away from you today?"

"Yes, I know," Elisha answered. "But let's not talk about it."

Then Elijah said to Elisha, "Now stay here; the LORD has ordered me to go to Jericho."

But Elisha answered, "I swear by my loyalty to the living LORD and to you that I will not leave you." So they went on to Jericho.

A group of prophets who lived there went to Elisha and asked him, "Do you know that the LORD is going to take your master away from you today?"

"Yes, I know," Elisha answered. "But let's not talk about it."

Then Elijah said to Elisha, "Now stay here; the LORD has ordered me to go to the River Jordan."

But Elisha answered, "I swear by my loyalty to the living LORD and to you that I will not leave you." So they went on, and fifty of the prophets followed them to the Jordan.

2 Kings 2:1–7

✠

Some awesome event is about to happen. Elijah knows it. The groups of prophets around the country sense it. The great prophet's time on earth is coming to an end, and he seems to be restlessly seeking the right place in which to die.

Elisha is faithful to the end. He refuses to be left with any of the groups of prophets they visit.

✠

Lord God, thank you for those who love us. And when we're unsettled, or facing some particular crisis, thank you for those who stay with us and see us through.

✠ ✠ ✠ ✠ ✠

November 11

Elijah and Elisha stopped by the river, and the fifty prophets stood a short distance away. Then Elijah took off his cloak, rolled it up, and struck the water with it; the water divided, and he and Elisha crossed to the other side on dry ground. There, Elijah said to Elisha,

"Tell me what you want me to do for you before I am taken away."

"Let me receive the share of your power that will make me your successor," Elisha answered.

"That is a difficult request to grant," Elijah replied. "But you will receive it if you see me as I am being taken away from you; if you don't see me, you won't receive it."

They kept talking as they walked on; then suddenly a chariot of fire pulled by horses of fire came between them, and Elijah was taken up to heaven by a whirlwind. Elisha saw it and cried out to Elijah, "My father, my father! Mighty defender of Israel! You are gone!" And he never saw Elijah again.

In grief, Elisha tore his cloak in two. Then he picked up Elijah's cloak that had fallen from him, and went back and stood on the bank of the Jordan. He struck the water with Elijah's cloak, and said, "Where is the LORD, the God of Elijah?" Then he struck the water again, and it divided, and he walked over to the other side.

2 Kings 2:7–14

✠

So Elijah is taken to be with the God he loved so well and served so courageously. The fact that he was carried up to heaven in a fiery chariot reminds us that God never intended mankind to die. Death is something that has come in because of our sinful nature.

Meanwhile, Elisha has his dearest wish granted. He has Elijah's cloak on his back and God's power in his life.

✠

Loving Lord, help us to live each day in such a way that when we die we may find ourselves caught up triumphantly into the life of heaven.

✠ ✠ ✠ ✠ ✠

November 12

Naaman, the commander of the Syrian army, was highly respected and esteemed by the king of Syria, because through Naaman the LORD had given victory to the Syrian forces. He was a great soldier, but he suffered from a dreaded skin-disease. In one of their raids against Israel, the Syrians had carried off a little Israelite girl, who became a servant of Naaman's wife. One day she said to her mistress, "I wish that my master could go to the prophet who lives in Samaria! He would cure him of his disease." When Naaman heard of this, he went to the king and told him what the girl had said. The king said, "Go to the king of Israel and take this letter to him."

So Naaman set out, taking thirty thousand pieces of silver, six thousand pieces of gold, and ten changes of fine clothes. The letter that he took read: "This letter will introduce my officer Naaman. I want you to cure him of his disease."

When the king of Israel read the letter, he tore his clothes in dismay and exclaimed, "How can the king of Syria expect me to cure this man? Does he think that I am God, with the power of life and death? It's plain that he is trying to start a quarrel with me!"

When the prophet Elisha heard what had happened, he sent word to the king: "Why are you so upset? Send the man to me, and I'll show him that there is a prophet in Israel!"

2 Kings 5:1–8

✠

Naaman may be the greatest soldier in the land, but his days are numbered. He has leprosy, which means he will slowly die. And anyone nursing him will catch the disease as well.

But in Naaman's stricken household is a bright little girl from Israel. She knows the power of God through his servant Elisha, and she plucks up courage to tell Naaman's wife that the prophet can certainly help.

✠

Lord God, we have problems which only you can solve. Help us to be quick to bring them to you – and to encourage other people to do the same with their troubles.

✠ ✠ ✠ ✠ ✠

November 13

So Naaman went with his horses and chariot, and stopped at the entrance to Elisha's house. Elisha sent a servant out to tell him to go and wash himself seven times in the River Jordan, and he would be completely cured of his disease. But Naaman left in a rage, saying, "I thought that he would at least come out to me, pray to the Lord his God, wave his hand over the diseased spot, and cure me! Besides, aren't the rivers Abana and Pharpar, back in Damascus, better than any river in Israel? I could have washed in them and been cured!"

His servants went up to him and said, "Sir, if the prophet had told you to do something difficult, you would have done it. Now why can't you just wash yourself, as he said, and be cured?" So Naaman went down to the Jordan, dipped himself in it seven times, as Elisha had instructed, and he was completely cured. His flesh became firm and healthy, like that of a child. He returned to Elisha with all his men and said, "Now I know that there is no god but the God of Israel; so please, sir, accept a gift from me."

Elisha answered, "By the living LORD, whom I serve, I swear that I will not accept a gift."

Naaman insisted that he accept it, but he would not. So Naaman said, "If you won't accept my gift, then let me have two mule-loads of earth to take home with me, because from now on I will not offer sacrifices or burnt-offerings to any god except the LORD. So I hope that the LORD will forgive me when I accompany my king to the temple of Rimmon, the god of Syria, and worship him. Surely the LORD will forgive me!"

"Go in peace," Elisha said. And Naaman left.

2 Kings 5:9–19

✠

Naaman may need help desperately, but he's still very proud. He comes in search of Elisha with gifts of money and clothes, and with a letter from his king.

But Elisha has other ideas. He sends a message telling the great man to go jump in the Jordan – or at least to dip himself seven times in its muddy waters!

When Naaman humbles himself to do it, God wonderfully heals him. So Naaman is cured not just of leprosy but of the terrible disease of pride as well. He takes some earth home, because he wants to worship the Living God on a little piece of the Promised Land.

✠

Lord, may we always be "little" people in our own eyes – not putting on airs or insisting on our rights. Instead, may we humbly enter in at the low door which leads to your kingdom of peace.

✠ ✠ ✠ ✠ ✠

November 14

Naaman had gone only a short distance, when Elisha's servant Gehazi said to himself, "My master has let Naaman get away without paying a thing! He should have accepted what that Syrian offered him. By the living LORD, I will run after him and get something from him." So he set off after Naaman. When Naaman saw a man running after him, he got down from his chariot to meet him, and asked, "Is something wrong?"

"No," Gehazi answered. "But my master sent me to tell you that just now two members of the group of prophets in the hill-country of Ephraim arrived, and he would like you to give them three thousand pieces of silver and two changes of fine clothes."

"Please take six thousand pieces of silver," Naaman replied. He insisted on it, tied up the silver in two bags, gave them and two changes of fine clothes to two of his servants, and sent them on ahead of Gehazi. When they reached the hill where Elisha lived, Gehazi took the two bags and carried them into the house. Then he sent Naaman's servants back. He went back into the house, and Elisha asked him, "Where have you been?"

"Oh, nowhere, sir," he answered.

But Elisha said, "Wasn't I there in spirit when the man got out of his chariot to meet you? This is no time to accept money and clothes, olive-groves and vine-yards, sheep and cattle, or servants! And now Naaman's disease will come upon you, and you and your descendants will have it for ever!"

When Gehazi left, he had the disease – his skin was as white as snow.

2 Kings 5:19–27

✠

Elisha had refused any payment for Naaman's cure. He wanted to make it clear that this was something God had done freely and for love. But Gehazi can't bear to lose sight of all that wealth, and his greed leads him first to lies, and then to disease and death.

✠

Dear Father, help us to give to others with the simple love and generosity that you so constantly show to us, through Jesus Christ our Lord.

✠ ✠ ✠ ✠ ✠

November 15

Hezekiah son of Ahaz became king of Judah at the age of twenty-five, and he ruled in Jerusalem for twenty-nine years. His mother was Abijah, the daughter of Zechariah. Following the example of his ancestor King David, he did what was pleasing to the LORD. He destroyed the pagan places of worship, broke the stone pillars, and cut down the images of the goddess Asherah. He also broke in pieces the bronze snake that Moses had made, which was called Nehushtan. Up to that time the people of Israel had burnt incense in its honour. Hezekiah trusted in the LORD, the God of Israel; Judah never had another king like him, either before or after his time. He was faithful to the LORD and never disobeyed him, but carefully kept all the commands that the LORD had given Moses. So the LORD was with him, and he was successful in everything he did.

2 Kings 18:1–7

✠

What a difference a king makes! Hezekiah set himself to follow the good example of King David. He cleared out all the hideous pagan shrines, and put an end to the mumbo-jumbo of worshipping the old bronze serpent.

It must have taken immense courage to do these things, for there would be many to say "We told you so" if he had then suffered defeat, illness or misfortune. But we read that God honoured Hezekiah's actions and kept faith with him.

✠

Lord God, help us to put you first in our worship, and to live our lives in the light of your truth.

✠ ✠ ✠ ✠ ✠

November 16

The Assyrian emperor sent a large army from Lachish to attack Hezekiah at Jerusalem; it was commanded by his three highest officials. When they arrived at Jerusalem, they occupied the road where the clothmakers work, by the ditch that brings water from the upper pond. Then they sent for King Hezekiah, and three of his officials went out to meet them.

One of the Assyrian officials told them that the emperor wanted to know what made King Hezekiah so confident. He demanded, "Do you think that words can take the place of military skill and might? Who do you think will help you rebel against Assyria? You are expecting Egypt to help you, but that would be like using a reed as a walking-stick – it would break and jab your hand. That is what the king of Egypt is like when anyone relies on him."

Then the official stood up and shouted in Hebrew, "Listen to what the emperor of Assyria is telling you! He warns you not to let Hezekiah deceive you. Hezekiah can't save you. And don't let him persuade you to rely on the LORD. Don't think that the LORD will save you, and that he will stop our Assyrian army from capturing your city."

2 Kings 18:17–21,28–30

✠

The armed might of Assyria is being thrown against Jerusalem, and it's clear that King Hezekiah and his people will be defeated. They could try making an alliance with Egypt, but it would probably be of little use – and the Assyrians know it. So why is Hezekiah so confident in the face of disaster? We know, don't we?

✠

Lord God, you are the creator of heaven and earth and your power is greater than any enemy we may have. Thank you that you invite us to trust you completely, whatever the odds; and that we are always safe in your care.

✠ ✠ ✠ ✠ ✠

November 17

As soon as King Hezekiah heard their report, he tore his clothes in grief, put on sackcloth, and went to the Temple of the Lord. He sent Eliakim, the official in charge of the palace, Shebna, the court secretary, and the senior priests to the prophet Isaiah son of Amoz. They also were wearing sackcloth. This is the message which he told them to give Isaiah: "Today is a day of suffering; we are being punished and are in disgrace. We are like a woman who is ready to give birth, but is too weak to do it. The Assyrian emperor has sent his chief official to insult the living God. May the Lord your God hear these insults and punish those who spoke them. So pray to God for those of our people who survive."

When Isaiah received King Hezekiah's message, he sent back this answer: "The LORD tells you not to let the Assyrians frighten you with their claims that he cannot save you. The LORD will cause the emperor to hear a rumour that will make him go back to his own country, and the LORD will have him killed there."

2 Kings 19:1–7

✠

King Hezekiah is confident on the outside, but in his heart he knows that he and his people are in terrible trouble. But like a true man of God, he takes his problem to the Lord. He puts on sackcloth to show that he is poor in God's sight, and sends important messengers to ask the prophet Isaiah to pray for them all.

What a wonderful glimmer of hope it must have been when Isaiah replied, "Don't worry – the Living God is in control and he will save you."

✠

Mighty God, help us to trust in your protection in the face of every enemy, however strong.

✠ ✠ ✠ ✠ ✠

November 18

Isaiah said to King Hezekiah: "This is what the LORD has said about the Assyrian emperor: 'He will not enter this city or shoot a single arrow against it. No soldiers with shields will come near the city, and no siege-mounds will be built round it. He will go back by the same road he came, without entering this city. I, the LORD, have spoken. I will defend this city and protect it, for the sake of my own honour and because of the promise I made to my servant David.'"

That night an angel of the LORD went to the Assyrian camp and killed 185,000 soldiers. At dawn the next day, there they lay, all dead! Then the Assyrian emperor Sennacherib withdrew and returned to Nineveh. One day, when he was worshipping in the temple of his god Nisroch, two of his sons, Adrammelech and Sharezer, killed him with their swords, and then escaped.

2 Kings 19:32–37

✠

We don't know precisely what happened to the Assyrian army that night, but the result was devastating. Perhaps a plague swept through the camp, killing so many thousands of soldiers that the Emperor was forced to retreat.

For King Hezekiah and his people it is a deliverance beyond their wildest dreams. God has stepped in with perfect power and timing, to show that he alone is able to save.

✠

Lord, we pray that you will save and deliver everyone who turns to you in their trouble today. And may we never forget to give you the glory for the great things you have done.

✠ ✠ ✠ ✠ ✠

November 19

Manasseh was twelve years old when he became king of Judah, and he ruled in Jerusalem for fifty-five years. His mother was Hephzibah. Following the disgusting practices of the nations whom the LORD had driven out of the land as his people advanced, Manasseh sinned against the LORD. He rebuilt the pagan places of worship that his father Hezekiah had destroyed; he built altars for the worship of Baal and made an image of the goddess Asherah, as King Ahab of Israel had done. Manasseh also worshipped the stars. He built pagan altars in the Temple, the place that the LORD had said was where he should be worshipped. In the two courtyards of the Temple he built altars for the worship of the stars. He sacrificed his son as a burnt-offering. He practised divination and magic and consulted fortune-tellers and mediums. He sinned greatly against the LORD and stirred up his anger.

2 Kings 21:1–6

✠

Manasseh reigned longer than any other king of Judah, and his rule was the worst of all. He encouraged many occult practices (occult means "hidden"), some of which are still around today.

The Bible tells us not to go to the stars or to fortune-tellers for guidance, because God alone is truth and his law is our perfect guide. Nor are we to seek help in magical arts, or by worshipping idols, because Satan can use these practices to bring us into slavery and fear.

✠

Lord God, help us to heed the warnings of scripture, and deliver us from evil.

✠ ✠ ✠ ✠ ✠

November 20

Josiah was eight years old when he became king of Judah, and he ruled in Jerusalem for thirty-one years. Josiah did what was pleasing to the LORD; he followed the example of his ancestor King David, strictly obeying all the laws of God.

In the eighteenth year of his reign, King Josiah sent the court secretary Shaphan, the son of Azaliah and grandson of Meshullam, to the Temple with the order: "Go to the High Priest Hilkiah and get a report on the amount of money that the priests on duty at the entrance to the Temple have collected from the people. Tell him to give the money to the men who are in charge of the repairs in the Temple."

Shaphan delivered the king's order to Hilkiah, and Hilkiah told him that he had found the book of the Law in the Temple. Hilkiah gave him the book, and Shaphan read it. Then he went back to the king and reported: "Your servants have taken the money that was in the Temple and have handed it over to the men in charge of the repairs." And then he said, "I have here a book that Hilkiah gave me." And he read it aloud to the king.

When the king heard the book being read, he tore his clothes in dismay.

2 Kings 22:1–5,8–11

Josiah was only eight when he became king, but he already knew right from wrong, and he aimed simply to please God. It's never too early to listen for God's will in our lives, and no one is too young to be able to please him.

One day, when Josiah is well into his twenties, a most precious book is discovered in the Temple. It's not that the Temple had been neglected – we know that there were people in charge of repairs. Nor was it that the Temple was deserted – there were priests in attendance and pilgrims visiting. But the heart of Judah's religion – obedience to God's laws – had been lost and forgotten.

✠

Lord God, maybe we need a spring-clean in our lives – in case we have allowed all the clutter of our busyness to squeeze you out.

✠ ✠ ✠ ✠ ✠

November 21

King Josiah summoned all the leaders of Judah and Jerusalem, and together they went to the Temple, accompanied by the priests and the prophets and all the rest of the people, rich and poor alike. Before them all, the king read aloud the whole book of the covenant which had been found in the Temple. He stood by the royal column and made a covenant with the LORD to obey him, to keep his laws and commands with all his heart and soul, and to put into practice the demands attached to the covenant, as written in the book. And all the people promised to keep the covenant.

Then Josiah ordered the High Priest Hilkiah, his assistant priests, and the guards on duty at the entrance to the Temple to bring out of the Temple all the objects used in the worship of Baal, of the goddess Asherah, and of the stars. The king burnt all these objects outside the city near the valley of the Kidron, and then had the ashes taken to Bethel.

2 Kings 23:1–4

✠

It sounds as though the Temple had become a junkyard of idols, without anyone realizing how far they were straying from God's commandments.

Now Josiah reads the terms of the Covenant to the people – to love God with all their heart, soul, mind and strength, and to open themselves to receive God's blessing and protection.

Now God's people can start all over again – thanks to King Josiah's own good example.

✠

Lord, help us to rid our lives of all the things which crowd out our love for you. Thank you that you are always willing for us to come to you and start again.

✠ ✠ ✠ ✠ ✠

November 22

King Josiah ordered the people to celebrate the Passover in honour of the LORD their God, as written in the book of the covenant. No Passover like this one had ever been celebrated by any of the kings of Israel or of Judah, since the time when judges ruled the nation. Now at last, in the eighteenth year of the reign of Josiah, the Passover was celebrated in Jerusalem.

In order to enforce the laws written in the book that the High Priest Hilkiah had found in the Temple, King Josiah removed from Jerusalem and the rest of Judah all the mediums and fortune-tellers, and all the household gods, idols, and all other pagan objects of worship. There had never been a king like him before, who served the LORD with all his heart, mind, and strength, obeying all the Law of Moses; nor has there been a king like him since.

2 Kings 23:21–25

✠

What a wholehearted person is King Josiah! He doesn't say, "Times have changed – we can't do that nowadays!" or "It's never been done before!" Instead, he looks into God's Law, and then sets out to obey it.

It must have caused a lot of heart-searching to tell people to throw out their favourite idols. And of course the people who made them were put out of work – and the fortune-tellers and mediums were sent away altogether.

But Josiah knew that if he was to please God, then hard decisions like this would have to be made clearly and carried out firmly.

✠

Dear Lord, may the leaders of our church and the leaders of our nation learn to be afraid only of you; for when we care about what you think and want more than anything else, we are well on the road to doing what's best for everyone.

✠ ✠ ✠ ✠ ✠

November 23

But the LORD's fierce anger had been aroused against Judah by what King Manasseh had done, and even now it did not die down. The LORD said, "I will do to Judah what I have done to Israel: I will banish the people of Judah from my sight and I will reject Jerusalem, the city I chose, and the Temple, the place I said was where I should be worshipped."

Zedekiah rebelled against King Nebuchadnezzar of Babylonia, so Nebuchadnezzar came with all his army and attacked Jerusalem on the tenth day of the tenth month of the ninth year of Zedekiah's reign. They set up camp outside the city, built siege walls round it, and kept it under siege until Zedekiah's eleventh year. On the ninth day of the fourth month of that same year, when the famine was so bad that the people had nothing left to eat, the city walls were broken through. Although the Babylonians were surrounding the city, all the soldiers escaped during the night. They left by way of the royal garden, went through the gateway connecting the two walls, and fled in the direction of the Jordan Valley. But the Babylonian army pursued King Zedekiah, captured him in the plains near Jericho, and all his soldiers deserted him. Zedekiah was taken to King Nebuchadnezzar, who was in the city of Riblah, and there Nebuchadnezzar passed sentence on him. While Zedekiah was looking on, his sons were put to death; then Nebuchadnezzar had Zedekiah's eyes put out, placed him in chains, and took him to Babylon.

2 Kings 23:26–27;25:1–7

✠

Despite the efforts of good King Josiah, the people continue to drift away from the Lord. At last, the disaster which has threatened for many years comes about, and the city of Jerusalem is besieged and captured by the army of King Nebuchadnezzar.

It seems that the people of Judah had thought God would never let them down. After all, his reputation was at stake – what with David's descendants ruling in Jerusalem, and a temple being there as well. It would look bad for God if Jerusalem were to fall . . .

✠

Lord, help us never to abuse your love – to call ourselves Christians but to behave in ways which insult your holy name.

✠ ✠ ✠ ✠ ✠

November 24

It looks like the end of the people of God. The Northern Kingdom of Israel has been captured and its people dispersed. Now the Southern Kingdom of Judah has been overrun, the city of Jerusalem destroyed, and her people marched away into exile.

But God never forgot his people. He continued to speak to them of his love, especially through the prophets Jeremiah and Ezekiel. It was Jeremiah who gave them the following loving message even in the dismay and grief of exile.

✠

The LORD's unfailing love and mercy
still continue,
Fresh as the morning, as sure as
the sunrise.
The LORD is all I have, and so I
put my hope in him.

The LORD is good to everyone who
trusts in him,
So it is best for us to wait in
patience – to wait for him to save us –
And it is best to learn this patience
in our youth.

Lamentations 3:22–27

✠

Lord, even when life is very dark, your love and mercy come like the sunrise. Thank you that we have only to turn to you to find that you are very close – ready, willing and able to save.

November 25

The prophet Jeremiah had a message of hope for the people in exile.

✠

The LORD says, "The time is coming when I will make a new covenant with the people of Israel and with the people of Judah. It will not be like the old covenant that I made with their ancestors when I took them by the hand and led them out of Egypt. Although I was like a husband to them, they did not keep that covenant. The new covenant that I will make with the people of Israel will be this: I will put my law within them and write it on their hearts. I will be their God, and they will be my people. None of them will have to teach his fellow-countryman to know the LORD, because all will know me, from the least to the greatest. I will forgive their sins and I will no longer remember their wrongs. I, the LORD, have spoken."

Jeremiah 31:31–34

✠

When God rescued the Hebrews from Egypt he made a covenant with them. He promised that he would bless and protect them, if only they would keep his law.

But of course the law could only tell people how to behave – it could do nothing to change their hearts. And to this very day we find it impossible to keep the Ten Commandments, for the simple reason that we don't really want to.

Here God makes a wonderful promise. There will

come a time when he will make a new covenant – and put it *inside* our hearts and lives, so that it comes naturally for us to keep it.

✠

Lord Jesus, you are the one who brings the new covenant. You are the way that God can come right inside our lives. We gladly give ourselves to you.

✠ ✠ ✠ ✠ ✠

November 26

God's people are dead and gone – scattered in exile like bones in a valley. But as Ezekiel listens to the voice of God, he realizes that the impossible is about to happen. When God's people listen to his word and are filled with his Spirit, they will become a mighty army once again.

✠

I felt the powerful presence of the LORD, and his spirit took me and set me down in a valley where the ground was covered with bones. He led me all round the valley, and I could see that there were very many bones and that they were very dry. He said to me, "Mortal man, can these bones come back to life?"

I replied, "Sovereign LORD, only you can answer that!"

He said, "Prophesy to the bones. Tell these dry bones to listen to the word of the LORD. Tell them that I, the Sovereign LORD, am saying to them: I am going to put breath into you and bring you back to life. I will give you sinews and muscles, and cover you with skin. I will put breath into you and bring you back to life. Then you will know that I am the LORD."

So I prophesied as I had been told. While I was speaking, I heard a rattling noise, and the bones began to join together. While I watched, the bones were covered with sinews and muscles, and then with skin. But there was no breath in the bodies.

God said to me, "Mortal man, prophesy to the wind. Tell the wind that the Sovereign LORD commands it to come from every direction, to breathe into these dead bodies, and to bring them back to life."

So I prophesied as I had been told. Breath entered the bodies, and they came to life and stood up. There were enough of them to form an army.

God said to me, "Mortal man, the people of Israel are like these bones. They say that they are dried up, without any hope and with no future. So prophesy to my people Israel and tell them that I, the Sovereign LORD, am going to open their graves. I am going to take them out and bring them back to the land of Israel. When I open the graves where my people are buried and bring them out, they will know that I am the LORD. I will put my breath in them, bring them back to life, and let them live in their own land. Then they will know that I am the LORD. I have promised that I would do this and I will. I, the LORD, have spoken."

Ezekiel 37:1–14

✠

Lord God, nothing is impossible for you. Please build your people today into a strong and united Church – powerful in fighting evil and energetic in reaching out to the world you love.

November 27

It was terribly hard for the Jews to live in Babylon. They had been brought up to know that the Living God is the King of Kings and Lord of Lords. But here was a great king, Nebuchadnezzar, who cared nothing for God. Instead he expected everyone to worship *him*.

✠

King Nebuchadnezzar had a gold statue made, twenty-seven metres high and nearly three metres wide, and he had it set up in the plain of Dura in the province of Babylon. Then the king gave orders for all his officials to come together – the princes, governors, lieutenant-governors, commissioners, treasurers, judges, magistrates, and all the other officials of the provinces. They were to attend the dedication of the statue which King Nebuchadnezzar had set up. When all these officials gathered for the dedication and stood in front of the statue, a herald announced in a loud voice, "People of all nations, races, and languages! You will hear the sound of the trumpets, followed by the playing of oboes, lyres, zithers and harps; and then all the other instruments will join in. As soon as the music starts, you are to bow down and worship the gold statue that King Nebuchadnezzar has set up. Anyone who does not bow down and worship will immediately be thrown into a blazing furnace." And so, as soon as they heard the sound of the instruments, the people of all the nations, races, and languages bowed down and worshipped the gold statue which King Nebuchadnezzar had set up.

Daniel 3:1–7

✠

Just imagine how you would have felt, with the herald shouting, the music playing, and a vast crowd of people doing homage to the statue. Would you give in and bow to it as well?

✠

Lord, help us to have the courage to stand up for you, whatever the pressures on us to do otherwise. Please be with all those who are being bullied or imprisoned for your sake today, and give them courage and hope in their troubles.

✠ ✠ ✠ ✠ ✠

November 28

It was then that some Babylonians took this opportunity to denounce the Jews. They said to King Nebuchadnezzar, "May Your Majesty live for ever! Your Majesty has issued an order that as soon as the music starts, everyone is to bow down and worship the gold statue, and that anyone who does not bow down and worship it is to be thrown into a blazing furnace. There are some Jews whom you put in charge of the province of Babylon – Shadrach, Meshach, and Abednego – who are disobeying Your Majesty's orders. They do not worship your god or bow down to the statue you set up."

At that, the king flew into a rage and ordered the three men to be brought before him. He said to them, "Shadrach, Meshach, and Abednego, is it true that you refuse to worship my god and to bow down to the gold statue I have set up? Now then, as soon as you hear the sound of the trumpets, oboes, lyres, zithers, harps, and all the other instruments, bow down and worship the statue. If you do not, you will immediately be thrown into a blazing furnace. Do you think there is any god who can save you?"

Shadrach, Meshach, and Abednego answered, "Your Majesty, we will not try to defend ourselves. If the God whom we serve is able to save us from the blazing furnace and from your power, then he will. But even if he doesn't, Your Majesty may be sure that we will not worship your god, and we will not bow down to the gold statue that you have set up."

Daniel 3:8–18

✠

The three young men aren't afraid of the king's rage, or of his blazing furnace. They know that God can save them from the fire if he chooses. And even if he doesn't, it would still be quite wrong to worship an idol.

✠

Lord God, when we fear you and you alone, then all other decisions become clear.

✠ ✠ ✠ ✠ ✠

November 29

Then Nebuchadnezzar lost his temper, and his face turned red with anger at Shadrach, Meshach, and Abednego. So he ordered his men to heat the furnace seven times hotter than usual. And he commanded the strongest men in his army to tie the three men up and throw them into the blazing furnace. So they tied them up, fully dressed – shirts, robes, caps, and all – and threw them into the blazing furnace. Now because the king had given strict orders for the furnace to be made extremely hot, the flames burnt up the guards who took the men to the furnace. Then Shadrach, Meshach, and Abednego, still tied up, fell into the heart of the blazing fire.

Suddenly Nebuchadnezzar leapt to his feet in amazement. He asked his officials, "Didn't we tie up three men and throw them into the blazing furnace?"

They answered, "Yes, we did, Your Majesty."

"Then why do I see four men walking about in the fire?" he asked. "They are not tied up, and they show no sign of being hurt – and the fourth one looks like a god."

Daniel 3:19–25

✠

There have been many occasions in history when God's people have been tortured or put to death because of what they believe. We call such people martyrs, and their faith and courage have inspired many others to trust in the Living God.

But sometimes God rescues his people from suffering – and this is one of those occasions. God himself meets Shadrach, Meshach and Abednego in the heart of the furnace and brings them safely through.

✠

Lord, whether we live for you or die with you, please use our lives as a clear message of your power and love.

✠ ✠ ✠ ✠ ✠

November 30

So Nebuchadnezzar went up to the door of the blazing furnace and called out, "Shadrach! Meshach! Abednego! Servants of the Supreme God! Come out!" And they came out at once. All the princes, governors, lieutenant-governors, and other officials of the king gathered to look at the three men, who had not been harmed by the fire. Their hair was not singed, their clothes were not burnt, and there was no smell of smoke on them.

The king said, "Praise the God of Shadrach, Meshach, and Abednego! He sent his angel and rescued these men who serve and trust him. They disobeyed my orders and risked their lives rather than bow down and worship any god except their own.

"And now I command that if anyone of any nation, race, or language speaks disrespectfully of the God of Shadrach, Meshach, and Abednego, he is to be torn limb from limb, and his house is to be made a pile of ruins. There is no other god who can rescue like this."

And the king promoted Shadrach, Meshach, and Abednego to higher positions in the province of Babylon.

Daniel 3:26–30

✠

At the end of all his rampaging, Nebuchadnezzar bursts into shouts of praise to God. It's because of Shadrach, Meshach and Abednego's courage and defiance that he is able to see clearly what a wonderful God they have.

Mind you, in other ways he's the same old Nebuchadnezzar – still issuing threats against anyone who disagrees with him. But at least he's changed his mind!

✠

Lord, help us to live without the defences of anger or worry. Instead, may we simply trust in your protection. And please make us a blessing to those who trouble us.

✠ ✠ ✠ ✠ ✠

A Psalm for
December

Praise the LORD!
   Praise the LORD, my soul!
I will praise him as long as I live;
   I will sing to my God all my life.

Don't put your trust in human leaders;
   no human being can save you.
When they die, they return to the dust;
   on that day all their plans come to
      an end.

Happy is the man who has the God of
      Jacob to help him
   and who depends on the LORD his
      God,
   the Creator of heaven, earth, and sea,
   and all that is in them.
He always keeps his promises;
   he judges in favour of the oppressed
   and gives food to the hungry.

The LORD sets prisoners free
   and gives sight to the blind.
He lifts those who have fallen;
   he loves his righteous people.
He protects the strangers who live in
      our land;
   he helps widows and orphans,
   but ruins the plans of the wicked.

The LORD is king for ever.
  Your God, O Zion, will reign for all time.

Praise the LORD!

Psalm 146:1–10

December 1

Now we turn again to the teaching of Jesus. Here we listen to what he told his disciples about the Last Days – the things that would happen between the time of his leaving them and his glorious return.

✠

As Jesus was leaving the Temple, one of his disciples said, "Look, Teacher! What wonderful stones and buildings!"

Jesus answered, "You see these great buildings? Not a single stone here will be left in its place; every one of them will be thrown down."

Jesus was sitting on the Mount of Olives, across from the Temple, when Peter, James, John, and Andrew came to him in private. "Tell us when this will be," they said, "and tell us what will happen to show that the time has come for all these things to take place."

Jesus said to them, "Be on guard, and don't let anyone deceive you. Many men, claiming to speak for me, will come and say, 'I am he!' and they will deceive many people. And don't be troubled when you hear the noise of battles close by and news of battles far away.

Such things must happen, but they do not mean that the end has come. Countries will fight each other; kingdoms will attack one another. There will be earthquakes everywhere, and there will be famines. These things are like the first pains of childbirth."

Mark 13:1–8

✠

The Temple was still very new. It had been started by Herod the Great, and the disciples are full of admiration for its splendour. Imagine their shock when Jesus predicts that it will very soon be reduced to rubble. (The Temple was indeed destroyed by the Roman armies of Titus in AD 70 – just forty years after Jesus' warning.)

Jesus goes on to tell his disciples that there will often be bad news of wars and natural disasters. From time to time people will even claim to be the Messiah. But in all this pressure, they aren't to be taken in, and they aren't to lose heart. Such events may be the beginning of the end, but the End itself is in God's control.

✠

Lord Jesus, when the world seems dark and the news fills us with dread, help us to look up to you. You are our Saviour and mighty Deliverer, and our times are in your hands.

✠ ✠ ✠ ✠ ✠

December 2

Jesus continued: "You yourselves must be on guard. You will be arrested and taken to court. You will be beaten in the synagogues; you will stand before rulers and kings for my sake to tell them the Good News. But before the end comes, the gospel must be preached to all peoples. And when you are arrested and taken to court, do not worry beforehand about what you are going to say; when the time comes, say whatever is then given to you. For the words you speak will not be yours; they will come from the Holy Spirit. Men will hand over their own brothers to be put to death, and fathers will do the same to their children. Children will turn against their parents and have them put to death. Everyone will hate you because of me. But whoever holds out to the end will be saved."

Mark 13:9–13

✠

Jesus tells his disciples that they will be arrested and put on trial because of their faith in him. But even this will be an opportunity to tell world leaders the Good News. And he promises that at such times, his Holy Spirit will be with them in a very special way, so that they needn't have any anxiety about what they should say.

There's nothing more difficult than when a family is divided over Jesus. If it should ever happen to us, let's be sure to love our brothers and sisters, parents and children – and to go on praying that God will draw us all together again.

✠

Lord, thank you for the gift of your Holy Spirit. When we find ourselves in conflict, may he give us his love and peace, his patience and self-control.

✠ ✠ ✠ ✠ ✠

December 3

Jesus concluded: "There will be strange things happening to the sun, the moon, and the stars. On earth whole countries will be in despair, afraid of the roar of the sea and the raging tides. People will faint from fear as they wait for what is coming over the whole earth, for the powers in space will be driven from their courses. Then the Son of Man will appear, coming in a cloud with great power and glory. When these things begin to happen, stand up and raise your heads, because your salvation is near."

Luke 21:25–28

✠

Jesus describes a cosmos in chaos, with the universe itself going wrong, and the whole of mankind paralysed with fear.

But when everything is at the very point of collapse, Jesus promises to return. We have no idea when these events will take place, and it's only natural to pray that it won't happen in our own lifetime. But if it does, we have Jesus' own word that he will arrive in time to save us.

✠

Heavenly Father, we pray for peace in our time. But if you do choose to bring in the End, please keep us safely in the times of stress.

✠ ✠ ✠ ✠ ✠

December 4

Jesus told his followers to be prepared for him to return at any time. And he told a story about five silly bridesmaids who missed their great moment because they got tired of waiting, and in the end they weren't ready.

✠

"At that time the Kingdom of heaven will be like this. Once there were ten girls who took their oil lamps and went out to meet the bridegroom. Five of them were foolish, and the other five were wise. The foolish ones took their lamps but did not take any extra oil with them, while the wise ones took containers full of oil for their lamps. The bridegroom was late in coming, so the girls began to nod and fall asleep.

"It was already midnight when the cry rang out, 'Here is the bridegroom! Come and meet him!' The ten girls woke up and trimmed their lamps. Then the foolish ones said to the wise ones, 'Let us have some of your oil, because our lamps are going out.' 'No, indeed,' the wise ones answered, 'there is not enough for you and for us. Go to the shop and buy some for yourselves.' So the foolish girls went off to buy some nd while they were gone, the bridegroom arrived. The five girls who were ready went in with him to the wedding feast, and the door was closed.

"Later the other girls arrived. 'Sir, sir! Let us in!' they cried out. 'Certainly not! I don't know you,' the bridegroom answered."

And Jesus concluded, "Be on your guard, then, because you do not know the day or the hour."

Matthew 25:1–13

✠

Lord Jesus, help us always to expect you soon, so that when you come you will find us with clean hearts, useful hands, and glad faces.

✠ ✠ ✠ ✠ ✠

December 5

When Jesus returns to this earth, it will not be as a baby being born in a hospital. He will come as a great king and judge, to examine the way we have spent our lives. And he will show that in all the world there are only two kinds of people: those who are on his side and those who aren't.

✠

Jesus said: "When the Son of Man comes as King and all the angels with him, he will sit on his royal throne, and the people of all the nations will be gathered before him. Then he will divide them into two groups, just as a shepherd separates the sheep from the goats. He will put the righteous people on his right and the others on his left. Then the King will say to the people on his right, 'Come, you that are blessed by my Father! Come and possess the kingdom which has been prepared for you ever since the creation of the world. I was hungry and you fed me, thirsty and you gave me a drink; I was a stranger and you received me in your homes, naked and you clothed me; I was sick and you took care of me, in prison and you visited me.'

"The righteous will then answer him, 'When, Lord, did we ever see you hungry and feed you, or thirsty and give you a drink? When did we ever see you a stranger and welcome you in our homes, or naked and clothe you? When did we ever see you sick or in prison, and visit you?' The King will reply, 'I tell you, whenever you did this for one of the least important of these brothers of mine, you did it for me!'"

Matthew 25:31–40

✠

Lord Jesus, help us to be kind and careful today – giving special attention to those in need. Thank you that it's in looking after them that we discover you and show you our love.

✠ ✠ ✠ ✠ ✠

December 6

Jesus continued: "Then he will say to those on his left, 'Away from me, you that are under God's curse! Away to the eternal fire which has been prepared for the Devil and his angels! I was hungry but you would not feed me, thirsty but you would not give me a drink; I was a stranger but you would not welcome me in your homes, naked but you would not clothe me; I was sick and in prison but you would not take care of me.'

"Then they will answer him, 'When, Lord, did we ever see you hungry or thirsty or a stranger or naked or sick or in prison, and would not help you?' The King will reply, 'I tell you, whenever you refused to help one of these least important ones, you refused to help me.' These, then, will be sent off to eternal punishment, but the righteous will go to eternal life."

Matthew 25:41–46

✠

Jesus says that we can see him in our world every day, if only we care to notice. Wherever anyone is in trouble or need, Jesus is there suffering with them. And when we give such people help, it's as though we're looking after Jesus himself.

✠

Lord Jesus, help us to care for those in need. And thank you that when we do so, we're able to show our love for you.

✠ ✠ ✠ ✠ ✠

December 7

Today we go back to the Old Testament to look at some of the prophecies which point to Jesus. The first is from Isaiah.

✠

The LORD sent another message to Ahaz: "Ask the LORD your God to give you a sign. It can be from deep in the world of the dead or from high up in heaven."

Ahaz answered, "I will not ask for a sign. I refuse to put the LORD to the test."

To that Isaiah replied, "Listen, now, descendant of King David. It's bad enough for you to wear out the patience of men – must you wear out God's patience too? Well then, the LORD himself will give you a sign: a young woman who is pregnant will have a son and will name him 'Immanuel'. By the time he is old enough to make his own decisions, people will be drinking milk and eating honey. Even before that time comes, the lands of those two kings who terrify you will be deserted."

Isaiah 7:10–16

✠

King Ahaz is in an agony of fear, and Isaiah begs him to put his trust in God. When Ahaz refuses to seek God's assurance for the future, Isaiah gives him a sign anyway!

A young woman will give birth to a baby boy and call him "Immanuel", which means "God with us". Within a few years of his birth, the whole nation will be enjoying a time of plenty and peace.

This little prophecy came to Matthew's mind when he wrote about the birth of Jesus. Mary was very young, her son Jesus was to be "God with us", and he would bring in a reign of peace.

✠

Lord Jesus, you are "God with us" – not just a distant creator or a stern judge, but a close and caring friend. Thank you!

✠ ✠ ✠ ✠ ✠

December 8

Here is another of Isaiah's prophecies about Jesus.

✠

The people who walked in darkness
  have seen a great light.
They lived in a land of shadows,
  but now light is shining on them.
You have given them great joy, LORD;
  you have made them happy.
They rejoice in what you have done,
  as people rejoice when they harvest
    their corn
  or when they divide captured wealth.
For you have broken the yoke that
    burdened them
  and the rod that beat their shoulders.
You have defeated the nation

that oppressed and exploited your
    people,
just as you defeated the army of
    Midian long ago.
The boots of the invading army
    and all their bloodstained clothing
    will be destroyed by fire.
A child is born to us!
    A son is given to us!
    And he will be our ruler.
He will be called, "Wonderful Counsellor",
    "Mighty God", "Eternal Father",
    "Prince of Peace".
His royal power will continue to grow;
    his kingdom will always be at peace.
He will rule as King David's successor,
    basing his power on right and justice,
    from now until the end of time.

The LORD Almighty is determined to do
    all this.

Isaiah 9:2–7

✠

Isaiah sings a hymn of praise to God. The Lord's blessing and victory are like the sunrise, dispelling the darkness and chill of night, and giving light and warmth and happiness.

And at the heart of God's Kingdom is God's King. Isaiah says that when God's King, the Messiah, is born, he will be perfectly wise and strong, and his peaceful reign will last for all eternity.

✠

Jesus, please come to rule as King in our hearts, King in our nation, and King in our world.

✠ ✠ ✠ ✠ ✠

December 9

The people of Isaiah's day looked back to King David's reign as a golden age of power, prosperity and peace. Would they ever see his like again? Isaiah says they most certainly will.

✠

The royal line of David is like a tree that has been cut down; but just as new branches sprout from a stump, so a new king will arise from among David's descendants.

> The spirit of the LORD will give him wisdom,
> and the knowledge and skill to rule
> his people.
> He will know the LORD's will and
> honour him,
> and find pleasure in obeying him.
> He will not judge by appearance or
> hearsay;
> he will judge the poor fairly
> and defend the rights of the helpless.
> At his command the people will be
> punished,
> and evil persons will die.
> He will rule his people with justice and
> integrity.

Wolves and sheep will live together in
peace,
and leopards will lie down with young
goats.
Calves and lion cubs will feed together,
and little children will take care of
them.
Cows and bears will eat together,
and their calves and cubs will lie down
in peace.
Lions will eat straw as cattle do.
Even a baby will not be harmed
if it plays near a poisonous snake.
On Zion, God's sacred hill,
there will be nothing harmful or evil.
The land will be as full of knowledge
of the LORD
as the seas are full of water.

Isaiah 11:1–9

✠

Isaiah prophesies the coming of a greater king even than David. This king will be so finely attuned to God's will, that there will be justice and protection for all mankind. And isn't it exciting to read that the animal kingdom and the rest of the world of nature will enjoy peace as well!

✠

Lord Jesus, thank you for coming to bring justice and peace, restoring the whole world to the perfect harmony God intended.

December 10

Isaiah says a time is coming when the world and all that is in it will be put to rights. To all who are sunk in tiredness, fear and gloom, Isaiah says, "Look! Here comes God!"

All who are discouraged or disabled will be helped and healed, the ravaged and polluted world of nature will be restored, and all who turn to the Lord will have their feet set on his highway of holiness.

✠

The desert will rejoice,
  and flowers will bloom in the wilderness.
The desert will sing and shout for joy;
  it will be as beautiful as the Lebanon Mountains
  and as fertile as the fields of Carmel and Sharon.
Everyone will see the LORD's splendour,
  see his greatness and power.
Give strength to hands that are tired
  and to knees that tremble with weakness.

Tell everyone who is discouraged,
  "Be strong and don't be afraid!
  God is coming to your rescue,
  coming to punish your enemies."

The blind will be able to see,
  and the deaf will hear.
The lame will leap and dance,
  and those who cannot speak will shout for joy.
Streams of water will flow through the desert;
  the burning sand will become a lake,
  and dry land will be filled with springs.
Where jackals used to live,
  marsh grass and reeds will grow.

There will be a highway there,
  called "The Road of Holiness".
No sinner will ever travel that road;
  no fools will mislead those who follow it.
No lions will be there;
  no fierce animals will pass that way.
Those whom the LORD has rescued
  will travel home by that road.
They will reach Jerusalem with gladness,
  singing and shouting for joy.
They will be happy for ever,
  for ever free from sorrow and grief.

Isaiah 35:1–10

✠

Lord God, we praise you for setting out to save us, and for the new thing you are doing through Jesus in our lives and in our world.

✠ ✠ ✠ ✠ ✠

December 11

These words were written many hundreds of years before Jesus was born, and yet they describe him perfectly. Jesus was God's Servant, doing everything according to God's will. And the Lord's plan was not just to bless the people of Israel, but to beam his light and truth to the whole world.

✠

Listen to me, distant nations,
  you people who live far away!
Before I was born, the LORD chose me
  and appointed me to be his servant.
He made my words as sharp as a sword.
  With his own hand he protected me.
He made me like an arrow,
  sharp and ready for use.
He said to me, "Israel, you are my servant;
  because of you, people will praise me."

Before I was born, the LORD appointed me;
  he made me his servant to bring back his people,
  to bring back the scattered people of Israel.
The LORD gives me honour;
  he is the source of my strength.
The LORD said to me,
"I have a greater task for you, my servant.
  Not only will you restore to greatness
  the people of Israel who have survived,
but I will also make you a light to the nations –
  so that all the world may be saved."

Isaiah 49:1–3, 5–6

✠

Lord God, help us to be your willing servants today – pleasing you in all that we say and do, and shining with your light and love.

✠ ✠ ✠ ✠ ✠

December 12

Here is another of Isaiah's prophecies in which we can hear Jesus himself speaking.

✠

The Sovereign LORD has filled me
with his spirit.
He has chosen me and sent me
To bring good news to the poor,
To heal the broken-hearted,
To announce release to captives
And freedom to those in prison.
He has sent me to proclaim
That the time has come
When the LORD will save his people
And defeat their enemies.
He has sent me to comfort all who mourn,
To give to those who mourn in Zion
Joy and gladness instead of grief,
A song of praise instead of sorrow.
They will be like trees
That the LORD himself has planted.
They will all do what is right,
And God will be praised for what he
has done.

Isaiah 61:1–3

✠

One day Jesus will use these words as his text for a sermon in Nazareth. God's Servant will tell the poor that God will provide for them. He will tell the broken-hearted that God will comfort them. He will tell the captives that God will rescue them and set them free.

When Jesus read these words to the people of Nazareth, he said, "All this has come true today – before your very eyes!"

Jesus himself is God's true Servant. Jesus himself, in his teaching and healing, in his death and resurrection, is Good News.

✠

Lord Jesus, thank you for meeting our deepest needs – turning our poverty into your wealth, and our sadness into your gladness.

✠ ✠ ✠ ✠ ✠

December 13

This is the famous prophecy which foretells that the Messiah will be born in Bethlehem. It was in this little town that Boaz and Ruth had lived, and that their grandson had been born – he who was to become the great King David. Now the prophet Micah looks forward to a greater king still. His name will be Jesus.

✠

The LORD says, "Bethlehem Ephrathah, you are one of the smallest towns in Judah, but out of you I will bring a ruler for Israel, whose family line goes back to ancient times."

So the LORD will abandon his people to their enemies until the one who is to give birth has her son. Then his fellow-countrymen who are in exile will be reunited with their own people. When he comes, he will rule his people with the strength that comes from the LORD and with the majesty of the LORD God himself. His people will live in safety because people all over the earth will acknowledge his greatness, and he will bring peace.

Micah 5:2–5

✠

Lord God, as we get ready for Christmas, we marvel again at the way you prepared the world for the birth of your Son. We see how you took ordinary people and places to work the beautiful tapestry of your perfect plan.

✠ ✠ ✠ ✠ ✠

December 14

At the beginning of John's gospel, the writer talks of Jesus as the Word. When we want to share an idea, we express ourselves in words. When God wanted to tell us about his love for us, he sent us a person – his Son.

And what was God's Son like when he walked this earth? John's gospel says Jesus was "full of grace and truth". All the same, there were many who wanted nothing to do with him.

✠

Before the world was created, the Word already existed; he was with God, and he was the same as God. From the very beginning the Word was with God.

Through him God made all things; not one thing in all creation was made without him. The Word was the source of life, and this life brought light to mankind. The light shines in the darkness, and the darkness has never put it out.

God sent his messenger, a man named John, who came to tell people about the light, so that all should hear the message and believe. He himself was not the light; he came to tell about the light. This was the real light – the light that comes into the world and shines on all mankind.

The Word was in the world, and though God made the world through him, yet the world did not recognize him. He came to his own country, but his own people did not receive him. Some, however, did receive him and believed in him; so he gave them the right to become God's children.

The Word became a human being and, full of grace and truth, lived among us. We saw his glory, the glory which he received as the Father's only Son.

John 1:1–12,14

✠

Lord Jesus, we want to be those who recognize you, welcome you and put our trust in you. Thank you for enabling us to become God's children.

✠ ✠ ✠ ✠ ✠

December 15

Today we read the beginning of Luke's gospel.

✠

Dear Theophilus,

Many people have done their best to write a report of the things that have taken place among us. They wrote what we have been told by those who saw these things from the beginning and who proclaimed the message. And so, your Excellency, because I have carefully studied all these matters from their beginning, I thought it would be good to write an orderly account for you. I do this so that you will know the full truth about everything which you have been taught.

Luke 1:1–4

✠

Luke wrote his gospel for a distinguished Roman called Theophilus.

Luke is a good historian, and he has done thorough research. He talked with people who knew Jesus well, and collected many of his stories and sayings.

To this very day experts are impressed by Luke's careful work, and many recent discoveries have borne out the truth of the story he had to tell.

✠

Lord, you care about truth. Thank you that Luke worked in a way which honours your name and commends your message.

December 16

During the time when Herod was king of Judaea, there was a priest named Zechariah, who belonged to the priestly order of Abijah. His wife's name was Elizabeth; she also belonged to a priestly family. They both lived good lives in God's sight and obeyed fully all the Lord's laws and commands. They had no children because Elizabeth could not have any, and she and Zechariah were both very old.

One day Zechariah was doing his work as a priest in the Temple, taking his turn in the daily service. According to the custom followed by the priests, he was chosen by lot to burn incense on the altar. So he went into the Temple of the Lord, while the crowd of people outside prayed during the hour when the incense was burnt.

An angel of the Lord appeared to him, standing on the right of the altar where the incense was burnt. When Zechariah saw him, he was alarmed and felt afraid. But the angel said to him, "Don't be afraid, Zechariah! God has heard your prayer, and your wife Elizabeth will bear you a son. You are to name him John."

Luke 1:5–13

✠

The first people we meet in Luke's gospel are an elderly priest and his wife – Zechariah and Elizabeth. Their great sadness is that they are unable to have children. In those days it was thought that you must have done something to displease God if you had no descendants.

However, God always stands by those who faithfully trust him. And one day (actually the very day that it was Zechariah's turn to lead the temple service) an angel appears with some exciting news.

Lord God, thank you for all those who have served you faithfully over many years and learnt to trust you in hard times. As long as we live may we always be alert to the new things you want to do in our lives.

✠ ✠ ✠ ✠ ✠

December 17

The angel said to Zechariah:

"John will be a great man in the Lord's sight. He must not drink any wine or strong drink. From his very birth he will be filled with the Holy Spirit, and he will bring back many of the people of Israel to the Lord their God. He will go ahead of the Lord, strong and mighty like the prophet Elijah. He will bring fathers and children together again; he will turn disobedient people back to the way of thinking of the righteous; he will get the Lord's people ready for him."

Zechariah said to the angel, "How shall I know if this is so? I am an old man and my wife is old also."

"I am Gabriel," the angel answered. "I stand in the presence of God, who sent me to speak to you and tell you this good news. But you have not believed my message, which will come true at the right time. Because you have not believed, you will be unable to speak; you will remain silent until the day my promise to you comes true."

In the meantime the people were waiting for Zechariah and wondering why he was spending such a long time in the Temple. When he came out, he could not speak to them, and so they knew that he had seen a vision in the Temple. Unable to say a word, he made signs to them with his hands.

When his period of service in the Temple was over, Zechariah went back home. Some time later his wife Elizabeth became pregnant and did not leave the house for five months. "Now at last the Lord has helped me," she said. "He has taken away my public disgrace!"

Luke 1:15–25

✠

Zechariah and Elizabeth are to have a son, and they must call him John. One day he will be known as John the Baptist – a strong, fearless preacher who will call God's people to turn from their wickedness and prepare themselves for the arrival of the Messiah. Zechariah simply can't believe what's happening to them!

✠

Lord God, we believe that you can do great things. Help us to expect that some of the great things you do will involve us, so that we don't hinder you by our surprise or unbelief.

✠ ✠ ✠ ✠ ✠

December 18

In the sixth month of Elizabeth's pregnancy God sent the angel Gabriel to a town in Galilee named Nazareth. He had a message for a girl promised in marriage to a man named Joseph, who was a descendant of King David. The girl's name was Mary. The angel came to her and said, "Peace be with you! The Lord is with you and has greatly blessed you!"

Mary was deeply troubled by the angel's message, and she wondered what his words meant. The angel said to her, "Don't be afraid, Mary; God has been gracious to you. You will become pregnant and give birth to a son, and you will name him Jesus. He will be great and will be called the Son of the Most High God. The Lord God will make him a king as his ancestor David was, and he will be the king of the descendants of Jacob for ever; his kingdom will never end!"

Mary said to the angel, "I am a virgin. How, then, can this be?"

The angel answered, "The Holy Spirit will come on you, and God's power will rest upon you. For this reason the holy child will be called the Son of God."

"I am the Lord's servant," said Mary; "may it happen to me as you have said." And the angel left her.

Luke 1:26–35,38

✠

How amazed Mary must have been at the angel's message – and how frightened, at least at first.

Suddenly she finds herself living out the words of the old prophets. It is she who is the young woman who will give birth to God's Son. Her baby will grow up to be a greater king than David, and his kingdom will never end.

She finds it hard to believe, for she is not even married yet! But God himself is to be the father of this child.

✠

Dear God our Father, thank you for Mary's faith and courage: her faith that everything is possible for you, and her courage in putting you first, whatever the cost to herself.

December 19

This was how the birth of Jesus Christ took place. His mother Mary was engaged to Joseph, but before they were married, she found out that she was going to have a baby by the Holy Spirit. Joseph was a man who always did what was right, but he did not want to disgrace Mary publicly; so he made plans to break the engagement privately. While he was thinking about this, an angel of the Lord appeared to him in a dream and said, "Joseph, descendant of David, do not be afraid to take Mary to be your wife. For it is by the Holy Spirit that she has conceived. She will have a son, and you will name him Jesus – because he will save his people from their sins."

Now all this happened in order to make what the Lord had said through the prophet come true, "A virgin will become pregnant and have a son, and he will be called Immanuel" (which means, "God is with us").

So when Joseph woke up, he married Mary, as the angel of the Lord had told him to do.

Matthew 1:18–24

✠

It was a scandal for Mary to be expecting a baby before she and Joseph were properly married.

Joseph is torn between his love for Mary and the clear evidence that she has been unfaithful to him.

But then Joseph receives his own assurance from God, in a dream. This baby has no human father. Mary is to be his mother, but his father is God.

✠

Lord, when we're distressed by a problem, help us not to act unkindly or hastily, but to listen for your wise guidance, and to find your perfect way.

✠ ✠ ✠ ✠ ✠

December 20

Soon afterwards Mary got ready and hurried off to a town in the hill-country of Judaea. She went into Zechariah's house and greeted Elizabeth. When Elizabeth heard Mary's greeting, the baby moved within her. Elizabeth was filled with the Holy Spirit and said in a loud voice, "You are the most blessed of all women, and blessed is the child you will bear! Why should this great thing happen to me, that my Lord's mother comes to visit me? For as soon as I heard your greeting, the baby within me jumped with gladness. How happy you are to believe that the Lord's message to you will come true!"

Mary said,

"My heart praises the Lord;
my soul is glad because of God my Saviour,
for he has remembered me, his lowly servant!
From now on all people will call me happy,
because of the great things the Mighty God has done for me."

Luke 1:39–49

✠

Mary and Elizabeth are cousins. How wonderful that they can spend time together – both unexpectedly pregnant, and both expecting very special sons!

It seems that the babies were glad to be near each other as well. Elizabeth feels her child "jump with gladness" – expressing the joy of greeting the Messiah.

✠

Lord, thank you for friends who understand us and support us, and especially for those who share our joy at all your goodness in our lives.

✠ ✠ ✠ ✠ ✠

December 21

The time came for Elizabeth to have her baby, and she gave birth to a son. Her neighbours and relatives heard how wonderfully good the Lord had been to her, and they all rejoiced with her.

When the baby was a week old, they came to circumcise him, and they were going to name him Zechariah, after his father. But his mother said, "No! His name is to be John."

They said to her, "But you have no relatives with that name!" Then they made signs to his father, asking him what name he would like the boy to have.

Zechariah asked for a writing tablet and wrote, "His name is John." How surprised they all were! At that moment Zechariah was able to speak again, and he started praising God. The neighbours were all filled with fear, and the news about these things spread through all the hill-country of Judaea. Everyone who heard of it thought about it and asked, "What is this child going to be?" For it was plain that the Lord's power was upon him.

Luke 1:57–66

✠

Old Zechariah may have been slow to believe what God was doing, but he's certainly full of faith now. He boldly and gladly looks forward to all that God has in store for them.

He and Elizabeth surprise everyone with their choice of name. When did we last decide that things can be different – never mind what the neighbours say?

✠

Lord, please awaken us afresh to your presence with us. Keep us from getting too set in our ways, blind and deaf to your call, or unable to respond to the promptings of your Spirit. May this be a day when we are especially alive to you and alert to your guidance.

✠ ✠ ✠ ✠ ✠

December 22

John's father Zechariah was filled with the Holy Spirit, and he spoke God's message:

"Let us praise the Lord, the God of
Israel!
He has come to the help of his people
and has set them free.

He has provided for us a mighty
    Saviour,
  a descendant of his servant David.
He promised through his holy
    prophets long ago
  that he would save us from our
    enemies,
  from the power of all those who hate
    us.
He said he would show mercy to our
    ancestors
  and remember his sacred covenant.
  With a solemn oath to our
    ancestor Abraham
  he promised to rescue us from our
    enemies
  and allow us to serve him without
    fear,
so that we might be holy and righteous
    before him
  all the days of our life.

Luke 1:67–75

✠

Suddenly Zechariah sees so clearly all that God is doing. He is keeping his age-old promise to his people. He is about to send his Messiah to rescue his people, and to draw them back to a life of freedom and holiness. What a wonderful God he is!

✠

Lord, thank you that in sending Jesus you were saying "Yes" to us. Thank you that you keep your promises throughout the generations, and that you want to bless us even more than we can ask or imagine.

✠ ✠ ✠ ✠ ✠

December 23

Zechariah said to John:

> "You, my child, will be called a
> prophet of the Most High God.
> You will go ahead of the Lord
> to prepare his road for him,
> to tell his people that they will be saved
> by having their sins forgiven.
> Our God is merciful and tender.
> He will cause the bright dawn of
> salvation to rise on us
> and to shine from heaven on all
> those who live in the dark shadow
> of death,
> to guide our steps into the path of
> peace."

The child grew and developed in body and spirit. He lived in the desert until the day when he appeared publicly to the people of Israel.

Luke 1:76–80

✠

Now Zechariah has a special word for his son John. The child will grow up to pave the way for the Messiah. Like a road-builder, he'll be making a highway for the great king to travel on – not a road of slabs and stones, but a highway through men's hearts and minds.

And John isn't only to make way for the Messiah, but to herald his coming by powerfully calling everyone to get ready.

✠

Lord Jesus, we open wide our hearts to you this Christmas time. Please come into our lives and direct all we do. And may we tell others about you: not just that you came as a babe to Bethlehem years ago, but that you are the Saviour of the world today.

✠ ✠ ✠ ✠ ✠

December 24

At that time the Emperor Augustus ordered a census to be taken throughout the Roman Empire. When this first census took place Quirinius was the governor of Syria. Everyone, then, went to register himself, each to his own town.

Joseph went from the town of Nazareth in Galilee to the town of Bethlehem in Judaea, the birthplace of King David. Joseph went there because he was a descendant of David. He went to register with Mary, who was promised in marriage to him. She was pregnant, and while they were in Bethlehem, the time came for her to have her baby. She gave birth to her first son, wrapped him in strips of cloth and laid him in a manger – there was no room for them to stay in the inn.

Luke 2:1–7

Mary and Joseph live in Nazareth – some eighty miles north of Bethlehem. How can it be that the baby will be born so far from home?

But then the Emperor's order arrives that a census is to be taken, and everyone must return to their family town to be counted.

How amazing that even the Roman Emperor has a vital part in this story. And how intriguing that the baby Jesus might have been counted in a Roman census as soon as he was born.

✠

Lord Jesus, you came to share our life as it really is. You didn't come to a place of privilege and comfort, but to the stark realities of homelessness and inconvenience. Today even the poorest and humblest can recognize you as a friend indeed. Thank you!

✠ ✠ ✠ ✠ ✠

December 25

There were some shepherds in that part of the country who were spending the night in the fields, taking care of their flocks. An angel of the Lord appeared to them, and the glory of the Lord shone over them. They were terribly afraid, but the angel said to them, "Don't be afraid! I am here with good news for you, which will bring great joy to all the people. This very day in David's town your Saviour was born – Christ the Lord! And this is what will prove it to you: you will find a baby wrapped in strips of cloth and lying in a manger."

Suddenly a great army of heaven's angels appeared with the angel, singing praises to God:

"Glory to God in the highest heaven,
and peace on earth to those with
whom he is pleased!"

Luke 2:8–14

✠

Shepherds are usually the last to get any news. They are with their sheep day and night. In Judah the shepherds were treated as outsiders because they never attended the synagogue services. Certainly they never went to the great religious feasts at Jerusalem.

But on this night of nights, it's to the shepherds that the good news comes. Good news from heaven to earth. Good news that the Saviour is born. Good news for outsiders.

✠

Dear God our loving Father, thank you for sending Jesus to be our Saviour. May he find a special place in our home today.

✠ ✠ ✠ ✠ ✠

December 26

When the angels went away from them back into heaven, the shepherds said to one another, "Let's go to Bethlehem and see this thing that has happened, which the Lord has told us."

So they hurried off and found Mary and Joseph and saw the baby lying in the manger. When the shepherds saw him, they told them what the angel had said about the child. All who heard it were amazed at what the shepherds said. Mary remembered all these things and thought deeply about them. The shepherds went back, singing praises to God for all they had heard and seen; it had been just as the angel had told them.

Luke 2:15–20

✠

No doubt the shepherds had seen babies before. No doubt they had tucked baby lambs in cattle troughs many times, to keep them snug and safe from the cold night wind.

But this baby is different from all others. The whole of heaven is rejoicing at his birth. And when the shepherds see for themselves, they praise God. And then they share their Good News with others.

✠

Dear Lord Jesus, you are the real Christmas present. Thank you that your joy and peace can be with us now and every day.

✠ ✠ ✠ ✠ ✠

December 27

Jesus was born in the town of Bethlehem in Judaea, during the time when Herod was king. Soon afterwards some men who studied the stars came from the east to Jerusalem and asked, "Where is the baby born to be the king of the Jews? We saw his star when it came up in the east, and we have come to worship him."

When King Herod heard about this he was very upset, and so was everyone else in Jerusalem. He called together all the chief priests and the teachers of the Law and asked them, "Where will the Messiah be born?"

"In the town of Bethlehem in Judaea," they answered. "For this is what the prophet wrote:

'Bethlehem in the land of Judah,
you are by no means the least of the
leading cities of Judah;
for from you will come a leader
who will guide my people Israel.'"

So Herod called the visitors from the east to a secret meeting and found out from them the exact time the star had appeared. Then he sent them to Bethlehem with these instructions: "Go and make a careful search for the child, and when you find him, let me know, so that I too may go and worship him."

Matthew 2:1–8

✠

The message in the stars is that a new king is born to the Jews. Naturally, the wise men call at the palace in Jerusalem to visit the baby.

But this is the first King Herod has heard of it, and *he* doesn't want a new king. Immediately he starts to plot the baby's death, if only he can find out where he is.

✠

Loving Father, may all who search for truth be led to Jesus. May all who long for life find life in him.

✠ ✠ ✠ ✠ ✠

December 28

And so they left, and on their way they saw the same star they had seen in the east. When they saw it, how happy they were, what joy was theirs! It went ahead of them until it stopped over the place where the child was. They went into the house, and when they saw the child with his mother Mary, they knelt down and worshipped him. They brought out their gifts of gold, frankincense, and myrrh, and presented them to him.

Then they returned to their country by another road, since God had warned them in a dream not to go back to Herod.

Matthew 2:9–12

✠

We don't know how many wise men there were, but they brought three gifts to the baby Jesus. The gold was for his kingship, the frankincense for his priesthood, and the myrrh for his death. These were indeed wise, thoughtful and generous gifts – faithfully offered to this little family who had so little money and were so far from home.

The wise men were looking forward to the whole of Jesus' life. And their gifts were tokens that one day all nations will offer themselves to God through Jesus.

✠

Lord Jesus, we bring to you the whole of our lives – our time, our talents, and our troubles – all wrapped up in our love for you.

✠ ✠ ✠ ✠ ✠

December 29

When the time came for the baby to be circumcised, he was named Jesus, the name which the angel had given him before he had been conceived.

The time came for Joseph and Mary to perform the ceremony of purification, as the Law of Moses commanded. So they took the child to Jerusalem to present him to the Lord, as it is written in the law of the Lord: "Every first-born male is to be dedicated to the Lord." They also went to offer a sacrifice of a pair of doves or two young pigeons, as required by the law of the Lord.

At that time there was a man named Simeon living in Jerusalem. He was a good, devout man and was waiting for Israel to be saved. The Holy Spirit was with him and had assured him that he would not die before he had seen the Lord's promised Messiah.

Luke 2:21–26

✠

There is no health clinic or baby store for Jesus, but there is a special ceremony in the Temple by which he is offered to God.

Jesus is circumcised to show that he is a member of the Jewish people, and that he shares in the covenant which God made with all the descendants of Abraham.

The sacrifice offered by Joseph and Mary – a pair of doves or pigeons – is a sign that they were quite poor, and that this was all they could afford.

✠

Lord Jesus, you came to be part of a family, part of a culture, part of a people. Help us to live fully and faithfully for you in our own time and place, and amongst our own folk.

✠ ✠ ✠ ✠ ✠

December 30

Led by the Spirit, Simeon went into the Temple. When the parents brought the child Jesus into the Temple to do for him what the Law required, Simeon took the child in his arms and gave thanks to God:

"Now, Lord, you have kept your
promise,
and you may let your servant go in
peace.
With my own eyes I have seen your
salvation,
which you have prepared in the
presence of all peoples:
A light to reveal your will to the
Gentiles
and bring glory to your people Israel."

The child's father and mother were amazed at the things Simeon said about him. Simeon blessed them and said to Mary, his mother, "This child is chosen by God for the destruction and the salvation of many in Israel. He will be a sign from God which many people will speak against and so reveal their secret thoughts. And sorrow, like a sharp sword, will break your own heart."

Luke 2:27–35

Some people have special insight, don't they? Simeon has been looking and longing for the Messiah all his life, and now his patient waiting is rewarded. He can die happy, for he has held the precious baby in his arms.

And he has another keen insight as well – that there will be great sadness and hurt for Mary in the years to come.

✠

Lord, thank you for those people who see things with your eyes and see them clearly. May we have sharp spiritual eyes and keen spiritual ears, so that we perceive what you're doing in our world and give our efforts to serving you.

✠ ✠ ✠ ✠ ✠

December 31

There was a very old prophetess, a widow named Anna, daughter of Phanuel of the tribe of Asher. She had been married for only seven years and was now eighty-four years old. She never left the Temple; day and night she worshipped God, fasting and praying. That very same hour she arrived and gave thanks to God and spoke about the child to all who were waiting for God to set Jerusalem free.

When Joseph and Mary had finished doing all that was required by the law of the Lord, they returned to their home town of Nazareth in Galilee. The child grew and became strong; he was full of wisdom, and God's blessings were upon him.

Luke 2:36–40

In Simeon and Anna we glimpse a whole network of people who have been waiting for God to act and who are now busy sharing this latest and greatest news. How does this compare with the way we behave as God's people today?

Meanwhile the little family returns to Nazareth, the north-country town where Jesus is to spend the first thirty years of his life. This is where he will learn to love and be loved, study God's Law, and master Joseph's trade. Here he will trace God's ways in the lives of his family and friends, and explore the wonderful world of nature in beautiful Galilee.

✠

Lord God, thank you for every ordinary day with its familiar routines, duties and chores. Thank you that it's in the ordinariness of every day that we discover and respond to your extraordinary love.

✠ ✠ ✠ ✠ ✠